The Gentleman's
INSTANT GENIUS
GUIDE

Also by Tom Cutler

A Gentleman's Bedside Book

The Gentleman's
INSTANT GENIUS
GUIDE

TOM CUTLER

Constable · London

Constable & Robinson Ltd
55–56 Russell Square
London WC1B 4HP
www.constablerobinson.com

First published in the UK by Constable,
an imprint of Constable & Robinson Ltd., 2011

A copy of the British Library Cataloguing in
Publication data is available from the British Library

ISBN 978-1-78033-057-0

Printed and bound in the EU

1 3 5 7 9 10 8 6 4 2

PEFC
PEFC/16-33-111
CATG-PEFC-052
www.pefc.org

To Ken Maycock,
my oldest chum and a genius, not to say walking encyclopaedia,
on many subjects (including ITV's lowbrow comedy *On the Buses*).

'What the world needs is more geniuses with humility; there are so few of us left.' Oscar Levant

Acknowledgements

All authors, and all geniuses, feed off other people but do not always thank them or even mention their names. This is a pity as the more people you include in your acknowledgements the more books you are likely to sell, for everybody loves to see his name in print. I therefore take especial pleasure in expressing my gratitude to the following, who helped me in various capacities as I wrote this book: Leo Hollis, for his editorial wisdom and continuous good sense; Carlos Castro, for his stylish illustrations; Laura Morris, for her unfailing agently cheer, constant encouragement and the occasional hilarious lunch; the Dark Star and Harveys breweries, for their life-affirming bitters; John Dowland, John Coltrane and Turlough Carolan for a sprinkling of perdurable music; Martin Bennett, for smuggling me into the cricket; Howard Watson, for copy-editing a mountain of ill-spelt and confusing twaddle into a beautifully readable book; Terry Burrows, for alerting me to song-poems; Dr Clive Bach, for decades of astute counsel and good humour; the late Audrey Hepburn, for looking so lovely; the man whose name I don't know, for finding my wallet and posting it back to me; Mr and Mrs Evans, for delivering my milk so happily for so long; and, most of all, Marianne, for squandering an awful lot of genuine affection on a fractious and desiccated toad. Thank you.

Contents

Part Two: THE INSTANT GENIUS'S WORLD OF KNOWLEDGE

Part Three: LISTS AND TESTS FOR THE INSTANT GENIUS

Quick information and enquiry for the time-poor gentleman 179

Part Four: THE DICTIONARY OF UNNATURAL BIOGRAPHY

Preface

Aren't you sick of all those self-help books that tell you how to become happy, rich, a sex-god and the most popular man in the world? I am. This book is a kind of antidote to all that and, though it will indeed make you an expert in everything in just fifteen minutes, it will not make any great demands on you. OK, there is a s-prinkling of excellent advice but, unlike other books of this kind, *The Gentleman's Instant Genius Guide* does not load your emotional shoulders with a burden greater even than the one you already strain to support, and are trying to relieve, for the truth is that love, laughter, wine, women and song are the true tools of gentlemanly self-help. *The Gentleman's Instant Genius Guide* supplies the laughter, you need only supply the rest (any women left over, please send them on).

So here, alongside the vital instant how-tos (learn how to waltz and draw the Union Jack – *at different times, obviously*), you will find a multitude of information that every genius ought to know, from the history of the blue-skinned people of Kentucky to the truth about the deadliest frog in the world, not forgetting everything you've ever wanted to know about the penis. Discover those amazing sporting facts you never hear about, and see compiled for the first time a list of that business jargon we all hate. You can even take a test or two – discover which sports car suits your personality, say, or work out your deathday, or test your sex drive to destruction.

As the man said, 'There's a fine line between genius and insanity,' and in this book I have attempted to erase it. If you end up crackers as well as brilliant, don't blame me.

Part One:

INSTANT GENIUS
HOW-TOS

*How to do everything
a gentleman should do*

How to live without self-help books

You may have noticed that the self-help racket has been going strong for many decades, and no wonder, because it causes punters to part with vast amounts of money – billions, actually – every year. Even those with pretty well-developed bullshit radar can sometimes be taken in by it, too. Just think of the various diets that come around periodically or the how-to books on every subject under the sun, from how to get pregnant to how to bring up children, to how to live a happy middle age, to how to die correctly. We've all probably got one of these knocking around somewhere.

The funny thing is that if you pause and think for a moment at the foot of the cliff-face of self-help tomes in the bookshop, you realize that there is a piquant paradox in the very epithet 'self-help', because if you are buying a book of somebody else's instructions about how to get out of debt, influence people or stop your children hating you, it isn't really self-help at all; the help is being transmitted from one party in the transaction to the other, that is to say – *they* are (allegedly) helping *you*.

On which point, I'm reminded of a book that came out a few years ago with the abominable face of its author grinning off the front cover. It was called *I Can Make You Rich* and became an unsurprising bestseller. But it really ought to have been entitled *You Can Make Me Rich*, because the author was getting richer and the reader – or, rather, 'purchaser', for nobody reads these books *in the library* or *at all* – was getting poorer to the tune of the book's cover price. There ought to be a 'money-back-if-you're-not-rich/slim/happy-in-five-years'-time' guarantee printed in books of this sort.

There are *two* perpetrators of the ridiculous self-help crime: the parasitic 'self-help' guru and the sad purchaser, who between them share a kind of secret understanding that the arrangement is not quite as it appears. The confident, well-turned-out self-help person appreciates the subtle neediness/idleness of his victims, while the seeker-after-somebody-else's-help is probably hoping for a quick and easy solution to his problems: a list, possibly, of simple instructions telling him exactly how

4

to fix his screwed-up life without having to work at it, and thereby absolving him of the horrible function of having to *think* about or do anything himself. Of course, he might also be hedging his bets so that if he doesn't become fitter, richer, thinner, everyone will see that it wasn't from lack of commitment on his part, it was all the fault of the particular self-help system or book; a win–win situation after all.

Anyway, this is all by way of an introduction to the crazy world of self-help. If you were hoping for an easy way out of your problems, let me reassure you that on other pages of this book you will indeed find lists of instructions telling you how to become rich, famous, popular, prestigious and so on, but I trust that you will have your bullshit detector turned up to eleven.

In fact, here's the first of those lists. Try the following to escape the gin trap of self-help:

- Think for yourself; you know more about you than the book's author does.
- Ask yourself: why did this person write this book? The answer can change your attitude to his or her advice rather quickly.
- Question what you are told. Maybe it's false. A very useful all-purpose attitude to adopt. Doubt is a vitally useful tool in understanding the world.
- Ask yourself: when and how will I be able to measure the success of this book? And:
- If it hasn't helped me, can I get my money back?

The answer to this last one is probably, 'No'! Anyway, good luck.

How to get on television

When asked what he watched on television, Noel Coward maintained that 'Television is for appearing on, not for looking at'. This was in the days when you only got on the telly if you were well known or important or a world expert in something or unusually gorgeous-looking or Richard Dimbleby. Nowadays there are trillions of TV channels and everybody, no matter how ordinary, dull or plug-ugly has their fifteen minutes of fame on the goggle box.

Naturally, you want to appear on a better-known channel. There's not much kudos attached to modelling scuba-diving gear on one of those blessed shopping channels. There are many ways to go about ensuring a higher profile. One is to commit some grisly murder and be caught. You will then appear at peak time on the news. Unfortunately, your whole upper body may be obscured by a grey blanket as you are hustled into a police station. But in due course photographs of you as a child, taken with primitive colour cameras, or looking sinister, or crackers, will appear on programmes along with your neighbours' announcements that you kept yourself very much to yourself. Let's face it, though, your mum isn't going to be impressed by this idea – especially if she was your victim.

A better way of getting on TV is to do something noteworthy and visually arresting. Dressing up as a chicken and abseiling down a national monument is good, so long as you keep your face visible – so all your friends know it's you – or swimming round the country, or eating worms for charity, or campaigning in some novel way against something that people hate anyway, such as dogs' excrement, or becoming an official nutcase and going on about how you've been abducted by aliens. Make a shaky video of some lights and you'll have an irresistible news story with this one.

You'll need to contact the broadcasters, of course, to let them know all about yourself and your story. You can find the names of the right people to talk to on their websites. Television programmes are desperate for material to fill the aching voids between the advertisements for cars and haemorrhoid cream, but unless you are growing another leg, or have discovered a cure for baldness that involves nude women rubbing your scalp with kittens, be prepared for some rejection.

Of course, you could always try to get on a quiz or game show, especially if you are good at storing and quickly recalling facts and figures and also look peculiar. Then there are those talent shows, which are ideal for people who cry easily and enjoy being humiliated by oafs. There are even websites now that publish requests for contestants and contributors to TV programmes. A list that I looked at not so long ago included predictable questions such as 'Do you want to share your diet stories – prime time?', 'Do you have a child aged 20–26? Is it time they flew the nest?' and 'Are you hiding a physical problem beneath your clothes which is destroying your self-confidence?' If you are steeped in popular culture, are somehow unusual or freakish and can talk about yourself incessantly, you are what's called 'a natural' for TV of this kind.

There again, if you fancy a career as a television presenter, you could do what others have done and get a degree in something like philosophy, Chinese, economics, history or English, then take a master's degree and then a doctorate, all the while working in your spare time in some chair-stacking position for your local radio station and smiling at important people. Next, travel somewhere weird for a year and, while away, set up a TV station there. Now write your CV and send it, with your showreel, to a thousand broadcasting organizations and maybe one of them will employ you in some menial role. Work your way up over the next few years, being as pushy as possible, until you find yourself in front of the camera. This takes a long time. If you don't fancy all that slog, try to have a parent who works in the industry – always a good bet.

Remember too, that sex sells and TV loves it. One of the world's most successful media pranksters, Alan Abel, has been on television countless times, insisting on protecting public decency by putting pants on animals, protesting against breast feeding (on the grounds that mothers are doing it for incestuous erotic pleasure) and describing in detail his *entirely imaginary* minuscule tallywhacker. See how you get on with that one.

How to be funny

I went to the psychiatrist the other day and I said, 'Doctor Finkelstein, I think I'm a dog.' He said, 'You'd better get on the couch.' I said, 'I'm not allowed on the furniture.'

That is what is known as 'a joke' and for every person who chuckles or smiles at one of those things there will be more than a few who sneer or remain entirely indifferent to its scintillating mirthfulness. As Dorothy Parker said, trying to be funny is a big risk because any fool can quite reasonably criticize you just by saying, 'You don't make me laugh'.

Nevertheless, chaps still seem to want to be funny, and those fellows who are able to laugh a girl into bed before you can say 'sausage on a stick' possess an undeniable advantage over those mere mortals who struggle to hold their own at some babe's barbecue.

With this in mind I thought I would pass on the benefits of my many years' experience of making people titter, which started at school when I used to put Sellotape over my mouth and blow out my cheeks like Dizzy Gillespie, causing a roar of approbation from the class. The drawback was that my parents were called in for a meeting with Mr Price, who was trying to teach us all German and wanted me to sit still and keep quiet. Three decades later, with Mr Price under the sod, I find it deeply pleasing that though I have long forgotten how to conjugate *wichsen*, *scheißen* and *ficken*, I now *get paid* for doing the things my teachers told me to stop doing. Plus my parents no longer get called up the school to explain my behaviour.

I am not going to suggest that to be funny you must do the Sellotape trick at your next cocktail party, because that would be a social gaffe worthy of my chum Colin who at some Belgravia ball asked a shimmering creature in pearls who she was and received the haughty reply 'I *live* here!' 'Oh you live 'ere do you?' said Colin, with his mouth full of crisps. 'No,' came the glacial response, '*Olivia*.'

Out in Internetland there is more advice about being funny than you can shake a stick at and I thought that before I let rip with my own comments I should see what others had to say on the subject. I have to report that I was unimpressed by the quality of the instruction on offer. Much of it appears to be written by people who don't have a clue. Nothing new there, then. Most of the advice we are ever given comes from people who don't know what they are talking about.

For example, one of the things they tell you is that being funny makes you the life and soul of the party, and that if you 'hang out with funny people' their *joie de vivre* will rub off on you. This reminded me of the story about the man who was so depressed that he went to the doctor. 'I tell you what,' said the doctor. 'Go and see Kropotkin the Clown, he's hilarious. He'll cheer you up, I guarantee it.' The man replied, 'But doctor, I *am* Kropotkin the Clown'. And it is true that, even if they are not deeply depressed, few comedians are funny all the time, especially at parties. Spike Milligan was hilarious when he was working, but he loathed parties and could be offensively rude and abrupt if you met him at one. On the other hand, people who have a reputation as hilarious life-and-soul types are, on closer inspection, often merely full of themselves.

I read somewhere else that being funny is 'an important part of job hires', and that you should 'see being funny as a positive way up the corporate ladder'. This how-to-be-funny website reported that '98 per cent of CEOs favour hiring someone with a sense of humour over someone who doesn't display such a sense'. But this is not my experience. When I worked as a drone for a well-known global business consultancy, 'being funny' went down with the partners like a mug of cold sick. If you displayed 'a sense of humour' they would give you a look as if their finger had just gone through the toilet paper and treat you thereafter as if you were radioactive.

Another thing I saw somewhere was that you should read joke books, 'and be prepared to put your foibles in the spotlight'. Well, I don't want my foibles put under any spotlight, they might get singed, and while the occasional well-told joke might be all right, jokes do not make you a funny person. This website also advised 'being witty', as if it were something you could just switch on. Wit was recommended as 'an impressive flirting tool!' though they warned rather disconcertingly that 'you might come off as a snob, or just plain weird!' They gave the following as an example of wittiness: 'Suppose a friend tells you his teacher is cross eyed [sounds unlikely], you can say "He's so cross-eyed that when he cries, the tears run down his back!"' I think Oscar Wilde would have fallen over laughing at that one. And it gets worse: 'Suppose someone says, out of the blue, "It's six o'clock!", you can say, "Thank you, Big Ben!" A playful smile and a raised eyebrow add a nice touch!' I think those exclamation marks tell you all you need to know about the sophistication of this advice-giver. Let us move quickly along.

Here is a secret: jokes are not the best way to be funny. People prefer stories from your own experience. Take the true story of Malawi's Justice Minister George Chaponda, who in 2011 announced that an anti-air-pollution bill included a provision to criminalize flatulence. 'Just go to the toilet when you feel like farting,' he said, rather bluntly you might think. Solicitor General Anthony Kamanga took issue with his interpretation of the law, telling journalists, 'How any reasonable or sensible person can construe the provision to criminalizing farting in public is beyond me.' In any case, Mr Chaponda did not explain how he was going to enforce the new prohibition.

In the end, you've either got it or you haven't. Many funny people are recognizably funny from an early age, and they are often also rather shy, disgruntled or otherwise unhappy. If you find that being funny doesn't come naturally, don't worry about it. Instead be grateful that you are not always desperate to be paid attention to, applauded and laughed at. However, if you still feel that you'd like to cause a chuckle now and again, here's a joke that is short, amusing and sounds like a personal story. I make you a present of it. 'I said to my newsagent, "Have you got a copy of *Psychic News*?" and he said, "You tell me." I said, "I had a premonition you were going to say that."'

How to persuade others

As well as being an overrated novel by Jane Austen, 'persuasion' is a method of argument, entreaty or expostulation intended to move another person or people to a belief, position or course of action. Persuasive people are highly valued by our society but the problem is that persuasion is often a con trick and persuasive people can wreak havoc, not by giving orders, but, with a variety of well-understood psychological techniques, by 'winning people over'. Politicians, salespeople and advertisers are masters of the art, but once you understand their game you'll spot them a mile off and will be better equipped either to resist their blandishments or to improve your own persuasiveness. Here are a few of their tricks – I mean techniques – which you can learn.

- Assume authority: people tend to obey authority figures. There is nothing like wearing a uniform bristling with medals to get off to a good start. Failing that, stand on a box.
- Be likeable: people are much more easily persuaded by people they like. This is the so-called 'Tupperware party' effect.
- Be handsome: in experiments, people responded much more strongly to advertisements fronted by handsome chaps than to those presented by ugly-mugs. A good haircut, a proper shave and an expensive suit will help, too.
- Be confident: in 1978, the beautifully dressed, good-looking founder of the People's Temple, Jim Jones, persuaded hundreds of otherwise intelligent men and women to poison their children and commit mass suicide mainly by assuming a supremely confident air. A good example of the power of persuasion.
- Use persuasive language: this is a big topic. Metaphors are very useful, especially if your position is weak. They are believable because of the analogy between a recognized, and often concrete, thing and the abstract or unattractive thing of which you are trying to persuade people. Better to say 'our steadfast progress to the sunny uplands of

11

recovery' than 'this hopeless period of economic downturn and falling salaries'. Don't be funny, because, as J. K. Galbraith said, 'Humor is richly rewarding to the person who employs it. It has some value in gaining and holding attention, but it has no persuasive value at all.' You are more likely to persuade people of a dubious proposition with a metaphor: 'Just as a razor is blunted by shaving, a mind is blunted by education.' It sounds believable as it flashes past your ears but it is rubbish when you think about it for a second. Next time you detect metaphorical language in an article or in an interview with a politician or business leader, you may find that it is the smell of a rat. (That was a typical one right there.)

- Be assumptive: begin with the thing you want to be accepted, and follow up with a desirable anodyne statement. For example, 'It's quite clear that global warming is a storm in a teacup so we can all relax a bit in this glorious sunshine and carry on enjoying our barbies and driving our cars.' Or, better, do it in reverse: 'Obviously you want to stay healthy for as long as you can and my new Elixir of Youth will keep you healthier for longer.'

- Use us-and-them words: use personal pronouns such as *I*, *we*, *you*, *us* and *them* to separate the good people – you and your followers – from the others – the un-people. Herr Goebbels was a master of this sort of thing: 'Some think we haven't noticed that the Jews are again trying to spread themselves all over our streets. The Jews ought, please, to observe the laws of hospitality and not behave as if they were the same as us.' Subtle and creepy.

- Use lists and contrasts: 'Punctuality, commitment and a can-do attitude is all we ask. Foot-dragging, idleness and necrophilia are not for us'. You can mix and match techniques, too. Here's an example of 'us-and-them' combined with 'contrast': 'We share a desire for peace. They share a lust for war.' Might be true, might not be true, but it is persuasive.

- Keep saying the same thing and people will believe it: repeated affirmation is persuasive. You hear this kind of trash trotted out all the time in political interviews, and politicians and lobbyists are trained to do it: 'Well, John, what I'm saying is, vote for Smith – the honest candidate, and I'm saying it because Smith *is* the honest candidate and it's why people are voting for Smith up and down the country. We all want an honest candidate and that's why Smith is the man to vote for. The real point is this, John: if you vote for Smith you'll get the honest candidate you want – the honest candidate everyone wants.' No evidence provided of Smith's purported honesty but the mantra kind of sinks in. See 'The best advertising slogans money can buy' on page 224 for more of this kind of thing.

■ Put your dynamite at the *other end* of the fuse: keep your big-bang stuff for the *ends* of your sentences. 'There is one simple thing for which every commuter secretly yearns – trains that run on time' is better for keeping its subject matter until the end. Winston Churchill's 'All the great things are simple, and many can be expressed in a single word: freedom, justice, honour, duty, mercy, hope,' would have been flabby like this: 'Freedom, justice, honour, duty, mercy, hope are simple, like all great things, many of which can be expressed in a single word'. Ending a sentence with the word 'word' is probably always a bad idea.

■ Promise and deliver: by letting people know you are going to tell them something interesting, and then keeping them in suspense, you can make them more subject to persuasion. Take this opening: 'Passing by Buckingham Palace today I saw the most incredible thing. Now, Buckingham Palace is interesting because they have experts there who are already using the kind of new gravel product that we've started producing. It's made from discarded weasel noses . . .' You can now talk about your new product for twenty minutes and your avid listeners will be paying close attention because they are dying to hear what the 'incredible thing' was that you saw.

■ Use advertisers' vocabulary: here's a list of powerful persuasion buzzwords that work – which is why they are clichés – guarantee, secure, healthy, strong, true, deserve, hurry, more, free, quick, discover, proven (a made-up word used only by advertisers and media professionals), best, you, us, them, certain, real, scientific, sure, now, improvement, sensational.

■ Threaten their emotional needs: sentences such as 'What would happen if your loved ones were eaten by lions?' cause an emotional reaction. When people are emotionally involved – laughing, crying, spitting fury – they are more open to persuasion. So, after raising the eaten-by-lions situation, you slyly mention your reassuring remedy: a guaranteed-strength lion protection spray or your low-cost lion insurance. Simple.

■ Ask them to imagine: 'What if . . . ?', 'Wouldn't it be nice if . . . ?' and 'Suppose for a minute that . . .' are powerfully persuasive formulations that overcome doubts and objections. 'Sorry I can't come out to dinner with you tomorrow; I'm washing my hair,' can be overcome by, 'What if me and my Italian brother-in-law with a bent nose came round and kicked your flippin' door in, lady?', which is subtly persuasive.

How to understand the British Isles

I have a friend who was born in the United Kingdom but not in Great Britain. He votes in English elections but isn't English and he has an Irish passport but wasn't born in the Republic of Ireland. Confused? You are in good company because everybody is confused when it comes to understanding what's what in the British Isles. Mistakes in terminology are easy to make, even if you're English, I mean British, or do I mean Great British, or United Kingdomish? It's terribly confusing.

If you have a look at the Euler (pronounced 'oiler') diagram below you'll see a clear illustration of the messiness of this problem.

In geographical terms, the British Isles are an archipelago (a scattering of islands) consisting of Great Britain *and Ireland* – two separate countries – and more than 1,000 surrounding islands, many of which are very small. Part of the difficulty in using the right terms for this mess is that the political

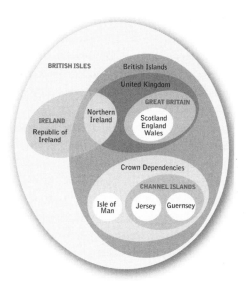

How the British Isles fit together. Geographical terms are in capitals, political terms in upper and lower case.

and geographic descriptions get confused and sometimes overlap. Also, of course, people use words loosely in everyday conversation.

Take 'the British Islands' for example, which is a legal term that nobody ever uses in ordinary speech. Considered as a unit, it consists of the United Kingdom, the Channel Islands of Jersey and Guernsey (much nearer France than England) and the Isle of Man (or just Mann). The Isle of Man and the Channel Islands are so-called 'Crown Dependencies', which are independently administered jurisdictions, with their own tax systems, that are not part of the UK although the British monarch is their head of state.

The UK, which is part of the British Isles and part of the British Islands, is sometimes wrongly referred to as Great Britain or Britain. Precisely speaking, the UK is the United Kingdom of Great Britain and

Northern Ireland, a constitutional monarchy that occupies the island of Great Britain, the north-eastern bit of the island of Ireland – not the same thing as the *country* of Ireland – and the other islands of the archipelago, except for the Crown Dependencies. The four countries of the United Kingdom are England, Scotland, Wales and Northern Ireland. The three countries of Great Britain are England, Scotland and Wales. Got all that? If not, have another look at the diagram.

'England' is often used by foreigners, and by some careless English people, to mean 'Britain'. Sean Connery, a Scot, is often referred to on American television as being 'English' or 'from England'. Look out if you make this mistake because he is a fire-breathing Scottish nationalist who will carefully explain things to you.

Now we come to Ireland, which is a sovereign republic (that is to say, a separate country, not run by, and nothing to do with, the UK). The Republic of Ireland, as it is often called so as to avoid confusing the political state with the geographical island, occupies the bigger, bottom left-hand bit of the island of Ireland. It is sometimes referred to by its Irish name, Éire, to avoid confusion (some hope), even though 'Éire' just means 'Ireland'. Not surprisingly, especially if you know anything about the history of these islands, people in the Republic often take exception to having their country referred to as part of the *British* Isles.

Northern Ireland, which is often called 'Ulster', mainly by Unionists (who wish to keep Northern Ireland as part of the UK), has its own unhappy history, which would require a whole book to go into. 'Ulster' is one of Ireland's four historic provinces, and consists of the nine northern counties. The United Kingdom, however, governs the six counties that are part of the UK, and the Republic of Ireland governs the other three.

By the way, that friend I mentioned at the beginning of this section was born in Northern Ireland and chose to have an Irish passport – though he's entitled to both British and Irish. He lives in London, so can vote in English local elections.

Time for a lie down by the pool.

How to mix a Manhattan

Traditionally, a gentleman does not drink any drink that contains more than two ingredients. Ice is an ingredient. This rather does for cocktails, doesn't it? However, if you don't care what people think you are supposed to do – how stylish of you! – then there's no reason you shouldn't drink a Manhattan if you fancy one or mix one for your friends.

A Manhattan is a brownish cocktail made with whisky (usually rye or bourbon), sweet vermouth and bitters. Bourbon is sweeter and fuller bodied than rye. Rye will lend the cocktail a drier character and a 'spicy' or 'fruity' flavour, which is sometimes compared to that of an Islay whisky (pronounced Eye-la by those who know). Islay is the southernmost of the Inner Hebridean Islands off the west coast of Scotland. There are eight or nine distilleries on the island producing Scotch with a powerful smoky-peaty flavour, for serious drinkers only. If you are trying to mix a Manhattan in Britain, and find yourself stuck for the basic ingredient, just use a Scotch of your choice (my chum Howard tells me this is called a 'Rob Roy'), though unless I had money to burn I wouldn't put a single malt whisky in a cocktail. The cocktail is generally garnished with a maraschino cherry with a stem. (But why?) Or it can be served on the rocks.

The cocktail is said to have been created in the 1870s at the Manhattan Club in New York City for Winston Churchill's mother, Lady Randolph Churchill, an American otherwise known as Jennie Jerome, although the story is probably false. Another claim is that it was named in honour of the city's water system, which ran rather brown at about this time.

Mixing cocktails is one of those activities that is seen by many, especially, perhaps, ladies, as sophisticated and sexy. Actually, mixing a Manhattan is about as sophisticated as making toad in the hole. Here's how.

Ingredients and equipment

1.69 fl oz (5 cl) rye or bourbon
0.68 fl oz (2 cl) sweet red vermouth
Dash of Angostura bitters

A maraschino cherry
Ice
Martini glass
Cocktail shaker

Method

1 Fill your glass with ice, to chill.
2 Half fill the cocktail shaker with ice and leave for a minute or two.
3 Strain any water from the shaker, then pour in everything except the cherry.
4 Shake well (try to look sophisticated, not as if you're having a seizure).
5 Empty the ice from the glass.
6 Strain the cocktail mixture into the glass.
7 Drop in the maraschino cherry.
8 Serve quick – it's getting warm.

How to stop frowning and start smiling

It takes more muscles to frown than to smile. Anyway, that's what people always say. Maybe it's true and maybe it isn't, so what? It takes more muscles to eat than it does to just lie there. Is that supposed to mean that you should lie there rather than eat? There is a lot of rubbishy unwanted advice of this kind around. 'Cheer up, it might never happen', that's another one. 'Have a nice day' is popular, too, and also rather irritating – suppose I have other plans?

There's this idea about that we are all supposed not only to *be* happy all the time but also that we must *look* happy. Happiness has become a compulsory emotion and one that we are obliged to wear on our faces all day long. The American 'Declaration of Independence' actually calls 'the pursuit of happiness' an 'unalienable right', without explaining what that might mean, but I think the chasing of happiness has resulted in a lot more frowning than smiling.

If you are having an operation or are suffering from some deadly disease, they tell you to think positive and act positive, and you sometimes get the feeling that if you get worse you are going to be blamed for not having smiled enough.

Members of the 'leave me alone – I like being miserable' club have their own misery-membership badge, and it is the frown. The frown is caused by the corrugator *supercilii*, a narrow pyramid-shaped muscle at the end of the inner end of the eyebrow, just above the *orbicularis oculi*. The corrugator draws the eyebrows downwards and inwards, producing the classic vertical upper-nose wrinkles of the frowning forehead.

Not all smiles are alike, though. There's the so-called 'Pan-Am Smile', that fake smile in which the zygomatic major muscle (which raises the corners of the mouth) is contracted, but the *orbicularis oculi* muscle (which raises the cheeks to form crow's feet at the corners of the eyes) is not. This smile is named in honour of the now defunct Pan American Airways, whose cabin crew treated each and every one of their passengers to one of their automatic 'Duchenne smiles', which itself is named after the French physician Guillaume Duchenne, who first identified it. Actually, it's not just cabin crew who dole these out. You get the feeling that many of the smiles you receive in everyday life are professional Duchenne smiles.

Nonetheless if you feel that you would much rather smile than frown – and I've nothing against it – here are a few simple tips for increasing their number.

1 Don't expect happiness. If it comes, accept it; if not, never mind.
2 Remember that most people are not happy a lot of the time.
3 Don't chase smiles. Pursuing happiness is like trying to catch fog in a sieve.
4 Lower your expectations and be content with less.
5 Nature cheers people up. Have a look at some of it.
6 Go fishing, or learn the lute, or plant some bulbs. Such activities promote smiles.

7   Don't let little things get to you. A tough one, this.

8   Have a laugh – you'll smile more afterwards. Try these one-liners:

- I want to die peacefully in my sleep, like my dad. Not screaming in terror, like the passengers on his bus.
- I went to the corner shop and bought three corners.
- Sex is not the answer. Sex is the question. 'Yes' is the answer.
- I'm on a whisky diet. I've lost three days already.

What do you mean they aren't funny? Honestly, there's no pleasing some people.

Self-confidence in a trice

I saw a strapline on the cover of a men's health magazine recently that said 'Ten tips to instantly become self-confident'. Whoever wrote that was certainly confident in himself to the extent that he didn't notice, or cared nothing about, that rather hideous split infinitive. Some of the articles you see in these magazines are a bit unrealistic, to be honest. I once saw one recommending that nervous chaps conquer their diffidence by sitting in the front row in public assemblies, wearing eye-catching clothing and speaking up in meetings. These are things of just the kind that the poor confidence-lacking man *wants* to do but *can't* because he lacks confidence. There's no point telling him just to do them, he needs a few techniques to help him banish his knocking knees, dry mouth and feelings of deep un-worth.

Somebody once asked Eleanor Roosevelt how on earth she managed to address audiences of thousands with such cool, confident composure and she replied, 'I wear my invisible crown'. There is great wisdom in this remark for confidence is often nothing more than a confidence *trick*. If you start by looking confident you soon move on to feeling confident. This is called behavioural therapy.

Anybody with an ounce of self-awareness is going to be a bit nervous in public situations. So the first thing to do is to recognize it. The second thing to do is to conceal it from everybody. Never admit your nerves to anybody else; you'll just make them jittery too, which helps nobody.

The third thing to do is to concentrate on your performance as a confident person. Think about the confident-looking people you admire, maybe it's the President or Prime Minister, your old headmaster or the Pope. Now take a leaf from their books. What are they doing that makes them ooze confidence? Probably they are standing erect yet somewhat relaxed, they are speaking in an easily audible voice and smiling a lot. What do you mean you can't smile? Start pretending, and before you can say 'zygomatic major' you'll be smiling like a man who has just won the lottery being massaged by nymphomaniacal teenagers while being told he's been awarded the Nobel Prize.

Stand with your legs somewhat apart and be deliberate in your movements. Nervous, jerky or hesitant moves not only fail to look confident, they make *others* nervous too. Keep movements to a minimum. High peripheral movement (HPM) is seen as a sign of weakness.

Next, make eye contact with people. If you find this almost impossibly difficult, join the club. Eye contact with unknown people can be profoundly threatening, as you'll realize if you've ever been stared at by a large dog or a group of strangers with knives. But if you consciously train yourself to look people in the eye and hold their gaze for a few seconds, you will find yourself being seen as very self-confident.

Smile frequently. High smile rates are generally regarded as a sign of confidence.

Try pausing every now and again, especially just before you speak. This causes people to wait for you, putting you in a psychologically dominant position. Not only will this make you seem more confident, it will – after some practice – make you *feel* more confident.

Before you approach a group take two or three deep breaths. This tends to relax you and will also help your 'good-afternoons' to come out with aplomb instead of with a squeak. If your mouth goes dry, bite the tip of your tongue. This is discreet and will give you enough saliva to speak normally.

Practise all of the above. You can't remember all this advice straightaway so practise it in small chunks in front of a mirror, then with a couple of friends down the pub, then with a group of people, then with larger groups of people you don't know and finally with an audience of violent football thugs in Wembley Stadium, and you'll be regarded as the most self-confident person in the entire world.

Of course, don't overdo it. You don't want to end up like one of those ghastly bombastic motivational speakers. That's not self-confidence, that's boorishness.

How to remember people's names

A couple of months ago I was asked to write something for an advertising agency. This is not a job for a grown man, but there you go. Anyway they invited me to meet the team. There were several of them there, none of whom had I met before, except for the boss, and it was important that I remembered all their names. 'Oh, why bother?' you might ask. 'Just remember the important people and forget the rest.' Fine, except that people move up fast in this business and you don't want to alienate the next MD, who is now a lowly account executive. Besides, it's good manners – although I do recall a chap once saying to me, 'I remember your name but I can't put a face to you', which I thought delightfully rude.

Anyway, the method I used to recall the names of the people I just mentioned is the one below. It works so well that I can tell you now, weeks later, what they were all called. In the order they were sitting, they were: Marc, Chris, Katie, Richard and Meg. I even remember the name of the guy who couldn't make it: Keith. That is only six people, but remembering just one name can be hard enough when people are asking you if you want tea, or would like to hang your coat up, how far you've come and so forth.

There are different ways of remembering different things. In the case of a shopping list, you might want to remember the items in order so you need a special technique for that. For names, all you need to do is link the person to his or her name by using some memorable feature. The link method is pretty easy so let me tell you how I used it in the case I mentioned.

The first two people who came in were Marc and Chris. I told them my name, shook hands and then smiled for England while I turned Chris into Christ by imagining him crucified in the sun. With common names, it is useful to have an image to hand and this is one I use a lot. With Marc, I imagined him with a huge black splodge (mark) on his nose. The more ludicrous, rude or extreme the image, the better you will remember it. Then came Katie. Although she bore little resemblance to CBS news anchor Katie Couric, I imagined her with TV makeup all over her face, reading the news to me. Meg became the children's character Mog the cat, and I imagined her with a cat asleep on her head during the whole meeting. Richard I knew and Keith, who couldn't make it, became bibulous TV chef Keith Floyd, who couldn't come because he was out cold on the kitchen floor.

I know what you are thinking: suppose you have to remember the names of a delegation from China or the Czech Republic? Well, I was once introduced to a chap called Orrin Springenatic so I imagined him pushing his oar into the water (oar in/Orrin) and springing out of the water – actually on springs – into his attic. I'm used to doing this now so I'm able to recall my own links, though you might find them obscure. You must invent links that work for you and are personal.

You can help yourself by asking the person to repeat his or her name, if there's time. Say the name aloud and remark on it if it is unusual and ask how it is spelled or where it originates. Use the name from time to time too and if you are going to meet again, jot down the name/s after you leave, for later reference.

If you use this technique, and if you practise it, you will find that at the end of a party, meeting, or whatever, you will have little trouble using people's names as you say goodbye. This will impress the hell out of them as they struggle to remember not only your name but possibly your face, too.

The more you do this, the better you will get at it. But you are only human and sometimes you will forget things. If you think you have forgotten a person's name you can either say, 'I'm sorry, I've forgotten your name', which people understand, or you can take a stab at it and say, 'Yes, that's right, Lucille'. If she replies 'Do you mind, this isn't a dress, as you seem to imagine; my name is Giacomo and I'm the Papal Nuncio', you have goofed badly.

How to distil single malt Scotch whisky

My Scottish brother-in-law likes the following joke: 'Is anything worn beneath the kilt? No, it's all in good working order', and he often tells me it after half a bottle of Laphroaig (which isn't so much a Scotch whisky as a spelling test). There's a big difference between good Scotch, like that one, and mediocre whisky, and it's all to do with the ingredients, the method of manufacture and the craftsmanship of the distiller. Here is a description of the basic process, which is a fascinating one.

The ingredients of malt whisky are just barley and water, with a little yeast for encouragement. Simple is always good. The first thing to do when you're making Scotch is to steep (soak) the barley grains in the water until they sprout. It's no good just running a hose from your bathroom because the quality of the water will have a significant effect on the final taste of the whisky. Distillers boast about the particular deliciousness of their local spring, loch or stream, and quite rightly. But if you want something that tastes a bit of swimming pools, then just turn on the tap.

Anyway, the germinating barley is now spread over the floor of a malting house (or a big garage, I suppose) so that it can sprout a bit over the next couple of weeks. During this process – to allow the air to get to it – it is turned regularly, either automatically or with specialist paddles. I guess you could even use a snow shovel. All this time the starch in the barley is turning to sugar and, after a bit, at just the right moment (you've got to know what you're doing), it is put into a drying kiln to stop the germination. Kilns used always to be peat-fired and the smoke from the smouldering peat would impregnate the barley, thus imparting that delicious peaty-smoky taste so distinctive of many good whiskies. Today, peat smoke is still used to flavour Scotch, but it may now be blown over the barley as it is dried by hot air. Hmm.

The dried barley is next milled to make a sugar-rich flour called 'grist', which is mixed with more water, this time hot, to create the 'mash'. This mash goes into a 'mash tun', a big metal tank, where it is stirred to let the sugar seep into the water. The resultant liquid, called 'wort', is then poured into giant wooden buckets called 'wash backs', where it is cooled. The solid leftovers ('draff') are fed to cows. You have to admit that, even if you don't like Scotch, the manufacturing business has a marvellous vocabulary.

The fermentation process is done in the wash backs by adding yeast, which feeds off the barley's sugar to create the magic ingredient, alcohol. No surprise then that the word 'whisky' comes from the Scots Gaelic *uisge beatha*, literally meaning 'water of life'. The fermenting liquid produces a vigorous foam with a smell reminiscent of brewing beer. It tastes the same, too, but contains only about 8 or 9 per cent alcohol.

It is at this point that several bucket-loads of gravy browning are stirred in, along with a few tins of anchovy fillets. Not really, I was just checking you were paying attention. What really happens is that the distillation now begins.

Two stills are used for the distilling the spirit, the so-called 'wash still' for the first distillation and the 'spirit still' for the second. Run-of-the-mill whisky manufacturers use a process called continuous distillation but under the Scotch Whisky Regulations of 2009 single malt Scotch must be distilled using pot stills. These copper stills have changed little over the centuries, having a gourd-shaped body and a long skinny neck, sometimes compared, unpersuasively, to that of a swan. Somewhat miraculously, different neck lengths and pot shapes have an effect on the character of the final Scotch.

Anyway, inside the still the liquid is heated to boiling point and evaporates to the top. There it goes through the long skinny pipe to be condensed into a liquid with an alcohol content of about 20 per cent, so-called 'low wine'.

The low wine is then distilled again. This second distillation is divided into three 'cuts'. The first stream to come off, so-called 'foreshot', which to me sounds like something from golf, is a very strong, undrinkable fluid full of methanol (poisonous wood alcohol). The stuff which comes off next, called the 'middle cut', is what the distiller is after and he collects this in a tank. The final part of the stream from the second distillation, the descriptively termed 'feints', does not contain enough alcohol for any practical use, so it is added to the next batch of low wine. The distillers being Scottish, nothing is wasted.

Because spirits earn the government so much tax money, the entire process is closely scrutinized by Her Majesty's Revenue and Customs. Any testing of the distilled spirit has to be done via something called the 'spirit safe'. The one I saw in a Scottish distillery had Revenue seals on it and looked like a sort of polished-brass and glass coffin.

If all the tests are OK, the spirit is now ready for maturation, a vital part of the process, which takes place in oak barrels that have been used to make American bourbon whiskey, sherry, rum or port. The casks are sealed and stored in a warehouse controlled by the Revenue. Scotch whisky must remain 'in bond' for at least three years and may not be described as whisky before three years are up.

Over time, the barrels imbue the Scotch with their own peculiar characteristics. Many malt whisky distillers on the west coast of Scotland boast of their open storehouses, which, they say, allow the sea air to transmit its salty, seaweedy flavour to the Scotch. Do I detect a whiff of marketing?

Each year some 2 per cent of the liquid from maturing barrels is lost through evaporation, and a twelve-year-old Scotch will have lost a quarter of its volume, the so-called 'angel's share', by the time it is finally poured into a glass by some man, with a nose that looks like a brain, beside his roaring log fire.

The alcoholic strength of bottled malt whiskies varies greatly, but is commonly less than 50 per cent. Some connoisseurs maintain that the more alcoholic Scotches are less flavoursome, owing to a greater presence of tasty by-products in the weaker drinks.

Old Scotch is often more expensive than young, though it is not necessarily superior. Indeed, much of the smoky flavour so delighted in by the Scotch cognoscenti is lost over time. If you like 'em smoky, drink 'em young.

How to hypnotize people (really)

Have you ever arrived somewhere after a long drive, slammed the car door and then realized that you can't remember having done the journey? This is known as 'highway hypnosis' and is akin to common hypnosis.

The term 'hypnosis' comes from Hypnos, the Greek personification of sleep. It was coined by the Scottish surgeon and hypnosis pioneer James Braid (1795–1860), in about 1841. He based his work on that of Franz Mesmer (1734–1815), who practised 'mesmerism' (unsurprisingly), in which he passed his hands in front of a subject's body, believing that something mysterious was flowing out of his fingers and affecting his subject. Under the influence of the 'Scottish School of Common Sense', Braid removed some of Mesmer's 'animal magnetism' nonsense from the theory and described hypnosis more plainly as 'a peculiar condition of the nervous system, induced by a fixed and abstracted attention of the mental and visual eye, on one object, not of an exciting nature'.

The military, who have studied hypnotism, have found no clear evidence that it exists as a definable phenomenon beyond 'ordinary suggestion, high motivation, and subject expectancy'. Irving Kirsch,

professor of psychology at the University of Hull, recently described hypnotism as a non-deceptive placebo, which openly makes use of suggestion and amplifies its effects. James Randi, a magician and professional sceptic, calls it 'a mutual agreement of the operator and the subject that the subject will cooperate in following suggestions'.

Hypnosis usually starts with 'hypnotic induction' (the softening-up bit), typically a series of preliminary instructions and suggestions. Subjects are not 'put to sleep' but are simply encouraged to focus their attention, and to become calm and relaxed. In this state they show an increased response to suggestion. The most influential induction technique was Braid's original 'eye-fixation' method, also known as 'Braidism', which he described like this:

Take any bright object (I generally use my lancet case) between the thumb and fore and middle fingers of the left hand; hold it from about eight to fifteen inches from the eyes, at such position above the forehead as may be necessary to produce the greatest possible strain upon the eyes and eyelids, and enable the patient to maintain a steady fixed stare at the object. The patient must be made to understand that he is to keep the eyes steadily fixed on the object, and the mind riveted on the idea of that one object. It will be observed, that owing to the consensual adjustment of the eyes, the pupils will be at first contracted: they will shortly begin to dilate, and after they have done so to a considerable extent, and have assumed a wavy motion, if the fore and middle fingers of the right hand, extended and a little separated, are carried from the object towards the eyes, most probably the eyelids will close involuntarily, with a vibratory motion. If this is not the case, or the patient allows the eyeballs to move, desire him to begin anew, giving him to understand that he is to allow the eyelids to close when the fingers are again carried towards the eyes, but that the eyeballs must be kept fixed, in the same position, and the mind riveted to the one idea of the object held above the eyes. It will generally be found that the eyelids close with a vibratory motion, or become spasmodically closed.

Braid ultimately abandoned the induction technique as unnecessary, and as the popularity of the swinging fob watch died off over the decades, verbal suggestion became the keystone of the hypnotist's art, science, hoodwinkery or whatever you like to call it.

Modern hypnosis is used for entertainment as well as therapy, and the field of erotic hypnotism, or so-called 'titnotism', is perhaps a combination of the two.

If you'd like to hypnotize someone – maybe a young lady who has just come back for coffee – then you will be interested to hear that it is easier than you might think. But first, the small print. When you hypnotize someone you need her (I'm going to assume your subject is female) to be agreeable to it. If she is hostile or frightened, it won't work. She must trust you and let you control the proceedings.

You are going to relax your subject, and there are various techniques you can use to ease the process. For one thing, you need to reassure her by not being hesitant. So speak in your normal voice but with confidence. Remain calm but authoritative. Don't scream like the regimental sergeant major but try to speak slowly and soothingly (without sounding like Vincent Price).

Before you begin the hypnotism make sure you are not going to be interrupted. It's going to be tricky if there's a dogfight in the street, or the baby starts screaming, or you are next to a busy bomb-disposal training facility.

1 Explain to your subject that you are not going to ask her to do anything illegal, embarrassing, harmful or against her principles (unless this is the girl I just mentioned who has come back for coffee). Tell her that she will remain conscious, but relaxed, and that it will not be like a Hollywood-style 'trance'. Reassure her that you can't make her do anything she doesn't want to, and that she can't get 'stuck' in a hypnotic state. Tell her that she will be aware of things going on around her, and will probably remember the whole thing afterwards.

2 Ask your subject to sit or lie down comfortably.

3 Say: 'Take a deep breath and release it slowly. As you let it out, close your eyes and begin to be aware of yourself relaxing.'

4 Every now and then tell your subject she's doing well. This is an odd situation and a bit of reassurance goes a long way.

5 Ask your subject to focus her attention on various parts of her body (polite ones only, please) and to relax them. You might begin by saying, 'Become aware of your arms. Focus on them. Relax the muscles. Feel them relaxing. Let them become more relaxed, and more comfortable. Let them become limp, and loose, and relaxed; more and more comfortable.' The mesmeric repetition is important. Progress to the neck, legs, back and so forth.

6 Keep going until you spot one or more signs of hypnosis, which include slower, deeper breathing, fluttering eyelids, light twitching of the fingers, arms or legs, general relaxation and a loosening of the muscles, including those of the face. (If her face actually falls off, you've gone too far.)

7 Now you can do the business: persuade her to give up smoking, suggest that she will feel a powerful urge to cook you a delicious dinner, or encourage her to believe that her interview for the job of president of the company tomorrow will be highly successful.

8 When you've finished the business, maintain the formality of the process by explaining that that you will count up to five. Say: 'By the time I reach five, your eyes will have opened, and you will be fully awake, feeling fresh and relaxed.' Allow your slow count to become firmer as you approach five. If she hasn't opened her eyes by number four she is probably very relaxed. Just say, 'When I count *five* your eyes will open and you will be awake, relaxed and refreshed. *Five* – eyes open, awake, relaxed and refreshed.' If she still fails to open her eyes she may be dead.

That's it. Are you feeling sleepy?

How to eat what you like and lose weight, too

I went on a special diet once that allowed me to eat anything I liked – cream cakes, pizzas by the dozen, steak, sausages, the lot – without putting on an ounce of weight. The trouble was that I wasn't allowed to swallow any of it. It was a tasty diet but not very satisfying. I tried other diets, such as the water diet (rather bland), the cucumber diet (like a green version of the water diet) and the cabbage diet (not for the faint-hearted), but none of them satisfied my hunger, though I did get thinner. I knew there must be a way round this; after all, the French are famous for their fantastic food, yet they are not a fat nation. So I looked up the latest research and I found a few easy tips – not a diet – that, if you follow them, will allow you to eat what you like and lose weight, too.

- Eat protein: protein makes you feel full and keeps you feeling full for longer than fat or carbohydrate. Eggs, milk, meat, fish and beans are all good at this. Gammon and eggs with bubble and squeak is a brilliant combination, and you can eat it for breakfast, lunch or dinner. Apologies if you are a vegetarian or religiously disinclined to eat meats of various kinds.
- Eat vegetables: vegetables contain plant cellulose (fibre), which is indigestible but important for keeping the gut scoured. Fibre absorbs water, fills you up and eases the passage of everything through the pipes at the same time.
- Eat soup: drinking a pint of water before a meal is supposed to fill you up and make you eat less. But it doesn't work because it goes right through the system. If, instead, you mix your food, say steak, mushrooms, gravy, potatoes and vegetables, with water to make a soup it will – surprisingly – take your body more time to digest everything than if you ate the steak, mushrooms, gravy, potatoes and vegetables separately. And will leave you satisfied for longer. Homemade vegetable soup will also fill you up and has almost no calories in it. If you *start* all your meals with soup you'll tend to eat a little less of everything else, too.

- Don't be a pig: during the war the British population ate whatever they could get hold of including generous amounts of beer, sugar and fat milk. But they stayed thin as rakes. This was because they didn't overeat. There's no reason you shouldn't eat anything you like, but you needn't be a pig about it. People tend to eat what's on the plate in front of them so, although there's no need to introduce government food rationing, try using smaller bowls and plates. It's that simple. As a rule when you're dining out, order the smallest available portion of everything. I'm not saying *small* portions, I'm saying *normal-size* portions. You'll find that the food that arrives will be plenty instead of enough for twenty fat giants, and you'll be saving money, too. At home, take enough and no more. That's not difficult, is it? And if you are at one of those awful functions with a buffet, don't go mad. The stuff on offer is likely to be pretty fattening anyway, so go for the chicken legs or other protein (to fill you up) and just have one sausage roll, not fifteen.
- Don't get hungry: I had a dieting friend who decided to eat nothing all day, and went to bed a proud man. He woke at 3 a.m. with a stomach rumbling like Niagara Falls but found nothing in the house except half a jar of honey, some flour, an egg and a bit of milk. Being creative, he made two pounds of honey pancakes and undid a whole day's starvation, ending up much fatter than if he had eaten normally.
- Eat dairy: the body works in mysterious ways and it is known that eating dairy products such as cheese and milk (especially lower fat ones) causes your body to excrete more fat (about double the amount) than if you don't, by binding to the fat so that more of it is eliminated and less ends up on the old tum. Plus its protein content will help to fill you up – a double whammy.
- Eat-diary: it has been found that knowing what you've eaten results in your eating about 10 per cent less overall. So keeping a diary of what goes down the old gravy tunnel will work even if all you do is scribble it on the fridge with your girlfriend's eyebrow pencil.
- Count calories: this might sound boring but being aware of roughly how much energy (calories) is in food helps you to avoid doing stupid

things. A carelessly snacked muffin is likely to outdo your entire lunch for calories. It's all there on the label, in case you're wondering. And you need to stay awake. Although something natural like a pint of freshly squeezed orange juice might sound healthy it is going to be groaning with fruit-sugar (more calories).

■ Exercise: oh gawd! It's all about using up more calories than you take in through the gob. You've got to spend more calories than you earn. So exercise is vital. One knackering sprint round the park may use up a vanishingly small number of calories, but the calorie-burning goes on well into the next day. And just moving around a bit, walking upstairs instead of going in the lift, washing the car, or even standing instead of sitting burn calories without you really doing much. Walking is brilliantly good, and simple, so walk to the restaurant and back. A very slimming exercise during dinner is to put your hands on the table-edge and *push away*.

■ Have a good laugh: an article in the *International Journal of Obesity* (2007) reported that chuckling for fifteen minutes a day burns enough calories to shift five pounds of flab over a year, and a belly laugh uses as much energy as walking half a mile. Anyway, it can't do you any harm.

■ Mind the booze: alcohol is packed with calories. Answer: don't drink quite so much of it. If you enjoy going on a bender, don't make it a daily occurrence, and when you stagger back into the kitchen at 2 a.m. don't eat all the leftover rice pudding and pizza in the fridge while you fry a big packet of sausages. Just have a cracker and a pickled onion. Who the hell do I think I'm kidding?

How to beat all your phobias in about ten minutes

Last night I was seated at my piano when a thought came to me, and it was this: I must get myself some lessons in how to play this thing. The trouble is that it would probably take me ten years of intensive training to get much further than 'Dance of the Pixies' and I fear the cost of those

1,000 lessons with Alfred Brendel would bankrupt me. Of course, that 'fear' is of a different sort to the feeling you get when you see smoke coming from the wing of your Boeing 747 or a knife-wielding maniac leaps out at you from behind some dustbins down a dark alley. Nevertheless, I'm now going to tell you how to conquer all your fears in about ten minutes.

I remember reading some research that a man called Bill Tancer did into fear, in a book called *Click: What Millions of People are doing Online and Why it Matters*, which at the time of writing is number 1,392,098 in Amazon's popularity rankings. Actually, I'm not sure that what anyone does online matters, but I looked Bill up anyway and according to his online biography he is the general manager of global research at 'Hitwise, the world's leading online competitive intelligence services'. I'm not sure quite what that means, if anything, or even whether the grammar is right, but Bill's research interested me because he'd found the top ten fears most searched for on the internet. These are those listed below. Beside each one I've given you the latest psychological wisdom on banishing it.

1 Flying: jazz guitarist Wes Montgomery was once asked to play at Ronnie Scott's Soho jazz club but declined because he was terrified of flying. So Ronnie personally flew out to California to hold his hand on the flight over to London. As they taxied to the runway the already heavily sweating Montgomery started to shake with terror. In his best reassuring voice, Scott said 'Look at it this way, Wes: when it's your time to die, it's your time to die.' 'I know,' replied Montgomery, 'but I don't want to die when it's the *pilot's* time to die.' Heavy sedation (try a few large Scotches) is the answer here.

2 Heights: I'm not very good with heights myself and my knees tend to go all wobbly. Once, coming out of the lift at the top of the Empire State Building, I looked down through the gap between the door and the floor and could see the sharply receding 'chimney' up which we had travelled. It gave me the willies – with knobs on – and I started to make mouse-like squeaking noises. On another occasion, I was persuaded to go up the not-all-that-high lighthouse on Plymouth Hoe.

34

Steeling myself, I bent double and squeezed into the narrow staircase, where I was immediately overcome by claustrophobia. I should have had a few large Scotches beforehand.

3 Clowns: clowns don't bother me, except for their not being very – or at all – funny. If you are frightened of them I suggest you just imagine them falling over, or having water poured into their trousers, or getting a custard pie in the face. That will stop them seeming so fierce. Hang on a minute, that is what happens to them anyway. I don't know what the problem is here. Just avoid going to the circus (*obviously*) or have a few large whiskies to calm your nerves.

4 Intimacy: if you are frightened of intimacy I suggest you simply avoid it. It's not compulsory and it can't spring out at you from a dark alley.

5 Death: listen, before you were born you had been effectively dead for billions of years. Did it bother you then? No, of course not. If you are, on the other hand, frightened of hellfire retribution from a vindictive deity, then you should either moderate your behaviour or stop believing such fairy tales.

6 Rejection: nobody likes rejection but it is a normal part of life, like indigestion. You can avoid it by never doing or saying anything and never meeting or talking to anyone, but that isn't a life. Best thing to do if rejected is lick your wounds, pick yourself up and try again. Either that or drown the humiliating memory with a bottle or two of Scotch.

7 People: yes, they can be horrible, but avoidance is hardly an option. I think our old friend the intake of several large whiskies is the answer here.

8 Snakes: move to Antarctica.

9 Success: I don't get this one at all. I can understand fear of failure, but *success*? What's the matter with you? Actually, I don't think anyone really fears success – it's one of those made-up psychiatric things that they use to label people they can't persuade to stay in ruinously expensive psychoanalysis for another ten years. 'You won't continue, Mr Smith? You're afraid of success, that's your problem. That will be £350, please.'

10 Driving: *other people's* driving is what scares me. My own driving is a model of exquisite perfection. Men in white vans, with 'clean me' scratched in the mud on their sides, who appear from nowhere and cut you up, boy racers who speed past you at ninety in built-up areas and little old ladies peering at you through the steering wheel as they go the wrong way down the M1, that's what scares me. I control my fear by always drinking a few large Scotches before I get behind the controls. You should try it; it's guaranteed to banish all fear and send you off into a lovely doze. (My publisher's Legal Department browned their trousers on reading this. It is a *joke*. Obviously, you should never drink and drive – *as if you would*.)

How to win prestige

'In my opinion, most of the great men of the past were only there for the "beer" – the wealth, prestige, and grandeur that went with the power.' So said the prestigious historian A. J. P. Taylor, who was so prestigious a historian that he used to present off-the-cuff half-hour talks on historical subjects on the TV entirely without notes, and impress the hell out of everyone. Unfortunately, his prestige was rather undermined by his turbulent private life, and it certainly wasn't enough to protect him against a car that rudely ran him down in 1984 as he crossed the road to buy some coffee.

According to American sociologist C. Wright Mills, prestige is 'the shadow of money and power', which I suppose is why people want it so much. It's hard to get hold of, so many people who regard it as worth having spend years chasing after it, and, though it doesn't cost anything, its accoutrements do. Nonetheless, if you'd like a bit of prestige yourself, here a few ways you might go about getting some of the stuff.

■ Dress smart: it's no good traipsing about in a cardigan full of holes; get yourself a proper suit and some decent shoes. A three-piece tailored suit is going to be expensive but it will do wonders for your prestige.

- Get a good haircut and maintain a scrupulous shave: there's no prestige in dreadlocks and stubble.
- Work for a prestigious organization: if you work for the United Nations or the World Bank, even in a lowly position, you can legitimately borrow some of their authority and an aura of prestige will naturally surround you. If, on the other hand, you work for a garbage disposal firm, even as the boss, it ain't gonna help your prestige any, even though you may be doing great things for street cleanliness. And neither, if it comes to that, are you going to smell too sweet when meeting the Lord Lieutenant in your noisome dungarees.
- Speak properly: I once knew a dentist who was desperate for the patients whom he regarded as prestigious to see him as prestigious himself. He had a polished brass plate, with his name and post-nominal letters engraved on it, put up outside his door; he had expensive wallpaper put up and he got himself a well-spoken secretary. But, having rather a common accent himself, he had to work hard to acquire what he thought to be prestigious pronunciation and grammar. When he was doing a bit of root canal work on posh patients he would always say, 'Open *widely*,' believing this to be more proper. He let down his guard with me, though, and just used to say, 'Open big'.
- Don't drive a beaten-up car: I know a glamorous, and rather interestingly unusual, magician called Fay Presto, who turns up to posh dos in a huge car, driven by a chap in a liveried uniform. People are unaware that she lives in a modest flat and has to change the car tyres herself. They read a huge amount into her fur stole and the prestigious Bentley. So take a leaf from her book.
- Be distant: familiarity breeds contempt, and as General de Gaulle, a very prestigious chap, pointed out, prestige doesn't work without distance. So maintain an air of mystery, and never apologize or explain yourself.

If you are ambitious for authority, prestige is going to be vital, especially if you are no good at anything useful. As someone said, if you want to make ambitious people waste time running errands, you must bait the hook with prestige. Then they will travel miles to give talks to bored audiences, write forewords to dull books and serve on mind-numbing committees, all for no fee. If they think it's prestigious, they will do it. Frankly I'm not interested in prestige. I'd rather put on my sweater with the holes in the elbows and shuffle in the rain to my local pub for a pint with my un-prestigious but *real*, and interesting, friends.

How to waltz (or bluff it, anyway)

If there's one thing every gentleman genius ought to be able to do it's dance. Of course, I do not mean wobble about on some ill-lit nightclub floor in a drunken stupor. Anybody can do that. No, I mean proper ballroom dancing. You may sneer, but just you wait until some wedding – maybe your own – at which everybody will be looking at you as you take the floor with your partner. You're either going to have to pretend to faint or learn a bit about how to do it. But don't worry, it's easy.

When I was at school they made us learn ballroom dancing. The man who taught us was an interesting fellow, whom I shall call 'Mr Nemo'. He used to come into school in a Land Rover covered in camouflage netting, and I remember he once took out of his jacket a black Luger pistol that he claimed to have removed from the body of some Nazi soldier whom he had, he said, strangled, commando style. We all thought he'd probably got it at some jumble sale. Mr Nemo was the first man I ever encountered who was an enthusiastic racialist. He once handed out posters at school emblazoned with some daft slogan about 'jungle bunnies'. 'If anyone asks where you found them, boys,' he said, 'tell them, in a telephone box. Yes, that's the ticket.' He finally disappeared off the scene after the police came knocking, when the corner shop, run by a charming fellow called Mr Singh, received a half-brick through its window. As the constabulary rolled up at Nemo's house with a warrant, about five pubescent boys were seen escaping over a back fence. The police added pederasty to the charges and not long afterwards Nemo was invited to become a guest of Her Majesty.

Anyway, he taught us ballroom dancing, with the help of a delightful classroom assistant whom he would swirl around the disinfectant-smelling school gym to the accompaniment of the 'Radetzky March' and the 'Blue Danube' waltz on an old record player, while we uncoordinated eleven-year-olds shambled about in extreme embarrassment, holding our partners as if they were radioactive waste. Here is a quick lesson in how to bluff the waltz, for the complete beginner.

- With your weight on your right foot, present your left hand to the lady.
- She now gives you her right hand and adopts a position slightly to the right of you.
- In a close hold, your body should make full contact down the lady's right side. Remember you may touch anything hanging off the sides of a lady but avoid things that hang off the central area. I'm going to assume that this is a social dance and that you do not know this lady well enough for a close hold. So: allow her to rest her left hand on your upper left arm while you position your right hand on her left shoulder blade. That's naked skin, that is.
- On the first beat of the music (it's 3/4 time, remember) start forward with your left foot. That's Step 1. OK so far.
- Step 2: move your right foot sideways, to the right. Simple.
- Step 3: close your left up to your right foot and put it down flat on the floor ready to move off, forward to the right. Couldn't be easier.
- During the first three steps you perform a quarter-turn. Remember that everybody will be dancing round the room in an anti-clockwise direction. Get this wrong and there's going to be a car crash. If you get a bit lost just keep going, and try to follow what the others are all doing.
- On the first beat of the second bar (am I blinding you with science?) step forward, this time with your right foot, slide your left foot sideways *to* the left, and close your right foot up to the left one (sort of reverse, kind of thing), shifting your weight accordingly. Got all that? Now just keep going, maintaining an air of confidence, especially as it all starts to go wrong.

Don't forget that dancing is sexist, in the sense that the man (that's you) leads and the lady follows. You lead the rhythm, timing and movement, and she is dragged after and pushed in front of you, doing it all backwards in heels, while trying to avoid you putting your great big feet on her hem and tearing off half a yard of pink silk.

They do say that dance is a vertical expression of a horizontal desire, so if you're bad, she's not only lumbered, but forewarned about the boudoir performance to come. Better practise.

How to write a bestseller

As the old proverb says, 'Success has many fathers; failure is a orphan.' Success is important in our culture and failure is regarded as toxic to popularity. Interestingly, though, it is fairly obvious that mistakes are vital for progress in business, science and other areas. All the same, there's no point in writing a book that you want to make you rich that sells only thirty-seven copies. So here are a few tips from a man who has written a number of bestsellers – *me*.

Not long ago I heard a psychiatrist talking about a would-be author, who was a patient of his, who was finding it impossible to finish writing the worthy books he had started. The psychiatrist discovered that what the fellow really wanted to write was bestsellers, and advised him to give up being literary and do just that. Today he is, I understand, a well-known bestselling author – but I'm afraid I do not know which one.

You'd imagine that writing a bestseller would be bound to make people admire you and earn you a bit of money into the bargain, but it's more complicated than that. Some bestselling authors are never asked for their autographs, or interviewed on telly, or invited to go to bed with models, or switch on the Christmas lights, because although their *books* are popular, *they* aren't. For example, few people could tell you the titles of the bestselling books by Dr D. G. Hessayon. He is the author of such corkers as *The Garden Expert* and *The Lawn Expert*, which have stayed in print for years and sold in vast numbers (fifty million so far).

When Katie Price (Jordan, as was) decided to write a bestseller – not a literary masterpiece, you'll notice – she had the distinct advantage of being famous for something else first, being described on the blurbs of her numerous books as 'an ex-glamour model, TV presenter, entrepreneur and mother'. Publishers know that being famous first is a huge bonus and if you look at the top twenty books in your local bookshop, or online, you will see that many of the names in the list are not authors in the old-fashioned sense but celebrities, famous chiefly for their well-knownness, who have also produced a book or two.

But though not having a famous face means you are down on points to start off with, don't be put off writing a bestseller just because you may not be able to bolt a sentence together and have no ideas. Instead, take a leaf out of the books of those TV personalities who don't write their stuff themselves. The celebrity subject – I'll spare her blushes – of one successful 'autobiography' shamelessly told a journalist that she didn't know exactly what 'they' had put in her book, because she hadn't read it. This is the right attitude.

Anyway, you've decided that you want to write a bestseller, so here is a short list of things to do and not to do to maximize your likely success. If you succeed, please don't thank me, just send a large cheque to my publisher, made out in my name.

Top ten bestseller dos and don'ts

1 Be famous to start off with.
2 If you're not famous, at least be visible: talk about yourself all the time. Remember: a high profile helps.
3 Use well-worn themes and subjects: military, ghost, sex, romance, science fiction, horror, suspense, misery and gangster subjects are all safe bets. Humour, philosophy and the taxonomy of bacteria are more difficult.
4 Don't worry about rambling plots, lack of decent characterization, vulgarity and obviousness: it didn't bother Harold Robbins, who sold 750 million copies of his books, in thirty-two languages. Imagine if he

only earned a royalty of $1 per book, that would still have been more than $9 million a year, from cradle to grave.

5 Get a really eye-catching but degenerate cover designed. Works wonders.

6 Don't steal other people's writing, you'll end up in trouble. But *ideas* are not copyright so you can pinch those willy-nilly.

7 Be well connected, then:

8 Be reviewed by all your friends in the newspapers.

9 Be interviewed by your friends on television.

10 Don't try to be high-brow. As Stephen King said, 'I am the literary equivalent of a Big Mac and Fries', and he's a bestseller's bestseller.

How to become rich and famous

A boy asked a rich man how he had made his fortune. 'Well,' said the old man, 'one day, when I was just a boy myself, I bought half a slab of toffee for a few pennies that I had carefully saved. I broke up the toffee with a hammer, wrapped the pieces in twists of paper, and sold them for a halfpenny each. By the end of the week I had made a profit of £1. Then the next week I bought *a whole* slab of toffee and did the same again, and I went on like that for a year, but I was still flipping poor. Then my dad died and left me a million pounds.'

Now, there is a great deal of wisdom in that joke and it is certainly true that choosing the right parents is the best way to start your journey to wealth for, if you want to make money, there is nothing to beat having some already.

On the other hand, as Mr Bernstein says in *Citizen Kane*, 'It's no trick to make a lot of money – if all you want is to make a lot of money.' For example, if you have chosen the wrong parents – which is to say, ones *without any money* – the next best thing you can do is to marry it. The easiest way to do this is to learn the disappearing coin trick in 'Magic for beginners' on page 80 and hang around a pub somewhere very expensive where you know the wealthy drink. Start doing the trick in the pub and get yourself a reputation, then, when you spot a likely lady, seduce her using the technique in 'How to seduce a woman: top ten tips' on page 45. Before long you will be a married couple, and you will be living off her fortune.

'But', I hear you cry, 'that's not very masculine.' Well, look, this is 'How to become rich and famous', not 'How to become masculine'. If you can't bring yourself to sink this low there is a third way to become rich, and that is to steal somebody else's money. 'Hold on,' I hear you cry again (incidentally, you've got to stop all this interjection or we'll never finish this), 'stealing is illegal.' In response, I would direct your attention to the global financial crisis of recent times, in which the banks legally 'walked away' with public money amounting to hundreds of thousands of millions of dollars. Do these squandering bankers still live in the nicest parts of Chelsea? Do they still roar around in smart cars while we grub about, desperately trying to pay off their disgraceful debt? I rest my case.

Failing a huge lottery win, working like a slave and becoming a successful footballer/rock star/actor, or receiving compensation for being turned into a vegetable in an industrial accident, the unromantic 'working-and-saving' method is the most likely route to wealth. I remember reading about a bus driver who had scrimped and saved for decades and then blown hundreds of thousands of pounds on his daughter's wedding, going from rich and unknown to poor and famous in one fell – and rather daft – swoop.

But if what you want is wealth *and* fame, you could try committing a big bank robbery. I should warn you, however, that although fame is not unlikely, lasting wealth is less so and, in any case, you might find that nobody likes you by the end of it. In 2006 Warren Buffett, one of the world's leading rich men, said he was going to give away almost his entire fortune. 'I know people who have a lot of money,' he said, 'and they get testimonial dinners and hospital wings named after them. But the truth is that nobody in the world loves them.' There's a lesson for us all there, surely.

Sincerity and how to fake it

Everyone knows that sincerity is the key to success – once you've learned to fake it, you've got it made. It's a wonderful skill, much used by politicians and other salespeople, but the trouble is that although people claim to admire sincerity, they don't really want you to be sincere all the time, just when it suits them. If you don't believe me try being sincere when your wife or girlfriend next asks you what you think of her new haircut, or whether you like her new dress, or does she looks fatter to you, or does her bum look big in those jeans. I tell you, any man who decided to give a sincere answer to these questions that was not also a paean of superlative praise would be playing with fire.

The problem is that sincerity is not in itself necessarily an admirable quality. The burglar who sincerely wants to steal your car, the friend who sincerely wants to go to bed with your wife or the colleague who sincerely loathes you is not likely to win your approval. Nonetheless, there is something to be said for people who speak their mind – at least you know where you are with them. We are all so fed up with politicians lying to us through their sincere smiles that any of them who came on television and announced that taxes were to be doubled and everybody then beheaded in the street would be cheered to the rafters just for their straightforwardness. I knew a bluff northerner once who used to say the rudest things to people, like 'Eh up! Tha's put on a bitta weeyat 'asn't tha!' and when you objected to his offensiveness would reply, 'I'm only sayin' what ah think. I'm only speakin' mah mind.' (I trust that northern readers will accept my apologies for the awful all-purpose 'northern' stereotype. At least I'm being *sincere*.)

Another thing is that sincerity is hard to fake. There used to be an oleaginous man on the television by the name of Hughie Green. He had a strangely deformed Canadian accent and his catchphrase was, 'I mean that most sincerely, friends'. Somehow you could just tell that he didn't mean anything sincerely, except, you suspected, when he was throwing a fit about his fee. His gargantuan insincerity became apparent after his death when it emerged that, despite the smarmy family-entertainer persona he liked to adopt, he was a serial adulterer who had fathered a string of illegitimate children, the first with an usherette when he was just seventeen. Green seems to have cuckolded whoever happened to be around at the time, including his producer, Jess Yates. Yates was known as 'the Bishop' and used to present a religious programme, *Stars on Sunday*, seated at an electric organ in front of a fake stained-glass window. The result of Green's shenanigans with Yates's wife was Paula Yates (sometime consort of Bob Geldof). Jess Yates only learned the interesting fact that Paula was Hughie Green's daughter, not his, after he read it in the papers.

But Yates himself was not the smiling holier-than-though Bishop character he played on television either, and when it was revealed that he also had been having a sincere relationship with a young actress, he had to be smuggled out of the TV studio in the boot of a car.

I was thinking that in this busy world, where people come in and out of your life so quickly, you should never miss an opportunity to tell them sincerely how important they are to you, but maybe this sincerity thing is overrated. Perhaps you should just do what Hughie Green and Jess Yates did, and pretend you are sincere instead. Better still, sit piously in front of a fake stained-glass window and then get fornicating behind a bit of scenery with some actress who is not your wife.

How to seduce a woman: top ten tips

In my local bookshop – the one that hasn't just closed down – the 'Personal Growth' section and the 'Mind, Body & Spirit' section are both huge and easy to find. The philosophy section (now called 'Feed Your Mind') is tiny and is in a cobwebby nook under the stairs. I wouldn't care except that the books in the Spirit and Growth sections are mainly self-help titles written by a bunch of silly fakirs who quite evidently don't know what they are talking about but are clearly raking it in. I saw one called *How to Develop a Natural Seducer's Mindset and Become Powerfully Magnetic*. Now, I'm sure the chap who wrote this rubbish didn't really explain how you could become an electromagnet overnight, but his lengthy title did give you a good idea of the quality of his book's insides. One of the imaginary exchanges he included made me smile.

HER: 'Hey, you're so interesting! Other men are real dull in comparison!'
YOU: 'Compliments like that won't make me into an easy target to get me into bed! I'm not easy, you know!!'
HER: 'Ha ha ha!!'

Now anyone who uses that many exclamation marks in three lines is going to suffocate his seductee. And, be honest, on hearing the foul grammar and unimaginative obviousness of his supposedly witty riposte, any woman worth her salt would not reply 'Ha ha ha!!' She would say something like, 'Goodbye'. If chaps are taking advice from books like this, no wonder they aren't getting enough horizontal refreshment. My guess is, actually, that these 'seduction experts' are writing their sad books as a kind of therapy for their own lack of success in this department. Don Juan, Errol Flynn and John F. Kennedy didn't bother with this tripe. No, they knew that the real secrets of seducing a lady are quite different to this prepared banter. Here are the top ten dos and don'ts. Why not tear out the page and keep it in your wallet for easy reference?

1   Do pay attention to your body language: this is the most important thing. Look into her eyes and point your body directly at hers. Stand in an exaggeratedly masculine pose, with your glances, voice and dominant bearing exuding sexuality. Your feet should be wide apart, fingers in belt and thumbs pointing towards your 'zone', like a cowboy full of spunk (well, you know what I mean). It may feel funny at first but she'll think you are the bee's knees – standing like this raises her temperature while saving on a lot of chat.

2   Don't bother with intensive grooming: there is no need to be handsome; this has little to do with it, despite what you might think. Better to be rich, actually.

3   Don't be too nice: the point is *not* to be charming and nice. Being

nice will get you nowhere in the seduction stakes. Indeed, being nasty is likely to increase your seductive power. Ever wondered why women fantasize about vampires? It's not because they are nice.

4 Do be a bit pushy: assertive and confident pressure are important, so be persistent.

5 Do touch her: don't grab hold of her bum or pull her hair. Instead, touch her lightly on the 'safe' areas – forearms are a good place. You'll have plenty of time later for grasping the other unsafe bits.

6 Don't try too hard: if you are trying hard it shows you care – which you shouldn't. Indifference is much more alluring. So maintain a cool, elusive, mysterious intrigue.

7 Do share danger with her: scientists have recently discovered that crossing a wobbly bridge or going on a fast toboggan ride with a man causes a woman to become attracted to him. Worth knowing. I mean, how much does a ride on a ghost train cost? It's a better investment than flowers. Creating tension will pay boudoir-dividends.

8 Do be funny (if you can): if humour comes naturally to you, then go for it as it has a similar effect to shared danger. After all, a guffaw is the orgasm she is allowed to have in public.

9 Do shut up about yourself: ask her about herself. 'What's your favourite sexual fantasy?' is a good question. Even 'Do you like screwing?' has been known to work, though it lacks style.

10 Do keep your eye on the ball: you'll know quickly (within seconds, actually) how interested she is. If you can't spot this you're lost, for now is the time to kick chivalry into the long grass and overwhelm her with the bold move.

The secret to getting the job you really want

I remember once, when I worked in an office, a colleague wanted my advice. He had been asked to provide a reference for the laziest man I have ever met. This chap used to swan in and spend the morning with his feet up on the desk reading the *Financial Times*. When he'd finished, he would pop out to 'get my hair cut', coming back hours later smelling of beer. He made no pretence of working but he was never admonished because his dad was on the board. Anyway, he finally got tired of the boredom and decided to move on, having nominated my colleague as one of his referees. 'What can I write, and still be truthful, and still make sure we get rid of him?' he asked me. So we sat down and came up with the following short and sweet reference: 'Whoever gets Charles to work for him will be very lucky.' It worked and he was gone.

If you've always wanted to flip burgers or clean public lavatories then you can probably get a job tomorrow. But for every action in jobs like these, there is an equal and opposite criticism, and the less important you are the more your lateness or absence will be noticed. When you try to balance out the terrible conditions and awful pay by sneaking off early you will inevitably meet the boss in the car park, while all your working late will go unnoticed.

So if you are looking for something more rewarding you are going to have to prepare a bit. The first thing to do is decide what you'd really like to do. If you don't know, you just need to look at your skills. People enjoy doing what they are good at. I knew a morose fusspot once and all he ever did was criticize and find fault. Everything had to happen exactly to schedule and nothing was ever good enough. He spent years in sales, pissing people off and failing to sell anything because he always went on about what was wrong with the things he was trying to sell. Then, one day someone suggested he go into procurement, and he found it was the perfect job for his demanding and critical personality. The quality of the components his company was buying went up because he insisted on drawing all their faults to the suppliers' attention and costs went down because he demanded it, and he became very popular. So if you enjoy being up-and-doing don't get a job as a night-time security guard in an empty building; if you're bad with people, avoid sales; if you enjoy cutting people up, then becoming a surgeon or a serial killer is the thing to aim for.

Having settled on what you want to do, research the companies or organizations that you'd like to work for. Don't wait for ads to appear in the paper, send them a letter telling them why you want to work for them, along with your CV, checked carefully for mistakes by somebody who knows what they're doing. Then you will *be visible*. That is vital.

When you are called for interview think beforehand about how you want to be perceived and then prepare. Difficult questions such as 'Why did you fail?' should be a doddle if you've thought about a positive way to answer them. Incidentally, the 'failure' question sometimes comes in the form, 'What are your weaknesses?' It's no good saying 'Being perfect', and it would be suicidal to admit, 'My main weakness among all of them is that I don't really know what your company does'. So, what you can do with the 'weakness' question is to choose a true personality trait of your own, maybe it's rudeness, say, then mitigate it and then put it far back in the past. You must then preface it with something positive and finish your answer by offering another positive statement, which turns your 'weakness' into a success.

For example, you could say 'I'm the kind of person who likes to get things moving [positive] and when I started fifteen years ago [the distant past] I tended to speak to people rather gruffly [your unbearable humiliating rudeness diluted to an acceptable level] but I soon learned that expecting others to be as dynamic as myself [boasting cleverly disguised as empathy] was unrealistic and that patience was a much more effective strategy [positive, plus it contains a buzzword], and I think I now manage people very well [a positive answer to a question they didn't even ask].' If you pretend to be sincere as you say this (see 'Sincerity and how to fake it', page 44) they will believe you – which is a weakness of interviews.

Once you settle into your lovely new job you will start to receive emails like the following, which was issued to employees by somebody at IBM, many years ago. I hope you enjoy it.

Re: replacing mouse balls

Mouse balls are now available as FRU. Therefore, if a mouse fails to operate or performs erratically, it may need a ball replacement. Because of the delicate nature of this procedure, replacement of mouse balls should only be attempted by properly trained personnel.

Before proceeding, determine the type of mouse balls by examining the underside of the mouse. Domestic balls will be larger and harder than foreign balls. Ball removal procedures differ depending upon manufacturer of the mouse. Foreign balls can be replaced using the pop-off method. Domestic balls are replaced using the twist-off method. Mouse balls are not usually static sensitive. However, excessive handling can result in sudden discharge. Upon completion of ball replacement, the mouse balls should move around smoothly.

It is recommended that each operative has a pair of spare balls for maintaining optimum customer satisfaction. Any customer missing his balls should contact the local personnel in charge of removing and replacing these necessary items.

Please remember that any customer without properly working balls is an unhappy customer.

How to become a memorable conversationalist

The *Oxford English Dictionary* defines 'conversationalist' as 'a person who is good at or fond of engaging in conversation'. But I think it's more subtle than that. For example, I know a lot of people who could win an Olympic gold for chatting. I also know a philosopher called Iain who can freeze an entire sofa of women by starting on about his area of philosophical expertise, the so-called 'naturalistic fallacy', which is a favourite topic. One girl of my acquaintance did prick up her ears once, but she thought he'd said 'naturalistic phallus'. So at one end of the conversational spectrum you've got the lightweight chat-bores and at the other you've got the heavyweight serious-bores. And then, of course, you've got *boor* bores – bores who boorishly and boringly go on about why the French/men with beards/capitalists/women/the Irish/social workers etc. should be in concentration camps. Often they have very red cheeks, these fellows.

None of these people is really a conversationalist, because though they may appear to be conversing, the traffic is one-way only. Furthermore, 'conversation' implies a lightness of touch. A flaming row about gay footballers or a frank exchange of views on the subject of female circumcision is less a conversation than an argument, in the first case, and a discussion, in the second, leaving people nervously clutching their gin and tonics and grinning at their husbands with one of those help-me smiles.

Oscar Wilde was a noted conversationalist, who had the felicitous phrase always on his lips. At one boring party he was asked whether he was enjoying himself and replied, 'Madam, there's so little *else* here to enjoy.' For Wilde, the right word was always to hand, or rather to mouth, because he spent hours preparing his witty remarks in his garage, before putting them in a bag and taking them to a party. Naturally he had one on the subject of conversation itself: 'Conversation about the weather', he said, 'is the last refuge of the unimaginative.' Not one of his best, is it?

I thought I'd browse the shelves in my local library, one of the few remaining, and still with a few books in it, to see what the experts have to say on how to be a memorable conversationalist. I was astonished at the rubbishy advice from these people, none of whom seems to have become famous for his conversational style or ability. They are more famous for their books. As my dad used to say, 'Those who can't do, teach. Those who can't teach, teach gym.' For years I thought he was saying 'Jim' so I didn't understand what he was on about. Which reminds me of the girl who was puzzled to hear the priest intone every Sunday, 'And now, let us say the prairie tortoise' (*prayer he taught us*, geddit?). Anyway, I've wandered off the point – never do that in conversation – the point being that these books about conversation are written by people who show no understanding of the subject.

In one book, subtitled 'How to be excellent company whatever the circumstances and improve your conversational skills to become a welcome sight at every social event you attend', which seemed long-winded to me, the following advice was given (the stuff in italics):

1 *Ask questions, as most people want to talk about themselves not listen to what you think.* Well, it hardly seems worth bothering with them. Asking a load of questions and not being allowed to interject doesn't sound like much of a conversation to me. Better steer clear of those people.

2 *Be a good listener.* This looks like the advice above in a different dress.

3 *Pay compliments. If someone has lost weight or has a new haircut, pay them a compliment.* This strikes me as a cynical approach, designed to make you look good. In any case, I was brought up to regard the making of personal remarks as offensive.

4 *Be ready to comment on the latest popular fiction and films, current affairs, politics, entertainment and sport, and watch the news.* I hate this one. Popular fiction and entertainment are nowadays largely mindless, as is the TV news. I notice it doesn't say listen to some music by Mark-Anthony Turnage, or seek out one of Ionesco's plays, or start a Physics degree, or learn some limericks, or learn how to play football, or take up cooking or first aid. Unless you are happy to chat about nothing but popular culture like some flaccid spectator this is really bad advice for the true conversationalist. Why limit yourself? Be interested in *everything*.

5 *Oppose the conventional and be provocative.* Facile advice. I can see the conversation really becoming interesting as you say something like 'I think we should kill old people who can't work', or 'Hitler meant well', or 'Jack the Ripper did a lot for British tourism'. Look, there's nothing wrong with driving on the same side of the road as everybody else.

6 *Laugh at other people's jokes even if you have heard them before.* Idiotic again. If you've heard a joke before, just say I've heard this one, I'm going to get another bottle of this disgusting alcohol-free beer from our charmless host.

7 *Don't mumble.* First bit of good advice yet. And bleeding obvious.

8 *Be cheerful happy and good-natured because nobody likes*

grumpy and miserable people. Wrong! At parties I prefer talking to intelligent people, who are often grumpy and always in the kitchen. Being a good conversationalist in the kitchen at parties involves nothing more challenging than the occasional grunt. Excellent!

How to look classy

When it comes to looking classy, few of us look like Sean Connery in *Goldfinger*. In fact, Sean Connery didn't look like Sean Connery in *Goldfinger* either, according to fellow actor Michael Gambon, who said he had been asked to audition for the role of Bond after Connery finished. He told producers that he was unsuitable because he had what he termed 'tits', but was informed that Sean Connery had them too and that they were 'shrunk' before the cameras rolled for a shirt-off scene by the judicious use of ice packs.

Of course, there's a lot more to looking classy than just freezing your moobs (man boobs), changing out of your grungy jeans and putting on a suit. With clothes it's a case of wearing the best you can afford, but wearing only what suits you. A good suit is, naturally, always elegant and classy, and put a wide-brimmed hat on top of that and you'll outclass them all. A silk-lined cape is a bit much, though, and a sword is just impractical these days, especially in a lift.

Anyway, classiness isn't really to do with wearing a lot of expensive clothes. I knew this fellow once who thought he was so classy he was going to win the Nobel Prize for classiness. But he wasn't really classy, he just had loads of money and could afford to spend hours having his hair cut in Jermyn Street and buy tailor-made suits by the armload. He used to insist on wearing a Rolex watch that cost an eye-watering amount and drove a sports car – which I rather liked, except that it was bogey-green in colour. He used to tap on the car door as we shot along country roads – the wind ruffling his silk scarf and playing merry hell with my map – and say, 'This is my fanny-magnet,' which I thought revealed an unattractively predatory side. He did have pretty girlfriends, but they were dim and tended to push off after milking him for a couple of skiing holidays, endless gorgeous dresses, startling jewellery and expensive dinners in restaurants I couldn't even afford to look at through the window. He is still a bachelor, this chap, but without liking it, and all he has to show for those ruinous meals and fast car rides is a bald head and a fat tum. The problem was that he didn't really have class so trying to look classy was never going to work. Lesson one: class comes from the inside.

By contrast, I had another friend who spent a normal amount on his glad rags and wore an ordinary watch on a leather strap. He didn't drive – he could but he didn't, preferring to go everywhere by taxi or in a huge hire car. He pointed out that this was actually *cheaper* than running a car himself. This fellow had real class and not only were his consorts pretty, they were intelligent and nice, too; in fact he ended up getting married to one. They were attracted to him because he wasn't pretending to be classy, he really was.

I remember he and I were once apologetically refused entry to an elegant restaurant because we were not wearing ties. Charlie, who was always beautifully spoken (another sign of class – you don't get far up the classy-graph if you talk like a rapper) smilingly said to the head waiter, 'Do you know what that Latin motto means above the door there?' 'Er, no,' said the man. So Charlie said, 'It means, "Do unto others as you would have them do unto you."' We were suddenly told that we could, in the circumstances, go in. Charles never boasted, so I asked him where he'd learned Latin. 'Didn't,' he said. 'I just made it up.' This was true class. Confidence is one of its hallmarks and if you can master the confidence trick, like Charlie, you've got it made.

My friend Jim always looks marvellous, and he equips himself from jumble sales and charity shops. This is a great tip if you want to look classy but are skint. Of course, you will reject most of the stuff, but amid the slag you will also dig out the occasional golden nugget. Jim has found such things as a handmade silk umbrella, a velvet smoking jacket (very classy), a Savile Row evening suit, an entire scuba-diving outfit and a box of 1940s silk ties. And he's picked them all up at a snip. Unless you want to pay through the nose, avoid the suppliers of so-called 'vintage' clothes and, for all that's holy, don't be seen rummaging about at a car boot sale; that's about as classy as tucking your shirt inside your underpants.

Of course, manners maketh the classy man, too. This means *no farting*, obviously. Politeness is highly valued by everybody and though a few people cultivate a rude personality, you will find that holding doors open, giving up your seat, and saying please and thank you will repay you a thousandfold – although this is not the reason a classy person does it. A genuine concern for others is a must, although this does not mean that you will allow people to trample all over you. If some boorish fellow starts taking advantage of your politeness or tries to muscle in on your girlfriend, challenge him to a boxing match – sexy *and* classy. The next one up is a duel, which, though classy, is rather camp.

Food and drink can be a tricky area, but when you are dining out, especially with a lady, there is no reason you have to eat pâté de foie gras or order bottles of cripplingly expensive Romanée-Conti burgundy. You are confusing classiness with snobbery. Egg and chips can be perfectly classy off a nice plate, though a mug of tea would be better if it were a proper pot of tea served in a decent cup and saucer.

Perhaps the classiest spontaneous thing a gentleman can do is recite a little poetry to his belle, though obviously not about women from various parts of the country. If you can do it in French, so much the better; you'll bowl people over – especially the ladies. For example, 'Une Charogne' by Baudelaire sounds marvellous when you recite it, but for goodness' sake don't translate it, because it's a poem about a maggot-ridden, foul-smelling, steaming corpse with its legs in the air 'like a lustful woman'. Which just goes to show that the French could do with a lesson or two in politeness, and certainly do not have the market in classiness cornered.

How to double the price of your home

No matter whether you are stinking rich or something of a pauper, your house or flat is likely to be the most expensive thing you ever buy. One day, though, you are probably going to sell it, and when you do you want to get as much money for it as you possibly can. This is called 'capitalism'. It is vital, when selling, to create the right impression, so you will need to become an Impression Management Genius. By understanding some simple principles, such as that bright lighting, light colours and small items of furniture create the illusion of a bigger space, you are halfway there. There are several things you can do to increase your property's value without bankrupting yourself. Here are some top tips:

1 First impressions count. The outside of your home is the first thing your prospective purchasers will see. You don't want them to be greeted by a car up on bricks or a rusting hot-dog van. So scoot down to the garden centre and get yourself a load of attractive flowers, which you can display in pots and window boxes. They will make a huge difference.

2 Paint the outside: paint exterior woodwork and slosh down outside walls. Wash those windows on both sides and keep them spotless while you are trying to sell your place.

3 Cut the grass – if you've got any.

4 See to the entrance hall. The first thing people will see as they enter your home is the entrance hall – if you have one. Banish the bicycles and muddy boots and do all you can to make the place look bigger. Brown may be cosy in the library but it's not right for a poky lobby. White is the most reflective colour and highest in tonal value and therefore is best for increasing the apparent size of your miserable hovel.

5 Paint the inside of your home. You needn't repaint the entire place but wash the walls and paint the woodwork, including doors and skirting. This DIY job will make the place sparkle. Painting a room in a variety of different hues will tend to 'shrink' it. So don't. One overall colour will make rooms appear larger.

6 Redo the electrics: get an electrician to replace your filthy light switches and plug sockets. This will make it appear that your

dangerous and ancient wiring is in tip-top condition. Bright lighting reflecting off small articles of light furniture increases the sense of space. Put maximum wattage bulbs into all your fittings and if necessary get your man to install some recessed downlighters in your kitchen and bathroom, where they will make your new taps sparkle (see No. 7 below).

7   Put some of your big furniture and other rubbish in storage: it's not until your purchasers try to force their rumps into your tiny chairs or attempt to relax under the glare of your broiling arc lamps that they will spot your sleight of hand. So don't let them.

8   Update your kitchen or bathroom. OK, this is going to cost some money but it will earn you a profit. Modernize the plumbing fixtures by tearing the pre-war hot water boiler off the wall and go for the most expensive taps and whatnot that you can afford. Redo knackered kitchen cabinets by chucking out the doors and putting on new ones. This is relatively cheap and easy to do.

9   Get the right mood in your master bedroom: piles of mouldering socks and underpants will do nothing to help you. Recessed downlighting and moody spotlights will create a cosy atmosphere, but not if your bed is unmade. And take the mirror off the ceiling.

10 De-clutter: tidy rooms appear larger and, unbelievably, there are now 'de-cluttering consultants'. So order a small skip and ruthlessly chuck out everything you don't actually need to keep yourself alive. Get rid of those Gainsborough oil paintings of your antecedents, your wedding album and all the other crappy impedimenta of life. If you can't bring yourself to junk Granddad's old harmonium put it in storage. Recycle whatever you can.

11 New blinds and curtains will give the place a real lift, as will new lampshades. If carpets are looking foul, get a chap in to steam-clean them. Roll up and hide those threadbare Turkish rugs and polish any wood floors.

12 Build an extension. After the location of your property – bad luck if you live between the sewage farm and the hospital for the criminally

insane – the number of rooms and their size are the two things most purchasers will be on the lookout for. An extension can add more to your home's value than anything else you do. It isn't cheap but why spoil the ship for a ha'p'orth of tar? A tastefully built extension will turn in a handsome profit because it creates an extra room.

13   Build a garage. On-street parking is increasingly expensive and hard to find, and if your place doesn't have a garage, and you have room for one, it may well provide a handsome return on investment – if petrol doesn't get any more expensive and we all have to get to work on skateboards.

14   If all else fails, or you are totally skint, just start a rumour that there is treasure buried in the garden/attic/under the floor. You'll be fighting off the bidders. Indeed, of all these suggestions, this is probably the only one that will actually *double* the value of your home.

How to become human again by using your hands

Once upon a time, Dad went off to work in a local office or factory. Mum handed over his lunchbox and kissed him goodbye at the door at 8.45, just like in *Bewitched* off the telly in the 1960s. At work he managed to do his job, take a coffee break and a lunch break – during which he ate his wife's scrumptious sandwiches – and got home by 5.15 for a pre-prandial glass of something friendly before kissing his little girl goodnight and sitting down to Mum's meat-and-potato dinner.

That was then. This is now.

Today Mum and Dad both get up at 5 o'clock on Monday morning, having been working on their laptops over the weekend. They drive to the station like maniacs and catch separate trains, travelling scores of miles to offices or airports or working breakfasts or client-meetings. They work like stink through lunch and spend the rest of the time screaming at their subordinates and being screamed at by their overseers, without having produced anything they can point at. At 6.45 they sprint to their separate stations and, missing their trains, have a couple of anaesthetizing drinks at two identical nauseatingly expensive and hideous station-bars, before getting the next available train back home, arriving at 9-ish (one of them having to get a taxi), after hold-ups for accidents, bent rails, dead horses etc., and stagger in to take over their screaming child from the stupendously expensive child minder. They then open a bottle of crappy wine and consume industrial quantities of it while eating a microwaved curry in front of something dreadful on the TV. They crawl off to bed an hour later, knowing that it will be the same tomorrow.

It doesn't have to be like this. There is a remedy – a way to become human again – by *using your hands*.

Once upon a time nearly everyone used his or her hands at work, whether you were a washerwoman, chimney sweep, fishmonger, midwife or gardener. Nowadays many of those artisanal jobs have disappeared and the ones that haven't have been outsourced to China or India, or have had all their practical bits computerized. Call-centre operators can't even feel like cogs in a machine anymore because they inhabit a nether world in which almost everything mechanical or three-dimensional has been abolished. Even their interpersonal relationships are fake, being scripted 'conversations' into a telephone headset.

To start using your hands in the office try introducing a plant and looking after it, or volunteering to fill the photocopier or sort the stationery cupboard. There is something deeply pleasing about fanning a ream of copier paper – which I learned to do when I worked for a printer – it meets a profound human need. Or you could sharpen a few pencils or carry some documents to a colleague upstairs instead of emailing them. You aren't wasting time; you are helping to create a happier workforce.

At home, why not take up origami, or bread-making, or carpentry? If you can actually produce something useful such as a rabbit hutch or some clothes you will benefit from an additional feeling of purposefulness. Alternatively you can make something useless, but entertaining. Here's a thing you can make in a twinkling – a six-foot paper tree.

First get yourself a newspaper, a glue stick, a rubber band, a pair of sharp scissors and a pair of hands. Now, open the paper flat and spread between six and ten sheets into a long strip on the floor. Carefully stick the bottom of the first sheet to the top of the next, overlapping them just enough to make a firm join, and keep going until you have made a strip running the length of the room. Once the glue has dried, roll the paper into a fairly tight cylinder, allowing enough room to poke your forefinger comfortably into the hole in the middle. Then glue down the loose edge. With a pair of *sharp* scissors, make two cuts down the opposite sides of the roll, to a point just over half way. It may all flatten out a bit at this point, but the next step will conceal this. Roll a separate sheet partly around your tube, attaching it with enough glue to secure it and make everything look neat and tidy.

You can now produce your tree to impress friends at the next dinner party you don't have time for. Make your entrance, rolling up your cylinder as if it's an unprepared sheet and secure it with the rubber band, which you have around your wrist. Tear the outer sheet with your forefinger, along the line of the cuts, and allow the strips of paper to flop down on either side. Holding the tree trunk in your left hand, put your right forefinger into the hole in the middle, and pull it up and out, twisting and tightening as you go. From the audience's viewpoint it looks as if all you did was to roll up a sheet of newspaper and produce an instant tree. Dead impressive, and so easy.

How to be a better dad

Mark Twain once remarked, 'When I was a boy of fourteen, my father was so ignorant I could hardly stand to have the old man around. But when I got to be twenty-one, I was astonished by how much he'd learned in seven years.' This, as every parent of teenage boys will agree, is a universal attitude and it's during the period when your son or daughter regards you as a stupid fool (most of your adult life before the Alzheimer years) that you have to be an especially good dad.

I like children – if they are properly fried – but you don't want to get off on the wrong foot with them. The best way round the problem is to give them a bit of your time – probably a rationed commodity – and do dad-ish things with them. Here are some amusing diversions suitable for boys as well as girls, which every perfect dad should have under his belt.

Colour a flower: this is great fun. First, cut a carnation or daffodil from your garden, or next-door's garden, or buy some from the supermarket – it doesn't matter where you get them. Now put them into a vase containing water, coloured with a few drops of a food colouring of your choice. Capillary action will draw the coloured water up the stem into the petals and tint the flower. It's a fascinating process that takes a little time. If you want to be really inventive, you can use a sharp knife to split the bottom of the stem lengthways for a couple of inches and put one half in a red liquid and the other half in blue. Now see what happens. It's weird.

Make an electromagnet: wrap a length of wire around a long nail. If you want a strong magnet you will require patience, because stronger magnets require more wire to be wrapped around the nail. Connect the two loose ends to a 6-volt battery and you should be able pick up some paper clips.

Unscramble the un-unscramblable: mix equal amounts of iron filings, sand and salt in a bowl. It looks as if a thousand pixies with tweezers couldn't separate those fine grains again, but *you* can. Here's how:

1   Use your recently made magnet (or a shop one) to take out the iron filings. This is easy and fun.
2   Add some water to the salt and sand mixture to make a thin 'soup'.
3   Run this through some filter paper (try the coffee machine), leaving the sand in the filter paper and collecting the saline solution in a non-stick pan. (Put the filter paper with the sand on it in the airing cupboard to dry off, but *take the cat out first*.)
4   Boil the remaining liquid in the pan until it has evaporated. Open the windows while you do this or it will rain on the inside of your kitchen.
5   Scrape off the salt residue, and Bob's your uncle. What's the point? I don't know but nobody can say you aren't being a good dad.

Finally, in case you are feeling a bit of a failure as a parent, as your son sits slumped in front of the TV showing no motivation to do anything more than grunt, read this letter that one poor father received.

Dear Dad

I have eloped with Brooklyn. She looks wonderful with all her tattoos and her glass eye, and the good news is she's pregnant. We are moving into her converted horsebox in the woods – our baby's new home. Don't worry about me, Dad, I'm pretty grown-up for fifteen and Brooklyn, being forty-three and a woman of the world, has taught me how to defend myself with just a knife. We are going into business trading homegrown marijuana for as much heroin as we can get, hoping that Pedro the Pimp will stop shooting at us from the trees, because it makes Brooklyn's syphilis flare up. I look forward to seeing you again one day, Dad, and introducing you to all your different-coloured grandchildren. Keep it real, ma gangsta. Your loving son, Tony.

PS: Actually Dad, none of the above is true. I'm at Grandma's, but I just wanted to remind you that there are worse things in life than my school report, which is on the kitchen table. Phone when it's safe to come home.

How to hold an audience

A small blue plaque on the wall of a fast-food restaurant, close to what was once 31–35 Sauchiehall Street, in sunny Glasgow, is the last physical reminder of the infamous Glasgow Empire, feared in showbiz circles for its reputation as the 'comedians' graveyard'. Though Bob Hope, Danny Kaye and Laurel and Hardy were all warmly welcomed there, English comedians such as Tommy Cooper and Morecambe and Wise were given the bird by the growling Glaswegians. English all-rounder Des O'Connor either fainted or pretended to, depending on who you believe, so as to escape the terror. They used to say that if the audience at the Glasgow Empire liked you they didn't applaud, they let you live.

Mercifully, most of us will never have to face the raspberries, flying orange peel and insults from the groundlings at the Empire, mainly because it isn't there anymore, having long ago made way for the charmless Empire House, one of those office-and-retail enormities. The worst *we* are likely to encounter is a bit of slightly drunken, and let's hope cheerful, banter from Uncle Charlie as we grimly stumble through our best-man's speech at some ghastly wedding or other.

Most people are, I read, more terrified of speaking in public than of death. But everybody ought to be able to learn to deliver a one-liner to their family over the cornflakes. Of course, it might be that you have ambitions to hold a crowd beyond the toast or the churning sea of relations at bleary family functions. But whether it's just a joke you're trying to tell in the pub, a couple of words about Auntie Violet at her funeral or actually chancing your arm at your local open-mic session, you are going to have to hold the audience, unless, of course, you want a reception such as the Glasgow Empire audiences so enjoyed doling out.

This is where it gets difficult. Naturally, the first thing you think you are going to need is a top-quality script. There are ads in the back of some magazines from people who offer to write a speech for you, laughs guaranteed. Maybe they are worth the money, I don't know, but, though good material can help, it is not the key to success in holding an audience.

The real secret is this: personality.

Now the idea of personality is something of which it is hard to get hold. What is it exactly? We all know a personality when we see one; and sometimes it's nice, sometimes it's nasty. At least 50 per cent of a person's personality seems to be there from birth, and to those who maintain that what your parents do to you makes you who you are, I would say look at a family of puppies. Within days you can see that they already have their own personalities: shy, boisterous, affectionate, daft and so on.

Being entertaining is certainly a function of personality and to hold an audience you must entertain them. There's nothing more sphincter-tightening than watching the lights go out in people's eyes as somebody who has waded beyond their depth keeps on with some dire joke or embarrassingly bad speech. But being entertaining doesn't mean that you have to be entertaining all the time. Some of the most entertaining performers I know are miserable, or even dull, when they are not trying to hold an audience. They come alive only when singing a song, telling a joke, doing impressions or pulling rabbits out of hats. So my first advice to you, if you want to hold an audience, is: be entertaining, which means: have the right personality, which means: have the right genes, which means: choose the right parents.

The best entertainers seem drawn to it, just as the best funeral directors, nurses or teachers seem to have exactly the right personality. Even if you are reserved in private, you must pretend to some confidence when trying to hold an audience. I saw a beefeater at the Tower of London giving a talk to some tourists. He was one of the most hilarious performers I've ever seen, and he knew how to hold his audience even while working under pressure. There was a lot of background noise, half his listeners didn't speak English very well, people kept wandering off, the unexpected kept happening and the next tour was due in twenty minutes. I remember at one point he used a joke: 'History', he said, 'is written by the winners . . .' People waited. '. . . which accounts for all those blank pages in French history books.' It got the biggest laugh of the day, and it wasn't the politically incorrect joke that did it, it was the man's ability to hold his audience with his personality. By the time he'd finished, people felt they'd learned something and been royally entertained into the bargain. They went away laughing, thinking that their money had been well spent.

Of course, this beefeater was a natural, but he used some learnable tricks, too, such as talking quietly to some boy next to him then suddenly raising his voice or telling short, snappy, suspenseful tales. He made lots of eye contact and he made sure that everybody could hear him. But what he did most of all was involve his audience. He produced an emotional response, laughter, by sharing something of his personality – of *himself*.

You don't have to be funny, of course. At a funeral, the joke about the Debonairs (you know the one I mean?) is going to go down like a rancid vindaloo, and some of the best performers have held their audiences with serious, indeed solemn, speeches – think of Winston Churchill or Martin Luther King. OK, you say, but they *wrote* superbly, which is true. But imagine if those speeches had been performed (the *correct* word) by other people – Donald Rumsfeld, say, or Donald Trump, or Donald Duck. No, the trick to holding your audience is:

1   KISS: Keep It Simple, Stupid
2   MaYoH: Make Yourself Heard
3   ChoRiPa: Choose the Right Parents, and, most important
4   SABOY: Share A Bit Of Yourself

How to die with dignity

Once upon a time in a land far, far away (my youth) I saw a terrible comedian die an awful death in a malodorous comedy club in one of London's less salubrious quarters. I remember a wit shouting, 'Someone put him out of his misery!' to which another replied, 'Put him out of *our* misery!' I stopped going to these clubs after a while because I got the feeling that I was watching a lot of people *rehearsing* their acts. Nowadays I occasionally recognize one or other of them on the television, where I can switch them off if I don't like them. Which I don't (like them, I mean).

Anyhow, on stage they often died and it was usually without dignity. It's hard to be dignified when people are yelling insults at you or, worse, standing there all silent. As some wise person once said, 'If it's going badly, get off. If it's going well, get off.' And let's be honest here, life often goes badly, especially towards the end, when bits of you tend to fall off, or stop working, or start hurting a lot. For some people the time comes when enough is enough and they opt to choose their moment and get off, rather than stand indefinitely in the I've-had-enough-of-this queue to be told when they are for the high-jump. I suppose they do this on the grounds that it is more dignified and less shabby to resign from life than to be fired.

But now the problems start, because doing away with oneself, or helping someone else to do away with him- or herself is, if no longer always illegal, still a taboo and fraught with difficulty. So-called 'medically assisted suicide', or euthanasia, is a lively topic and right-to-die-ers are often to be seen on news programmes fighting their controversial corner as best they can against so-called 'pro-lifers'. I bet all these right-to-die-ers are as pro-life as anyone else. What they are probably against is drawn-out, preventable human suffering. It's worth noting, I suppose, that the only people who ever get into trouble for killing themselves are, for obvious reasons, the ones who botch it. Perhaps they should introduce the death penalty for attempted suicide. Discuss.

There is now a well-known clinic in Switzerland named Dignitas, which uses a simple and kindly method to help people to die, assist their suicide or kill them, whichever term you prefer. Here is the method they use. First they give the person (I don't think 'patient' is the right word') an anti-emetic to stop them vomiting when they take the large overdose of the drug that will make them die. Then they wait about half an hour. What do people do in the meantime? Paint their nails? Do the crossword? Check their investments? Have a last look at the trees and sky, that's what I'd do. When the thirty minutes are up the Dignitas people give the person who is to die an overdose (I won't say how much, although I know) of a common barbiturate called Pentobarbital, powdered up and dissolved in a glass of water or fruit juice. (I'd have mine in a pint of Harveys' best bitter, which, as well as tasting delicious and being the ultimate valedictory glass, would increase the barbiturate's potency, because of its alcohol content. Although in the volume of poison given, this would be unnecessary.) Death never happens suddenly for any of us; it is a process. The drug works by depressing the central nervous system and it takes a little time, though not much. After about ten minutes the dying person becomes drowsy and falls asleep – the death many of us hope for – with anaesthesia progressing to coma as breathing becomes increasingly shallow. Death is ultimately the result of respiratory arrest (you stop breathing) about thirty minutes after swallowing the drug.

In 2008, Dignitas tried using helium gas as a way of helping people to die. I don't think this can have been very good idea. I mean, suppose they

66

had second thoughts halfway through? Who would have taken them seriously as they shouted, 'No! No! I've changed my mind,' in a hilarious chipmunk-style squeak? Still they could have filled a few party balloons at no extra cost.

As a final note I should mention Jack Kevorkian ('Dr Death', as he was stupidly named by the tabloids). Kevorkian, who died in 2011, was (you may be interested to learn) an Armenian-American painter, composer, instrumentalist and pathologist with a very strong belief in people's right to choose how and when to shuffle off this mortal coil, as Hamlet put it in that soliloquy. He had a quote for every occasion, that fellow. So strong were Kevorkian's beliefs that he endured years in prison as punishment for taking part in so-called 'physician-assisted suicide' of the terminally ill, pointing out that 'Dying is not a crime'.

You can't argue with that really, but, unless you are in desperate straits yourself, I shouldn't worry too much about how to die with dignity because for many of us it's *living* with dignity that's the problem. Laughter is a great life-enhancer, of course, so if you are feeling a bit low, I suggest you watch something or read something that you know really makes you laugh. But be careful, you don't want to overdose and die laughing.

How to become successful by doing what you're good at

I was having my house painted recently by a real craftsman, named Andrew. One day as I was passing his tea up the ladder he told me that his son had hurt his back while flying an enormous kite – something he was very keen on and good at doing. I learned that he was just about to apply to a famous university to do computer science and that he was also an accomplished tap dancer. I remarked that he sounded an interesting Renaissance-man-type man, to which Andrew replied that he himself had done a variety of things, including painting, by which meant canvases not walls.

When I thought about this I realized that the best way to be successful is to do what you are good at. The happiest people aren't the ones with big houses and nice cars, but those who love what they do because they do it

67

well. We are all good at different things and enjoy doing them. Actors enjoy acting, architects love architecting and dentists simply have to dent. The problem is that it can be hard to get a job doing the thing you are good at, which is why some people end up doing jobs they hate. But often these chaps compensate by spending their spare time doing a hobby they love. If you are one of the fortunate people whose job is also his hobby, you are almost bound to be a success. If you are already in a job you hate, and admit that you loathe it and are going to stop it and start doing something you love instead, you have taken the first step on the road to recovery.

Children have fun playing and playing is really learning in disguise. Some children even decide what job they want to do when they are still quite young. People admire this, but you have to be careful; you might decide as a child that you'd love to be a fighter pilot, say, but then find that you hated it and wish you hadn't chosen to do a job picked for you by an immature boy. Nevertheless, if you can find a job doing something you regard essentially as playing in disguise, you'll be on the launch pad to success.

Parents and teachers aren't much help, though. They go on at length about getting a good job – that is, one that pays big bucks and probably also one that is regarded as prestigious. If you tell most people you are a brain surgeon, rocket scientist or corporate lawyer, you can bet they will go 'Ooooh!' But who cares what other people think? Deciding to do what *you* want to do, not what other people tell you to want to do, is likely to make you successful and happy in the long run (but unpopular in the short run).

I suppose you can understand parents' emphasis on 'getting a good job'; after all, what father wants to hear his daughter say, 'Dad, I'm going to become a stripper', or his son say, 'Dad, I've decided to become a street sweeper'? But wouldn't it be better if parents encouraged their children to do what they loved rather than kept going on about 'good jobs' or 'something to fall back on'? That training that your dad says is supposed to give you something to fall back on is probably going to be for something you hate and would be like falling back on a sack of spanners.

Oh, you say, it's all very well for those people who have a rare talent, like brilliant footballers or bestselling authors, but what about the rest of us ordinaries? Well, the first thing you need to do is *not* ask yourself the question most people ask: 'How am I going to make money?' Instead ask yourself: 'What work would I most enjoy doing?' This will be something you'd do even if you weren't paid for it. By the way, it doesn't count to say you'd like to become a whisky- and cigar-tester, or spend your life lying on a Mediterranean beach being paid to fornicate with beautiful women while they feed you caviar. Hedonism wears off rather quickly and you get bored, or so I'm told. Working hard on a project you love produces pleasure of a more fulfilling kind.

Finally, you need to grasp every opportunity that presents itself. Decades ago, my friend Martin was walking in the country when he noticed a man struggling to take a huge 'picnic basket' off his car roof. He gave him a hand with it and discovered that this man was a balloonist. To thank him for his help the man took him up in his balloon and, looking over the majestic landscape, Martin asked how he could take lessons himself. 'I'll teach you,' said the balloonist. Now it turned out that this man was the British champion and, being taught by the best, Martin became an extremely good balloon pilot. In fact, he ended up so good that Richard Branson heard about him, rang him up and asked him to pilot him across a particularly treacherous bit of terrain, which he did very successfully. 'Did you enjoy that?' I asked him. 'Yes,' he said, 'I *loved* it.'

Fifty ways to become important

How often have you been brushed past, passed over, overlooked or looked inferior? Many times, possibly. How much more lovely it would be to be one of the important people, those who swan through life, never having to hold their own umbrella, make the bed or go shopping at Tesco. If you would like to become important and have bowing servants leap out of your way and open doors for you, it's not so difficult: it's mainly a matter of *acting* important.

The way you look and behave is vital and there is nothing like sitting on a dark stallion looking remote in a peaked cap and a uniform bristling with a fruit salad of medal ribbons to cause people looking up at you to believe you are a VIP and go, 'Oooh'. Very impressive – *if you're twelve* – as the comedian Mort Sahl amusingly pointed out. Sometimes – often even – it's all an act. Just think of Bernie Madoff, who went from very important 'financial genius' to very unimportant prisoner number 61727-054 in a twinkling. And if he can pretend to be important, so can you.

But, I hear you protest, I'm a nobody, I'll never be important. Not so! Just think of Disney's largest shareholder, Steve Jobs, who was adopted into a working-class family and dropped out of college because he couldn't pay the tuition fees, before co-founding Apple in his mum's garage. He is now worth $3 billion and so important that when he gets a cold Apple's share price wobbles horribly.

One thing that important people share in common is self-confidence – *with knobs on*. Low self-esteem – if you suffer from it – must be concealed, for an air of unshakable assurance is vital, especially if you are faking it. Here are a few practical tips to get you on your way up the greasy pole of importance.

1   If you want to be treated as an important, *act* important.
2   Wear a high-ranking uniform. People believe the evidence of their eyes.
3   Speak in a measured, slow, low-pitched voice. Avoid 'singing'.
4   Be erect – standing, I mean, or sitting.
5   Maintain firm eye contact – a sign of self-assurance and importance.
6   Chin up.
7   Chest out.
8   Clasp your hands behind your back. This shows fearlessness from attack.
9   Maintain LPM. LPM is Low Peripheral Movement. Important people tend to keep still.
10 Contrive a firm palm-down handshake.
11 Carry an expensive, impossibly thin leather briefcase, containing one or two documents only.
12 Move precisely and handle your props nicely.

13 Get a minion to be your favoured bag-carrier and door-opener. He'll feel spoilt and you'll look important.

14 Do not speak, move or express yourself hesitantly.

15 Walk purposefully.

16 Stand behind subordinates occasionally as you speak to them.

17 Be late. Let *them* wait for *you*.

18 Never explain; never apologize.

19 Smile frequently.

20 Never suck down – up only.

21 Maintain an authoritative emotional distance.

22 Wear reflective sunglasses.

23 Use reflective or smoked glass in office and car windows.

24 Have a desk big enough to land helicopters on.

25 Be handsome.

26 Be tall.

27 Failing that, raise yourself physically above others so that they have to look up at you. Horses are good.

28 Stand on a dais or, in an emergency, on a box. Never put yourself at a disadvantage.

29 Have a hardback classic such *The Brothers Karamazov* on your desk.

30 Flash your cash.

31 Use exclusive credit cards and bank accounts.

32 Wallets of the finest leather only.

33 Never travel by bus. Obviously.

34 Be driven when you can.

35 If driving, choose the right car: Jaguar, Bentley, Rolls-Royce will all do.

36 Have two black folders marked 'Most Private' on your desk.

37 Wear stupidly expensive aftershave. Get it free by going into a nice place and asking to sample some.

38 Talk as if you just expect things to be done.

36 Wear very good, expensive shoes and keep them spotlessly clean and shiny.

40 Get a really good haircut.

41 Wear really good suits. Tailored obviously.

42 Always be ready for a road accident. Make sure your *entire* shirt is ironed, not just the bits you can see, and discard socks with holes.

43 Use the 'steeple' finger position. Fingers spread and fingertips touching, elbows on chair arms.

44 Bribe waiters in advance to treat you as a much-valued regular when you dine with others.

45 Never drink instant coffee.

46 Know your wines.

47 Cultivate exquisite table manners.

48 Have a classical education (or fake it).

49 Know nothing of popular culture.

50 Never, ever, break wind. Well, maybe when alone on a blustery cliff.

ESP for beginners

The trouble with 'initialisms', as they are sometimes called, is that they can easily confuse people. Take 'MA', which can stand for 'Master of Arts', the state of Massachusetts or the self-explanatory 'Marijuana Anonymous' support group. When you put 'MA' after your name on your next job application, who knows what your prospective employers are going to think? 'ESP' suffers from this same problem and might stand for a number of things, such as the 'Empire State Plaza' in Albany, New York, the 'Empire State Pullers', a truck and tractor pulling sanctioning body(!), or 'extrasensory perception', which really ought to be 'EP' if you are going to spell it as only two words like that.

Extrasensory perception is the acquiring of information without the use of the five senses. The term was popularized by J. B. Rhine (1895–1980), a botanist who got all interested in ESP and did a number of ESP experiments at Duke University in Durham, North Carolina, during the 1930s. Amazingly nobody with ESP ever predicted that Rhine was going to do this.

ESP consists of telepathy (mind reading), precognition (knowing things before they happen) and clairvoyance (knowing things, like that your great-granddad is dead, without being told about them), but the problem with ESP is that, as everybody knows, you can't acquire information without using your boring old five senses. Even those who claim to have ESP have to ask their husbands what they want for dinner and read the paper to find out what's happening in the news rather than use telepathy and precognition. No one has ever become a prizewinning journalist-photographer who sends himself a day in advance to the places where volcanoes are going to erupt, trains crash dramatically, tsunamis flood towns, presidents get assassinated and so forth. No one successfully predicts daily stock market results or racing winners and no one has ever been the cause of the headline 'Psychic wins lottery'.

As you may guess, I'm not convinced by this ESP business, but only because there isn't any evidence for it; I am remaining open-mindedly sceptical.

So how are you going to wow everyone with your expertise at ESP then? Simple! You are going to do what others have done: cheat. Here is a piece of (fake) thought reading that is very simple to do but which has a huge impact – so long as you present it with sufficient mystery, as if you really believe it yourself. I first saw this bit of chicanery explained on the back of a cornflakes packet but don't let that put you off, because it's a real winner. People will believe you really are an ESP master. I'll describe the effect.

You first ask your host or hostess to get a couple of sheets of paper, ordinary A4 will do fine, a pen, a clean tea towel and an opaque mixing bowl (or something similar – in the old days it would have been a hat). Ask for five volunteers and after an intriguing mini-ESP history lecture, tell them that you will shortly leave the room and that four of them are then to choose the name of living people – one each. They can be famous or people you don't know. The fifth volunteer is to choose the name of a dead person, preferably famous. Tell them that they must each write their selected name on a slip of paper, fold it so that it can't be seen and drop it into the bowl. Nobody must know what is on any of the slips but their own.

You tear the two papers into identically sized pieces, hand them out and leave the room. Once they have finished writing and have dropped their pieces into the bowl, they call you back in, where they blindfold you with the tea towel. This usually provokes a bit of fun but you should remain solemn. You then take the folded pieces out of the bowl one at a time and hold them to your head, as if concentrating hard. You announce somewhat dubiously that the first has on it the name of a living person, and drop it unopened on the floor. You do the same with the second and so on until you finally bring out a piece which you hold to your head, and, with proper build-up to maximize dramatic suspense, you announce that you are receiving a strong emotional vibration that your last slip is inscribed with the name of the dead person. You dramatically tear off your blindfold and ask who chose the name of the dead subject. You then ask what that name is – let's say Winston Churchill (a common choice!). You slowly unfold the paper and reveal the name. It is indeed the dead subject. You take your applause.

Method

There's nothing wrong with the blindfold, you really can't see, and neither do you know the names of the people on the papers, even after you take them out of the bowl. The trick works by using a device so astonishingly simple that when I tell you what it is you may well say, 'Oh, nobody's going to fall for that'. But they do.

The blindfold is there for dramatic purposes only because, although it does effectively blind you, this doesn't matter. You do the trick by touch alone. When you tear each A4 paper into three you do it by folding it into thirds and tearing along the creases. It is important at this point that you know who is to choose the dead name. When you explain the trick you can nominate that person. Say something like, 'You four are to choose the names of living people – one each – and you [pointing] are to choose the name of a dead person. You then hand the papers to your volunteers. It is vital that the person choosing the dead name gets the middle piece of one of the sheets and that you retain the middle piece of the other sheet in order to demonstrate the folding process. Why? Because two of the pieces from each sheet will have three straight-trimmed edges and one torn edge. The middle piece of each sheet will have two trimmed edges and two torn edges. This is the key to working the trick. Demonstrate as you hand out the last (different) piece how the pieces should all be folded, using the middle piece from the other sheet. You do this by folding it once in half and then in half again, *so that the rough edges now form the short ends*. Check that your volunteers understand this. When they have said yes, you can put the extra slip – the sixth – into your pocket. If you have fewer people, just use one sheet of paper and demonstrate the folding with the middle bit, then hand it over.

When you put your hand into the bowl to pick out the pieces you will feel that four have two long folded edges, one short straight edge, and one short, rough, torn edge. Only one piece of the five will have two long folded edges and two rough, short, torn edges. Save this one until last, or nearly last – for dramatic reasons, of course.

Sometimes cheeky volunteers will not tell you the name of the dead person. If this happens, you just say, 'Well then, this is going to be that much more suspenseful,' and open the paper slowly so that only you can see it. Finally turn it round to show everybody that you were right anyway.

The effect will depend on your build-up and the appearance that you are really serious about this ESP thing. This is a trick that is all effect and little method, so put all the dramatic build-up into it that you can muster. Women particularly like it.

How to become as popular as your dog

My friend Jo told me that she will not let her husband Gary out of the house with their dog unless she goes with him. 'Why on earth not?' I asked. 'Because that dog is a babe magnet,' she told me. It's bad when your dog is more attractive to women than you are, but there's no denying that dogs just are popular – on the whole I mean. Obviously, nobody likes a dog that savages children or befouls suburban pavements.

Nonetheless if you could be as popular as your dog you'd be well ahead.

There's no doubt that popularity is popular, and popular people are particularly popular; possibly the most popular popular people are the *very* popular. But don't be fooled: popularity is not the same as happiness (see 'The secret of happiness and how to discover it' on page 88). Take Michael Jackson, who was hugely popular as a performer but was a drug-sozzled crazy offstage, sitting alone with a monkey in his fairground cup. He had once been a normal-looking boy but ended up like a Picasso gone wrong, possibly in an effort to become more popular than he was already, which was probably more popular than most people were to start off with.

Anyway, I've warned you. But, if you're determined to become popular, here's how.

1   Stop thinking about yourself. This is a very powerful insight and not only will it tend to make you more popular, it will increase your happiness into the bargain. Be honest, those people who think about themselves all the time are bores – or sometimes psychopaths.

2   Be cheerful. People like happy people. If you can't be cheerful, try pretending for five minutes. It might grow on you.

3   Stop moaning. Be less critical – and less self-critical. This one is related to the two above.

4   Ask questions of people, and really listen to what they are saying. Again this one is about thinking of others, not yourself. People like people who like them, and if you are interested in them, it shows that you like them. Good questions might be 'Have you ever played naked leapfrog?' or 'Do you want to see a trick I learned in prison?' Not if you're talking to the vicar, of course.

5   Relax a bit. Don't be so tense, you're upsetting people.

6   Do people a favour occasionally.

7   Be warm. I don't mean literally, though that won't do any harm. I mean compassionate, friendly, sympathetic and generous. If you are none of these things don't try doing them for the first time all at once, you might burst something.

8 Be rich. Sorry, but it helps. The best way to become rich is to have some money already. Also consult 'Get rich quick: others do it, so can you' on page 91.

9 Don't try too hard. People sense those parasitic souls who are desperate to be liked, and flee from them like a seasick atheist running from a nun with jellied eels. Popular people don't try to be popular, they just are, as a kind of by-product of their cheerful, warm personalities. If somebody doesn't seem to like you, never mind.

10 Don't pretend to be someone you are not – related to the above. People have an uncanny ability to see through this kind of thing. On the other hand, if you are genuinely bonkers and think you are Napoleon, put on your bicorn and go for it.

11 You don't have to be gorgeous. Joseph Merrick, the so-called 'Elephant Man', was very popular because he was a genuinely nice guy. That doesn't mean you shouldn't comb your hair though.

12 Be confident. Diffidence is one thing but those wet blankets who speak inaudibly and shake hands as if they are picking up a tapeworm don't endear themselves to others. It's a kind of passive aggression and people hate it – quite rightly.

13 Be able to speak. It's unnecessary to have the felicitous phrase always on your lips but if you can fill the gap when it all goes embarrassingly quiet people will warm to you. Share a bit of yourself. Have a self-deprecating amusing story or two ready to go, like the time you sawed off your leg or reversed over your grandma.

14 Be bothered. This is another important one. Make a bit of an effort: take a small gift or flowers when you call upon a lady, don't eat your lunch from a can, take the vacuum cleaner round before you have visitors, have a wash occasionally and don't defecate out of the train window. It's common sense really.

15 Join in a bit. If you don't like mixing with people, you could try to become popular online. Even trainspotters are popular amongst themselves.

16 Lower your expectations. If you have three good friends, count your

blessings. You don't want to be popular with the entire town, do you? And you definitely can't be liked by the entire world.

How to be idle without worrying

In his delightful book *Idle Thoughts of an Idle Fellow*, Jerome K. Jerome points out that it is impossible to enjoy idling thoroughly unless you have plenty of work to do. You cannot take pleasure in being idle if you are vastly rich and never need to roll your sleeves up, otherwise none of the wealthy would do a stroke of work. But they all do, just as lottery winners often go back to their jobs – if they enjoyed them – or take up some new occupation, such as counting their money and cackling like Fagin.

One of the best ways of idling at home is to announce a project, such as washing the car or clearing the scrub from the end of the garden. You can then spend ages putting your boots on, fiddling about with buckets, shovels and spades, cloths and brooms, all the while drinking gallons of coffee and listening to the radio. Since it is up to you how long a project will take, you can extend the idleness to last as long as you please. A good ploy is to introduce a few coffee breaks, during which you can take pictures of the dog with your phone (remember when you took pictures with a camera and used the phone for talking to people?) or sit on a wall texting jokes to your friends. The great beauty of this is that whenever your other half looks out of the window you will appear to be doing something – carrying a rake, rinsing a cloth, having a well-deserved tea break – and she will be unable to give you a hard time, as she would if you were reading the sports news or watching television.

Procrastination is a skill related to idleness, and may even be a form of it. Creative people are superb procrastinators. The cartoonist Posy Simmons once said that she would do anything, including the dishes, to put off getting down to her cartoon for the *Guardian*, and Douglas Adams, author of *The Hitchhiker's Guide to the Galaxy*, was a procrastinator par excellence. He would take long baths to put off the task of actually writing and was entirely unperturbed by his idleness. He once said, 'I love deadlines. I like the whooshing sound they make as they fly by.' You should take a leaf from his book. His editors tried everything, including booking him into hotels and sitting there watching him write, but after ten years' 'work' on his novel *The Salmon of Doubt* he didn't even have a complete first draft, when he suddenly – and inconveniently for his publishers – died. This was a master of the art.

Dr Johnson (see 'Dr Johnson: a man, his dictionary and his Tourette's' on page 282) was not so much a procrastinator as a notorious slowcoach. In 1756 he published his *Proposals for Printing, by Subscription, the Dramatick Works of William Shakespeare*, which maintained that Shakespeare had been badly edited and needed fixing up. But his progress on the book was sloooooooow and in 1758, as a way of avoiding finishing it, he began *The Idler*, a weekly series which ran until 1760. This is called 'doing the *wrong* job instead', and is another classic idler tactic – one you should try adopting. In *The Idler* Johnson explained that, 'The Idler, who habituates himself to be satisfied with what he can most easily obtain, not only escapes labours which are often fruitless, but sometimes succeeds better than those who despise all that is within their reach, and think every thing more valuable as it is harder to be acquired.' This is not only delightfully true, it is also one of the longest good sentences ever written.

But remember, idleness is not the same thing as laziness, and is nothing of which to be ashamed. There's no point in being busy – especially at work – if all you are doing is using up more photocopier paper, sending more emails and having more meetings without actually *producing* anything. Politicians always praise schemes that, they say, create employment, but you could create employment by getting the unemployed to shovel earth from Land's End to John o'Groats or by encouraging drivers to knock down pedestrians. And what does a local council's recently advertised 'Performance and Partnerships Manager' actually do for his/her £40,000 a year?

As Dr Johnson once pointed out, all intellectual improvement arises from leisure. When you are idling you have the time to think. More interesting, useful and even money-making ideas have come from idleness than from pointless graft, even if you allow for Mr Edison's clever remark that 'Genius is one per cent inspiration and ninety-nine per cent perspiration'. There may be a scintilla of truth in that comment, but, on the other hand, nobody likes a smart-arse.

Magic for beginners

> LORD LOAM: By the way, Brocklehurst, can you do anything?
> LORD BROCKLEHURST: How do you mean?
> LORD LOAM: Can you do anything – with a penny or a handkerchief, make them disappear, for instance?
> LORD BROCKLEHURST: Good heavens, no.
> LORD LOAM: It's a pity. Every one in our position ought to be able to do something.
>
> J. M. Barrie, *The Admirable Crichton*

Every gentleman genius ought to have a magic trick or two up his sleeve to impress a lady or divert a nephew. Of course, you don't want to have to drag around a trunkload of pigeons, rabbits and multiplying wine bottles. Impromptu close-up magic using ordinary things is what you should go for and the following impressive but simple trick is an ideal one with which to start.

The real secret of magic lies not in the way tricks are done, but in being entertaining. Furthermore, if people like your personality, they'll like your magic. So choose tricks that are genuinely magical but also easy to do, so that you can concentrate on entertaining people without having to strain to remember what it is you are meant to do next or bother with hiding elephants up your sleeve. The following simple trick has an effect much bigger than you'd imagine – *if you present it properly* – and embodies several important magical principles.

The elbow coin-vanish and production

The elbow coin-vanish is an old, old trick that relies for its effect on a number of well-understood principles of magic. Let me describe what happens.

1 Sitting at a table – this is good in a restaurant or pub – you ask whether one of the company will lend you a coin – a 2p or 10p piece are both fine but a pound coin is even better. You extend your left hand (if you are left-handed just reverse all these instructions) and ask your victim – I mean assistant – to place the coin on your palm. You display it in this position to those on your left.

2 Next you pick up the coin with your right hand and display it on your extended right fingers to the spectators on your right, allowing the left hand to relax into a loose fist and turn down on the table (Fig. A). Simple so far.

3 The next moves happen almost simultaneously. You pick up the coin with your left hand by pinching it with the thumb against the inside of the left fingers (Fig. B). There's nothing fancy about this, it's a normal way to pick up the coin. At the same time the fingers of your right hand curl inwards to form a loose fist and you place your right elbow down on the table edge with your right fist lifted until the fingernails are close to your right collarbone.

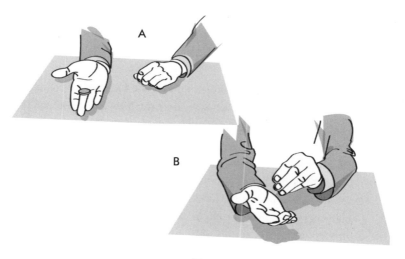

4   Your left fingers now press the coin against the right elbow a couple of inches above the table and release the thumb. Now rub the coin slowly up and down against the elbow but let it fall out onto the table, *apparently by accident* (Fig. C).

5   Pick it up apologetically with left hand and display it as before on the extended left fingers.

6   You do the same moves exactly as before but this time when you rub the coin on the elbow it appears to melt away into nothingness.

7   You now remove your shoe and tip the coin on to the table, returning it to the lender. Cue tumultuous applause.

Until no. 6 in the instructions above, you do exactly as described. However, it is not quite true that you repeat the same moves. Here is what you actually do after extending the left hand to display the coin (no. 5, above).

I   Your right hand does indeed pick up the coin but does not display it. Instead it is briefly pinched between thumb and fingers and then grasped by the closing right fist as the right hand is lifted and the elbow placed on the table, as before, except that this time there is a coin in the fist that the spectators will immediately forget is there – *yes, it's true.*

II At exactly the moment your right hand lifts away the coin, the left thumb presses down on the left fingers as if grasping a coin (there's no coin there), and the left hand, turning by ninety degrees, moves straight to the right elbow exactly as if it held a coin (Fig. D). The left thumb is released, as before, just as if the left fingers are holding the coin against the elbow. This subtlety might sound outrageous to you but the spectator's brain is suffering from a number of impediments. First, the whole point of going through the trick until the moment when you *pretend* to drop the coin, which is what you do at No. 4 above, is to accustom your victim to the actions while he is paying proper attention, so that when you repeat the moves – almost – he will think that you have done the same again and will be in a less vigilant frame of mind. Second, from the moment your right fingers lift the coin from the left hand and the left hand moves to the right elbow, the coin is out of sight, and the hands and arms are making big movements that obscure the smaller ones, such as the right hand secreting the coin. All the spectator can remember is that the hands came together as before and that the right fist was lifted, as before, and the left hand moved across to the right elbow, as before. Therefore, thinks his poor old brain, it must be holding the coin.

D

III Another way you make the trick believable is to use what magicians call 'misdirection'. Actually, the preceding sequence contains much subtle misdirection and all it really means, at this moment, is that you fog the spectator's brain a bit by getting him to think about something irrelevant while you do the funny business. Magicians have a saying concerning the timing of a bit of funny business: 'Do it when they aren't looking'. It is something a young child showing you a trick understands when he says, 'Close your eyes'. You've got to be a bit more subtle, that's all. So, *just before* your hands come together for the last time, look straight at your spectator. You will have been talking the whole time (some 'patter' is suggested below) but now your eyes drill into him, even if he doesn't return your gaze, and you say, 'Can you remember the date on this coin?' Now this is a naughty question, because you never showed him the date on the coin so he is going to have to divert his attention from what you are doing, so as to think about this. It doesn't matter what he replies; the point is to force him to think about something else just as you do the dirty. Whatever he says, you say something – anything. 'We'll look in a second' would do.

IV To get rid of the incriminating coin in your right fist wait until you have finished rubbing your elbow with your left fingers, lifting them away to show that your left hand is empty and the coin gone. Look momentarily at your spectator, then lift your right elbow and point at the table, saying, 'Completely melted' (Fig. E). As you do, all attention will be on the table. At this moment grasp your collar with the index and second finger of your right hand and drop the coin down inside your shirt. Now wave *both* hands unostentatiously above the table in an innocent motion, saying, 'Gone'. Do not, whatever you do, look at your empty hands or draw attention to them by saying, 'Look, nothing here,' or anything like it.

V Now say, 'Just a minute.' Stand and put your left foot on your chair. Unlace your shoe and carefully remove it, then tip it up slowly and out will fall the coin (Fig. F).

Actually, of course, it's a duplicate coin that you put in there before you began. You've got to think ahead in this game. Pick it up and look at it. Say, 'Ah yes, 1998,' or whatever it is. Then return it. When you ask for a coin at the beginning, specify one of the same value as the coin in your shoe or you'll be in trouble. And don't forget to link this request to your patter.

Tricks are a lot more enjoyable for your audience if you tell a story while you do them. You could start this one by displaying the coin and saying, 'You may have heard of the 'philosophers' stone', the *lapis philosophorum*, a legendary alchemical substance that was supposed to transmute base metals into gold. Let me see if I can turn this metal – gold only in appearance – into something more noble, using only *my elbow* . . .' A story gets people interested and it helps you misdirect them. So write yourself some simple patter and learn it.

Now practise the trick over and over with your patter until you can do it without thinking. Next, show it to a critical friend so as to iron out the wrinkles, then, finally, you can perform it.

Good luck.

How not to screw up the English language

Everyone seems to have his own favourite hates when it comes to English misusage, and I'm no different. There was a boy at my school who frequently referred to the leaves on the trees as 'foilage', which showed that he didn't really understand what the word meant. 'Foliage', the word he was after, is from the Middle French *foille*, meaning 'leaf'. That's why printers call the page numbers on the *leaves* of a book 'folio numbers'. But anyone can make a mistake and it never really bothered me. Neither was I upset when my milkman said he was delivering less pints of milk than last year. What he meant was 'fewer' pints or, even better, 'less milk', but who cares? Likewise, I never worried about that split infinitive, '*to boldly go* where no man has gone before', because it was perfectly acceptable usage and the words would have been worse in any other order.

But some people ought to know better. Years ago, now, I heard the presenter of a children's TV programme say, 'Which house has the most amount of windows?' This error needs half a page to go into, but what he was after was either, 'highest *number* of windows' or, better, 'most windows'. Anyway, 'amount' was just wrong. I felt that he should, as an 'educator', not only have spoken better English, but also have been ashamed of contaminating the brains of the impressionable young viewers with ugly English and spreading the disease of carelessness.

There are so many ill-written blogs and web-pages out there now that it's hard to escape this stuff, but you do expect better from national newspapers and broadcasters. I read on the BBC News website yesterday that 'In another scenario, doctors were asked to imagine that either themselves or a patient was infected with a new case of bird flu,' and it made me shudder. Some journalist – for whom words are tools of the trade – was paid money to write that clumsy, wrong and gormless sentence.

Politicians are especially bad at screwing up the English language. In 2003, Boris Johnson, now Mayor of London, said, 'I could not fail to disagree with you less,' though he might conceivably have been joking. The incredible Sarah Palin invented 'squirmish' when she meant 'skirmish', and conflated 'refute' and 'repudiate' into the unique 'refudiate', which resembles the commonly used, and wrong, 'irregardless'.

It sometimes seems as if the politicians who are worst at this do understand how to speak but have no inkling of the way in which the noises coming out of their mouths relate to the real world. Indeed, from time to time, the malady appears to be an index of a deeper, more general, ignorance. George W. Bush and Donald Rumsfeld were both gifted when it came to screwing the language. Bush, whose finger was on the button, used to refer to something he called 'nucular weapons'. His attempts at eloquence were always coming unstuck, too, and his 'Families is where our nation finds hope, where wings take dream' reminds me of that Martian cobbler who tried to make a shoe after hearing shoes described, but never having seen one. Apparently, Bush's 'The French have no word for "entrepreneur"' is made up, but it sounds *so* convincing.

Here are a few more political classics from the two front-runners. You can avoid creating this kind of confusion yourself by taking these examples apart like a broken motorbike and putting them back together properly so that they make sense. This exorcise would help you to not make more worse English one's self.

George W. Bush

- 'You teach a child to read, and he or her will be able to pass a literacy test.'
- 'I know how hard it is to put food on your family.'
- 'One of the great things about books is sometimes there are some fantastic pictures.'
- 'Anyone engaging in illegal financial transactions will be caught and persecuted.'
- 'Most imports are from outside of the country.'
- 'Our enemies are innovative and resourceful, and so are we. They never stop thinking about new ways to harm our country and our people, and neither do we.'
- 'I am mindful not only of preserving executive powers for myself, but for predecessors as well.'
- 'I know what I believe. I will continue to articulate what I believe and what I believe – I believe what I believe is right.'
- 'I think we agree, the past is over.'
- 'Rarely is the question asked, "Is our children learning?"'
- 'They misunderestimated me.'

Donald Rumsfeld

- 'I believe what I said yesterday. I don't know what I said, but I know what I think, and, well, I assume it's what I said.'
- 'I would not say that the future is necessarily less predictable than the past. I think the past was not predictable when it started.'
- 'Well, first of all, we don't know if he's in a cave. When I get up in the morning, I picture him in a cave. But he may not be in a cave.'

- 'Reports that say that something hasn't happened are always interesting to me, because as we know, there are known knowns; there are things we know we know. We also know there are known unknowns; that is to say we know there are some things we do not know. But there are also unknown unknowns: the ones we don't know we don't know.'
- 'Don't speak ill of your predecessors or successors. You didn't walk in their shoes.'
- 'We do know of certain knowledge that he is either in Afghanistan, or in some other country, or dead.'
- 'Learn to say, "I don't know." If used when appropriate it will be often.'
- 'Few are able to see what isn't there.'

The secret of happiness and how to discover it

You may never have had it so good but are you really happy? Many people aren't, or don't seem to be, so here is my short guide to making yourself at least a bit happier than you are now, if that is what you would like.

It has been known for some time that people have a sort of background happiness level, and that those people who win the lottery or become paraplegic tend to be about as happy afterwards as they were before. It is now also beyond doubt that money and the things it can buy you will not make you happier, unless, of course, it transforms you from a starving pauper to somebody who can feed himself. In *The Conquest of Happiness*, one of Bertrand Russell's witty potboilers, he says, 'To be without some of the things you want is an indispensable part of happiness,' and, indeed, happiness has been shown to have no link to high pay. One happiness expert has described keeping up with the Joneses as 'toxic to happiness'. Although *earning more than people around you* can make you feel better *for a bit*, it is an effect that diminishes over time.

Just to show that this isn't a new idea, here is one of the best recipes I've ever read for happiness. It appears in Jerome K. Jerome's side-splitting book *Three Men in a Boat*, which was published in 1889:

Let your boat of life be light, packed with only what you need – a homely home and simple pleasures, one or two friends, worth the name, someone to love and someone to love you, a cat, a dog, and a pipe or two, enough to eat and enough to wear, and a little more than enough to drink; for thirst is a dangerous thing.

What a wonderful piece of advice that is, especially the bit about drink.

In the United States and Britain, economic growth has meant an average rise in income but at the same time reported happiness hasn't budged. Nonetheless, laughter is still free and will banish a bad mood in a twinkling. I recommend watching a funny film or putting a tea cosy on your head and doing a stupid dance in the kitchen, though not if you're expecting the vicar for tea. A friend of mine recommends soaking a loaf of white bread in a sink of water overnight and dropping it from a second-storey window into a street full of expensive cars, where it will splatter in a most satisfying way. If you are a bit of a sadist, practical jokes can be good encouragers of cheerfulness. Jumping out and going boo at people is great for making me smile and the old whoopee cushion on a chair is a real winner. I cannot guarantee, however, that this will increase your popularity.

It's interesting, isn't it, that depressed and moany people are always talking about themselves? One route to happiness is to stop thinking about yourself for five minutes. Doing somebody a good turn, cancelling a grudge and meeting up with an old friend all make you happier. These activities share in common the quality that you must stop just thinking about yourself in order to do them. Research also shows that self-absorption diminishes if you grow a plant or care for a pet. These activities have a strong tendency to make you happier if you are lonely. A hobby, too, can be a great way of becoming absorbed in something other than yourself. Again Bertrand Russell put it succinctly: 'The time you enjoy wasting is not wasted time,' he said, glibly.

Exercise also helps cheer you up and the jogger's high is well understood, resulting as it does from the body's releasing happy-hormones into the blood stream. Of course, it is also a good distracter. There's no way you can wring your hands with misery while you are putting the shot, tossing the caber, running a marathon or falling down a mountain.

Like hobbies, work is vital to happiness. Unemployment, especially in men, has been shown to be very bad for wellbeing. A recent report by the British New Economics Foundation found that unemployment is so disastrous to happiness that governments could do well to make it more of a priority than it is. On the other hand, you don't want to be overworking. Another of Bertrand Russell's happiness quotes is apposite here: 'One of the symptoms of an approaching nervous breakdown', he said, 'is the belief that one's work is terribly important,' and how true that is. I should nonetheless point out, after all these blasted Russell quotes, that although Russell went on endlessly about how to be happy, he managed by his awful behaviour to make lots of people very miserable, including his family. I think it was the sex maniac Lady Ottoline Morrell (known to her friends as Lady Utterly Immoral) who said about the aged Russell, 'To sit in the back seat of a taxi with Bertie is to court disaster. Only a few moments go by before one hears a dry rustle as of dead leaves, as he slides across . . .'

One final piece of advice if you are miserable and also travel a long way to work is this: stop it. A recent study indicated that the longer your journey to work is, the more unhappy you will be.

This reminds me of a friend of mine who used to drive from Brighton to North London every day. As well as his horrible commute, he often worked late and one morning he was so exhausted he could barely face the two-hour journey. But he set off and a while later, just as he was joining the M25, he heard on the news that a car had been reported travelling the wrong way near junction 8. 'Hang on,' he thought, 'that's *here*. And it's worse than they're saying – it's not *one* car, it's hundreds of them.'

Get rich quick: others do it, so can you

The California Goldrush (1848–55) caused about 300,000 people to move to San Francisco, where a few of them recovered gold worth the equivalent of thousands of millions of dollars in today's money, but many went home poorer than they arrived. So how did the get-rich-quick guys get rich quick?

One thing is now clear: the entrepreneurs and tradespeople who sprang up made far more money than most of the miners. For example, a pushy newspaper publisher and loudmouth named Samuel Brannan opened the first shops in Sacramento and elsewhere. His idea was simple. He quickly bought up all the gold-pans, spades and other prospecting tools and equipment in the San Francisco area and resold them at a gigantic profit. This is called giving the customer what he wants (not to mention having a monopoly). A fellow with a related idea was Levi Strauss, who started selling denim overalls in San Francisco in 1853. I wonder what happened to him and his products.

As usual food, sex and services sold well. Laundry, clothing repair, transport and accommodation all flourished, as did light entertainment – and dark entertainment, too. Brothels, often with saloons and gambling establishments attached, were predictably profitable. These businesses were, for obvious reasons, often run by lady women of the female sex.

But, short of a gold rush, how are *you* going to get rich? Well, one way is to be dishonest, unscrupulous and abrasive. Robert Maxwell MC (1923–91), born Ján Ludvík Hoch in Czechoslovakia, rose from poverty to build an influential British publishing empire and become one of the richest people in the world. His way of getting rich was to tell fibs. As early as 1969 a British government department wrote, 'notwithstanding Mr Maxwell's acknowledged abilities and energy, he is not in our opinion a person who can be relied on to exercise proper stewardship of a publicly quoted company'. Then one day in 1991 he fell, jumped or was encouraged off his boat near the coast of Tenerife and floated ashore dead, the seawater having turned his suspiciously jet-black hair orange. His companies' finances were soon revealed to be a fairy tale of black holes and ectoplasm. But hey, he was rich, with helicopters and everything.

But if you insist on doing it legally, what about this? I once met a student who had an extravagant lifestyle and used to travel in taxis wearing tailor-made suits until one day he realized he was seriously in debt. He told me that instead of working two jobs around his studies he decided to try something easier. What he did was borrow a bit more money from his bank to pay for a small ad, which he ran in various national publications, reaching a readership of a million or so. This read, 'Get rich quick. I did it, so can you. For details of my foolproof, quick, legal scheme, send a pre-paid self-addressed envelope, along with a cheque for £9.99 to . . .' and there followed a central London accommodation address. At the bottom of the ad was printed, 'If you aren't in profit within a month, I will refund your money. Guaranteed!' This chap said that when the money started to roll in, as it did, he returned to the senders a cheaply printed A5 sheet that said, 'To get rich quick just like me, simply put a small ad in three high-circulation publications worded, "Get rich quick. I did it, so can you. For details of my foolproof, quick, legal scheme, send a pre-paid self-addressed envelope, along with a cheque for £9.99 to . . .' Did anyone complain?', I asked. 'Yes,' he said, 'a few. I refunded their money.' I asked how much he had made. He said that if I assumed that five out of every hundred readers had perused his ad, and that 5 per cent of that number had sent a cheque, the sum would look like this: total readership = 1,000,000; divided by the number of people who read the ad = 50,000; divided by the number of people who sent a cheque = 2,500; multiplied by £9.99 = £24,975. 'The trick,' he told me, 'is to charge them only what they are prepared to lose. When they receive the leaflet most realize, ruefully perhaps, that I've been truthful (though possibly not strictly honest) with them, and that if they do what I suggest they are pretty certain to make a profit, even after subtracting the cost of the newspaper ads. But most are lazy and want something for nothing. They will probably not bother to take my advice, but they won't bother to complain either, because even the little effort to which they have to go to reclaim their £9.99 is too much for them, and it's an amount they are anyway prepared to write off. For those very few who do ask for a refund, I return the full amount with a nice letter, and I pay the postage. That way everyone's happy. You don't want unhappy customers.'

So there you have it. I've never wanted to get rich quick myself, so there's no need to send me any money for this advice. Unless you want to, of course.

Part Two:

THE
INSTANT GENIUS'S
WORLD OF KNOWLEDGE

*A compendium of gentlemanly
must-know facts*

1 The Human Body

The history of false teeth from the Etruscans onwards

It is a well-known fact that George Washington wore wooden dentures. As with many well-known facts this one is false – like the teeth. George Washington was indeed an early adopter of dentures, but they were made – I'm told – of hippopotamus ivory and, subsequently, china.

False teeth have been around for almost as long as dental caries (tooth decay). In 700 BCE, or thereabouts, the Etruscans of Ancient Italy (modern-day Tuscany) made partial dentures from human or animal teeth. They didn't last long but were a doddle to make and remained popular for centuries until more sophisticated carved-bone or ivory models took over. In Europe, dentures were made by harvesting teeth from human cadavers or from the poor, who would sell a couple when the car needed a new head gasket or it was their daughter's wedding.

The resultant primitive dentures were attached to any remaining teeth with bits of silk or metal but tended to fall out at inconvenient times. Full sets had to be removed at meal times to avoid being accidentally eaten. Elizabeth I is said to have put white cloth in the gaps between her teeth for cosmetic purposes – the equivalent of the modern tooth-whitening process, I suppose. This was fine until she tried to eat spare ribs. Other rich people went for falsies of silver, gold or mother-of-pearl.

The oldest surviving complete denture was made in fourteenth-century Japan, where the Buddhist priestess Nakaoka Tei, known as

Hotokehime or Lady of Buddha, carved a set for herself out of a lump of cherry wood. These false teeth are of a similar shape to modern dentures and would have been kept in place by the vacuum caused by the Lady of Buddha periodically sucking on them.

The earliest dentists were often ivory turners, goldsmiths or novice barber-surgeons and the first recorded use of the word 'dentist' comes from 1752. London's Peter de la Roche is believed to be one of the first of these tooth specialists. The most famous early denture wearer was George Washington, who had some fitted in about 1764.

By the end of the eighteenth century people had become fed up with ivory teeth and in about 1770 the pharmacist and early dental experimenter Alexis Duchateau made the first china false teeth, in which the whole denture, teeth and gums, was made of porcelain. In 1785 Dr John Greenwood of New York City introduced the first porcelain teeth into the United States. George Washington was one of his patients. Porcelain teeth were more hygienic but they didn't fit well and smashed easily. Moreover, the colours were unrealistic and people laughed at them.

Parisian dentist Pierre Fauchard tried making upper and lower sets of dentures joined with steel springs, but these played merry hell with a wearer's mouth when he tried to close them. Nonetheless, Fauchard's compatriot Nicholas Dubois de Chemant began selling spring-fastened dentures in 1792. These were none of your rubbish – the china paste was provided mainly by Wedgwood and they were a much better fit because de Chemant had solved the problem of shrinkage during firing. In 1804 he was firmly established in London, already claiming to have made 12,000 false teeth.

By 1820 goldsmith Claudius Ash was manufacturing top-quality porcelain dentures attached to eighteen-carat gold plates. Moulds of the mouth were made from plaster so that dentures became a better fit. Demand was strong and Claudius Ash was established as a company in 1829. It is still going strong today. By the middle of the nineteenth century the base into which the porcelain false teeth were set was increasingly made of cheap and flexible hardened rubber (vulcanite).

The twentieth century was a period of rapid development. Acrylics and other plastics increasingly became the materials of choice while, at the same time, improvements in dental care led to reduced demand for false teeth and a higher demand for cosmetic treatments.

Today dentures are so realistic that they can be hard to spot. The only problem is the loony price. You can still get hold of cheap ones here and there, but these still have a disconcerting tendency to look blue in unfavourable lighting conditions.

Feeling blue: a look at the blue-skinned people of Kentucky

In 1960 Madison Cawein, a young haematologist, had just begun working at the University of Kentucky's Lexington medical clinic when he began to hear stories about Kentucky's remote, and wonderfully named, Troublesome Creek. He learned of a blue woman who had come into the American Heart Association clinic for a blood test, in not-so-far-away Hazard, announcing that she was one of the 'blue Combses' of Ball Creek. She seemed entirely unconcerned that her face and fingernails were 'almost indigo'.

Cawein heard that around Troublesome and Ball creeks lived a number of other people whose skin was blue. Apart from their unusual coloration, the health of these mysteriously blue people appeared to be robust, many of them living into great old age. Madison Cawein made it his mission to track down other members of the blue-skinned community and try to identify, if he could, what was going on.

One day, two of the blue people, Patrick and Rachel Ritchie, arrived at Cawein's clinic. He examined them and asked whether they had any other blue relations – possibly the oddest question any doctor has ever asked a patient. The blue people belonged, it seemed, to just a few local families, notably the Fugates, and Cawein suspected that they were exhibiting a hereditary condition known as methaemoglobinaemia, caused by raised levels of methaemoglobin in the blood. Methaemoglobin is a blue form of haemoglobin that accounts for the blue tinge of the veins on the back of a white hand. Cawein tested the Ritchies for abnormalities in their haemoglobin, one of the condition's chief causes, but drew a blank.

Though methaemoglobinaemia is a very rare disorder it was not unreported in the medical literature. Cawein found references going back to the turn of the century as well as a recent (1960) report in the *Journal of Clinical Investigation*. This was written by E. M. Scott, who suspected that the red blood cells of people with methaemoglobinaemia were lacking the protective enzyme diaphorase, which turns methaemoglobin into haemoglobin. He also decided that the condition was probably the result of an inherited recessive gene. A recessive gene is one that is present but not visible. To display the symptoms a person would have to inherit a methaemoglobinaemia gene from both Mum and Dad. Somebody with just one gene would not display the symptoms but could pass on the gene to their own children.

Gradually, Cawein began to uncover the branches of the Fugates' family tree. In 1820, Frenchman Martin Fugate had emigrated from his homeland to Kentucky. No record of the man's skin colour existed but Cawein suspected that he was carrying the blue gene. Against all the odds, Fugate married Elizabeth Smith, a non-blue woman who also carried the recessive gene. They had seven children. Four of them were blue.

For 200 years six generations of the blue Fugates lived in the same remote area of Kentucky, a settlement so isolated that it lacked even roads. Over the years, the inhabitants started families with members of other families nearby, including the Combses, the Ritchies and, inevitably, with their own cousins and other blood relations.

The Ritchies took Cawein to see a blue uncle, and Zach Fugate, the seventy-six-year-old head of the family, introduced him to his blue Aunt Bessie. A test on all this new blue blood did indeed reveal a lack of diaphorase, the protective enzyme mentioned by E. M. Scott that normally keeps methaemoglobin at less than 1 per cent of total haemoglobin. The blue people of Kentucky had accumulated so much of the blue molecule that it had overwhelmed the red of their haemoglobin.

The doctor now initiated a surprising treatment. At Patrick and Rachel Ritchie's house he injected each of them with 100 milligrams of methylene blue, a very blue liquid normally used to treat malaria. Within minutes the blue faded from the Ritchies' skin and for the first time in their lives they were pink, like everybody else around them. But Cawein warned them of a weird side-effect: their urine would turn blue, an effect made famous in an episode of *M*A*S*H* when methylene blue is used in a harmless prank to colour a character's urine. Because the effect on the Ritchies would be temporary, the doctor prescribed them methylene blue pills to take every day.

Years passed – as they say in books – and the remote areas of the United States began to become increasingly developed. As the blue-skinned people of Kentucky took to the newly built roads for the first time and began driving away from their communities to settle in far-flung places and marry strange new people, the blue gene began to be diluted among genetically dissimilar families, and its effects died away. In 1999, a young student, Benjamin Stacy, perhaps the last identifiable descendant of the blue-skinned people of Kentucky, sent an email to a website which was discussing hereditary methaemoglobinaemia. He said: 'I have had no major health problems related to the disorder and simply try to live an average life in spite of being "blue",' which seems to me to be a good way of going about your life no matter what colour you are.

Spontaneous human combustion

Before retiring to bed one night in April 1731, the sixty-two-year-old Countess Cornelia di Bandi of Cesena, in Italy, was behaving sluggishly. When she failed to get up the next morning her maid went into her bedroom, where she discovered her body on the floor, reduced to a ring of ash, along with three charred fingers and her lower legs (stockings intact). Some of her head also remained unburned and her skin – such of it as was left – was coated with a 'greasy and stinking moisture'. Under her blackened remains was an *empty* oil-lamp.

Looking around the room, the maid noticed that two candles on a nearby table had lost all their fat and had only their naked wicks remaining. A malodorous yellow grease was running down the window panes and the furniture was covered with a moist soot; the air was full of it, too. A piece of sooty bread offered to the Countess's dogs was refused. The fire which had apparently broken out seemed to have been peculiarly localized and the bed in which Countess Cornelia had been sleeping was unburned.

This is the first, classic, recorded instance of what has come to be known as 'spontaneous human combustion'. Over the course of the last 300 years, only a couple of hundred cases have been recorded, but they share in common several extraordinary features. Typically, an intense and unexplained fire appears spontaneously to overtake the victim, incinerating much of the body and leaving an ashy substance in the chest cavity and abdomen. Other parts remain strangely intact – often just a leg or two. Surroundings are likewise undamaged except for a fine layer of soot and 'grease'.

Several photographs have been knocking around for years showing remarkably similar pictures of the victims of spontaneous human combustion. The strangest characteristic – apart from the startlingly disembodied legs, with shoes sometimes on the feet – is possibly the intensity of the fire, which is hot enough to destroy much of the body, but which does not spread beyond it.

Paranormal and weirdo explanations naturally abound. One fellow maintained that, since the remains of several burnt bodies were found to contain quite a bit of alcohol, this could have caused the victim to catch fire. But that would be like trying to ignite a sherry trifle. Somebody else said that emotionally distressed people might cause nitrogen in the body to explode. (Why? How?)

If one looks at the photographs or reads autopsy reports, several fairly obvious things become clear. There is often a heat source very nearby, in some cases an open fire, in others, cigarettes and matches. Always the victims are alone, frequently they are old and more than sometimes they are

101

found to have been drinking heavily. Indeed, the London Fire Brigade has identified poor, old men, living alone, as a target risk group. Why? Because they have a few beers and then fall asleep in the armchair with a cigarette between their fingers. Indeed, several photographs of victims of spontaneous human combustion show their remains eerily seated in a chair.

Hang on a second, you say, a cigarette is not enough to incinerate a body and leave the flat intact. But – aha! – you may not have heard of the 'wick effect', which causes clothing that is in contact with a body to smoulder, liquefying the body fat and absorbing it, thus acting as a wick and keeping the very hot but localized fire going. Unclothed body parts remain intact. In these cases, the fire is started by clothing coming into contact with a flame, possibly when the victim collapses unconscious from illness, or as a result of the 'falling-down-liquid' effect.

In 1999, forensic scientists John DeHaan and Said Nurbakhsh decided to try to replicate the wick effect. They wrapped a large pig carcass in a thin cotton blanket and set fire to it. The body burned away merrily for four hours, fuelled only by its own fat, which seeped into the charred blanket, causing it to act as a wick, just as predicted, after a time exposing the bones of the thorax and limbs. Four-and-a-half hours into the test, the carcass burned into two pieces and the test was stopped. During this whole time, the room temperature remained low enough for experimenters to wander in and out at will.

So it seems likely that the Countess (remember her?) got out of bed feeling ill (or drunk), lit the oil lamp and collapsed or fell over, setting fire to her nightclothes, which produced the wick effect overnight, coating the walls and furniture of the closed room with the characteristic fatty airborne soot, and causing the household to get the decorators in.

Blind artists and deaf musicians

You would think that if you were deaf you couldn't be a musician, and likewise if blind that you couldn't be a painter (canvases I mean, not drainpipes and architraves, although the same applies really). But this is not true. I once heard a double-bass player named Gary Karr talking about a stone-deaf musician he was teaching. Apparently he could feel the music through the vibrations. Beethoven was famously deaf and Vaughan Williams also used to sit there with an ear trumpet in half the time. The Who's Pete Townshend is completely deaf in one ear from years of noisy concerts and an explosion when Keith Moon blew up his drum set onstage. 'It hurts, it's painful, and it's frustrating,' he says.

All these fellows suffered loss of hearing over time, but they are knocked into a cocked hat by Scottish percussionist Evelyn Glennie, who is the first person in musical history to make a full-time career as a solo percussionist. What's more, she's been profoundly deaf since the age of twelve. Glennie maintains that deafness is misunderstood. 'People have thought that deafness means silence, and music is sound, so how can you experience music?' she says. 'For me, hearing is also what I'm seeing and also what I'm feeling.' She explains that she taught herself to hear with parts of her body other than her ears, feeling different frequencies in different places. She picks out feet, legs and tummy for special mention, and regularly plays barefoot so as to *feel* the music – *literally*. Sounds perfectly feasible to me. Whatever the case, she's a superb musician – you should have a listen (if you are not yourself deaf; if you are, have a *feel*).

Well, OK, you say, but if you're *blind* there's no way you could be a painter. But don't count on it, because there are actually several blind painters who make a living at it. Eşref Armağan is a Turkish artist who was born without eyes. Incredibly, he produces figurative paintings – paintings of *things* – that not only look like what they are supposed to be, but are sort of decorative and balanced. I saw a portrait he'd done and recognized it immediately as Bill Clinton. 'How on earth did he manage that?' I wondered. In case you are interested, what he does is ask a sighted person to trace a photograph, pressing down hard. He then turns the paper over and feels the line, transferring what he feels onto another sheet of paper (back-to-front presumably). He then applies oil paints with his fingers, one colour at a time to avoid making a brown mess. After three days the paint has dried and he can go on to the next colour. I hope he then has a lie down with a stiff drink. And he doesn't just do portraits. I saw one he'd done of a leaping dolphin, and his landscapes have perspective, as well as differing points of view; it's all very strange – a sort of blind painting by numbers.

Sargy Mann takes a different approach. He is an English painter who was diagnosed with cataracts when he was thirty-six and eventually became completely blind. Interestingly, he once played drums in a jazz trio with Dudley Moore tickling the ivories and, before he got married (Mann, not Moore), he lived for eight years with Kingsley Amis and his wife at their house in Hertfordshire, painting the countryside whenever he could. In case the company was insufficiently interesting, Cecil Day-Lewis, who was the Poet Laureate and Daniel Day-Lewis's dad, used to come round.

Like the Impressionist painter Claude Monet, Sargy Mann underwent cataract operations, which improved things a bit, and infused his paintings – afterwards I mean – with a blue light.

In 1988 he began working full time as a painter, knowing that his sight was likely to get much worse. On his sixty-eighth birthday Sargy woke up with a pain in his left eye. He had suffered a detached retina, reducing his sight to almost nothing. But, by squinting through an adapted telescope with his remaining (very knackered) eye he continued to paint, often going off with his paints, brushes and white stick. He was soon described as 'probably the best blind painter in Peckham'.

Mann described beginning to paint while almost completely blind as 'one of the strangest sensations of my life. I "saw" the canvas turn blue as I put the paint down,' and, looking on the bright side – let's face it, he had little choice – Sargy told Tim Adams, who wrote about it in the *Observer*, 'I had about twenty-five years' apprenticeship for going blind. It was a bugger, but I kept working out how to paint over those twenty-five years, and my brain kept finding new ways to see the world, if you like.'

His paintings are wonderful and you should see them if you get a chance. I often complain about human beings, but sometimes some of them do such marvellous things that I can't help but have a sneaking admiration for them.

Last turkey in the shop: everything you've always wanted to know about the penis

The penis is a reproductive intromittent copulatory organ that functions also as the urinal duct in male placental mammals. The word 'penis' comes from the Latin for 'tail', and the word 'glans' – the term for the head of the organ – is Latin for 'acorn'. The human penis is the largest among the primates, both in proportion to body size and absolutely. An adult chimp's erect penis is about 3 inches (8 cm) in length and a gorilla's is only half that.

Although the blue whale has an impressive popular reputation, the barnacle holds the world-beating penis-to-body-size record. A barnacle's willy can grow to up to forty times its body length such that it can reach females who live round the corner of the rock, without Mr Barnacle having to get up from the TV. For a 6-foot(1.8-m)-tall man this would be the equivalent of a 240-footer (73 m), about the length of the perimeter of a basketball court. Imagine that – you'd need a low loader to drive it round.

From tip to root, a flaccid human penis generally measures between 3 and 4 inches (8.5 to 10.5 cm). There are two types. The first (called a grower) gets a lot bigger during erection while the second (called a shower – rhymes with mower not power) looks big most of the time but doesn't increase in size all that much during arousal. Reportedly, 79 per cent of men have growers, while 21 per cent have showers.

Interestingly, penises ('penises' and 'penes' are both correct plural formations) are pretty much the same size as one another when erect, though a small tool can double its length, while a larger member will get only about a third longer. Most erect penises measure 6–7 inches (15–17.8 cm) in length, with the average being about 6½ inches (16.5 cm). Who did the measuring? Jonah Falcon has the biggest (known) penis in the world. It measures an impressive 13½ inches (34 cm) when off duty. In 2010 Mr Falcon announced the interesting fact that he can envelop a doorknob with his foreskin. I read recently that he is unemployed and living with his mother.

Smokers might like to know that the habit is harmful to the John

Thomas and can shorten the old chap by damaging the blood vessels that are so important in erectile function. This you don't want because it's going to interfere with one of the main jobs of your nudger – sexual intercourse. Let's face facts, you can't open a door with a sock of blancmange. According to German researchers the average tallywhacker takes a mere two minutes and fifty seconds to complete a typical intercourse session. On the receiving end, women, the researchers discovered, perceive it as lasting five minutes and thirty seconds. That sounds like the opposite of time flying while one is enjoying oneself.

The average male orgasm lasts six seconds, which is seventeen seconds shy of a woman's twenty-three seconds. That's effectively four times the amount of orgasming (if that is a word) of gentlemen. I think, chaps, that in this world of sex equality, there's credit in the bank here and we are owed something. Incidentally, the furthest any man has been measured firing his salute is an astonishing 18 feet (5.5 m) – a bit more actually. The gunner's name: Horst Schultz. I don't know what crazy research project this formed a part of but I hope they wore safety goggles. Lucky he didn't have somebody's eye out with that one.

There are fifty million sperm in the average emission, but there can be as many as 300 million, though it would be a tedious job counting them. The better the quality and the higher the number of the sperm you produce, the more attractive you will be to women. I know this because some Spanish scientists measured the quality and counted the number of the sperm produced by some men and then showed some women their photographs (the *men* not the sperm). The ladies were instructed to choose the most handsome and they mainly picked the healthy-sperm producers.

Finally, on the subject of scientific research, doctors have been growing skin for burn victims from the foreskins of circumcised babies. Just one foreskin can produce 250,000 sq feet (23,000 sq m) of new skin, which is the area of the Information Technology Center of the Nanjing Olympic Sports Center in Nanjing, China.

For a list of interesting slang words for penis, see '125 slang terms for the penis' on page 228.

All about stomach ulcers

After a midday 'hotel-session' with her boyfriend, Marion Crane, the unfortunate character played by Janet Leigh in Alfred Hitchcock's *Psycho* (1960), says, 'I better get back to the office; these extended lunch hours give my boss excess acid.' So what? I hear you cry. Well, back in the 1960s and 1970s it was thought that indigestion and stomach ulcers were caused by lifestyle stress – a problem of high-flying executives and the bosses of secretaries taking long slap-and-tickle lunches with their boyfriends.

But in 1982, Dr Barry Marshall and Dr Robin Warren of Perth, Western Australia, discovered a spiral-shaped bacterium, now called *Helicobacter pylori* (*H. pylori*), living in the stomachs of patients with stomach ulcers. This was a surprise as the environment of the stomach contains acid similar in strength to car battery acid and was thought to be too hostile for bacteria to set up home. The two doctors suggested that the bacterium might be *causing* the ulcers and tests proved them right. Their creative thinking won them the Nobel Prize, and the treatment of stomach ulcers rapidly and dramatically changed.

It is now known that some 80 per cent of stomach ulcers are caused by *Helicobacter pylori*, which inflames the lining of the stomach or duodenum, 'wearing a hole' in the mucus barrier. Nowadays, the treatment is much easier and better than it was in even the fairly recent past. A combination of acid-lowering pills and antibiotics generally leads to swift relief of the symptoms and a complete cure in 95 per cent of cases.

I am reminded of the story of the medical research student who thought he would try vindaloo curry as a novel treatment for a stomach ulcer patient. To everyone's great surprise the treatment was a complete success and the researcher published the results in a paper, which he boldly entitled 'Vindaloo Curries Cure Stomach Ulcers'. Administering the same treatment to his next patient, he was shocked when the man promptly died and, realizing the significance of this result, he published another paper, which he entitled 'Follow-up Study Reveals Vindaloo Curries Cure 50% of Stomach Ulcers'.

A stomach (or gastric) ulcer is a type of peptic ulcer – a wound occurring in a variety of places in the digestive tract, leaving a small red crater. The most common kind is the duodenal ulcer, which crops up, unsurprisingly, in the duodenum, at the top of the small intestine. The symptoms are generally a burning or gnawing pain in the abdomen, sometimes drilling into the back. In some people, however, their ulcer causes no symptoms.

Ulcers can affect people of any age, including children, but are most common in people over sixty. Despite the stereotypes, women are just as prone to them as men.

Ulcers can also occur iatrogenically, that is to say as the result of medical treatment for some other problem. Twenty per cent are the result of the regular taking of aspirin, ibuprofen or other painkillers, which can disrupt the stomach's mucus barrier.

As often happens in medicine, the old suspect, stress, is now being reconsidered as a player in the stomach ulcer drama and researchers are looking at the way that it might promote *H. pylori* infection. The bacterium thrives in an acidic environment, and stress is known to cause the production of excess stomach acid. Indeed, a study in mice has shown that long-term stress and *H. pylori* infection are *both* associated with the development of peptic ulcers.

In case you fear that stress will give you an ulcer, here is a useful stress-management technique that I use myself:

1　Picture yourself beside a stream.
2　Listen to the birds twittering in the cool air. Nobody knows your secret place.
3　You are in total seclusion, away from the insanity and chaos of everyday life.
4　Listen to the gentle stream as it fills the air with its soothing babble. It is so clear and serene that you can, quite easily, see the bulging eyes of the bastard you're holding under the water, as he fights for breath.

Doesn't that make you feel better?

Men's diseases

A new place called 'Nibble-fish' opened near me recently. I thought it was a café but apparently women go there to have small fishes chew their toes for some reason. Men and women are different. Women regard their bodies as outcrops of their emotional selves and love to pamper and decorate them. Men, on the other hand, see their bodies as the thing hanging off the bottom of their head that gets them to work or down the pub. Few men spend hours massaging fragrant oils into their thighs or want fish to nibble their feet. Neither do they sprint down to the doctor's when they feel ill. It usually takes weeks of nagging from a worried woman to get them to drag themselves down there.

Men suffer from a whole load of illnesses that women don't (*can't*) get. These are mainly to do with the wedding tackle and connecting pipework. But chaps also tend to suffer more than women from certain illnesses that anyone can get, often because of their behaviour. Some of these – mainly predictable – conditions are listed below.

The leading causes of male ill health and death in this country are, in descending order, heart disease and cancer, accidents – including car crashes, poisoning, falls and drowning – lung disease, stroke, type-2 diabetes, suicide, flu and pneumonia and, finally, kidney disease. No, wait, there was another one but I can't remember what it was – oh yes, Alzheimer's disease.

The happy news is that many of these conditions are preventable – especially suicide. For example, stopping smoking, not eating a load of rubbish and actually moving around a bit will greatly improve your chances when it comes to heart-disease and cancer roulette. These two conditions together account for half of all male bucket-kickings. Not smoking, doing a bit of exercise and eating some vegetables with your steak will also reduce your chances of having a stroke, getting diabetes and suffering lung diseases. The evidence is now mounting up that Alzheimer's too has links to lifestyle. Other changes to your male behaviour, such as not driving everywhere at 80 mph (200 kph), not being a knife-wielding gang member

and not walking along roofs carrying a load of bricks, with no hard hat on, will help to cut down on accidents. Flu, pneumonia and kidney disease are going to have to look after themselves. Here are a few of the other interesting ones.

- **Gout:** less common predominantly male conditions include gout, which is usually depicted as a symptom of rich living as exemplified by the fat eighteenth-century gentleman in a powdered wig with his bandaged foot up on a stool. Men account for more than 90 per cent of all gout cases but too much food and drink are not altogether to blame. Gout is actually a form of arthritis, which affects joints and usually the big toe. Famous sufferers include King Henry VIII, Samuel Johnson and Benjamin Franklin. Treatment is available to relieve symptoms.
- **Testicular cancer:** though much talked about, testicular cancer accounts for only 1 per cent of all male cancers and is most commonly found in chaps between the ages of fifteen and thirty-five. It has a high cure rate if found early, so get down to the doctor's and start talking balls.
- **Hangover:** the hangover is one of those male conditions that women are increasingly trying to muscle in on. A cold shower followed by a hearty breakfast and a pint of 'hair of the dog' have long been said to be the best remedy. But doctors have discovered that sleep and a few of those fizzy pills you drop in a glass of water are the best bet.
- **Abdominal herniation:** hernias are another predominantly male condition and happen when a small piece of the underlying pipework comes through the abdominal muscle, producing a bump, often as a result of lifting a heavy weight. The most common type is the inguinal hernia or 'rupture', as it used to be known. Surgery is

successful and no more does a chap have to lumber about wearing a truss, euphemistically referred to as a 'gentlemen's abdominal support'.

- **Male pattern baldness:** baldness is one of those conditions that you can accept or attempt to disguise. Frankly the most dignified thing to do is to cut the hair short and recognize that women find baldness attractive. What nobody finds attractive is the comb-over or, worse, the toupee. A man in a wig? That's not masculine.

The flayed cadavers of Honoré Fragonard

We've all got black sheep in our families, indeed *I* am the dark meat in my own, and Jean-Honoré Fragonard (1732–1806) was no different. Fragonard was a French artist, whose 550 paintings in 'saucy' Rococo style were already old hat while he was churning them out. They have been described as 'hideous chocolate-box rubbish', but I shan't pass comment, because it's his mad cousin, Honoré Fragonard (without the 'Jean-'), whom I'm interested in.

Jean-less Honoré Fragonard (1732–99) was an anatomist, who is now mainly remembered for his flayed cadavers, or *écorchés* in French, some of which you can see in the Musée Fragonard d'Alfort in suburban Paris if it's not too warm a day. He was born in Grasse on the French Riviera and in 1762, after studying surgery, was recruited by Claude Bourgelat, who had started the world's first veterinary school, in Lyon.

Not to be outdone, Louis XV started up his own vet school in Paris in 1765, which is now the École nationale vétérinaire d'Alfort, in Maisons-Alfort. Fragonard spent six years as the college's first professor of anatomy, but was expelled in 1771 on the grounds of insanity, owing to his penchant for cutting up and posing – for theatrical effect – preserved cadavers, at the rate of about two a week. I like this fellow already. Of the 3,000 works he created during his lifetime, there remain twenty-one *écorchés*, including the amusing 'Human foetuses dancing a jig', which consists of three human embryos, doing just that.

After being sacked, he was obliged to do his dissections at home, which must have annoyed the neighbours – especially in the summer – and earned his keep by selling his 'artworks' to the aristocracy, many of whom, as today, had more money than sense.

Fragonard never explained his preservation methods, but he is likely to have used well-known anatomical techniques, preserving bodies by soaking them in alcohol, mixed with pepper and herbs, rather like the ancient Egyptians. After stripping them of skin to expose muscles, blood vessels, nerves, bone and connective tissue, and while they were still soft, he probably – there are no definite records – injected their veins, arteries and other miscellaneous bodily tunnels with wax or animal fat mixed with turpentine and pigment. To position them in the various poses he devised, he is likely to have stretched them on frames and left them to dry. I can think of worse ways of making a living – working in a call centre, for example.

After the death of Fragonard's fiancée, posh Parisian cafés and fancy Parisian cocktail parties were rife with rumour that the figure on the back of the horse in his *Horseman of the Apocalypse*, based on Albrecht Dürer's print and consisting of a figure on a galloping horse, surrounded by human foetuses riding sheep and horse foetuses, was actually the exhumed corpse of his betrothed, who had succumbed to grief after her parents forbade their marriage. I am given to understand, however, that if you have a look in the lap of the rider, you can see quite clearly that this rumour is false in one important respect.

In 1793, along with his painterly cousin, Fragonard became a member of the Jury national des Arts, but died six years later, rather disillusioned, on 5 April 1799.

All about Hansen's disease

If you go down the doctor's with funny light-coloured sores on your skin that feel a bit numb and don't heal, or you have numb hands, arms, feet, legs or muscle weakness, your doctor might diagnose a case of Hansen's disease. But he or she probably won't, because Hansen's disease is another name for leprosy, which, though it has been known since biblical times, is now very rare in this country.

Records of Hansen's disease go back to ancient Egypt, China and India, and afflictions that may well be leprosy are referred to in the early books of the Bible. During the Middle Ages leprosy was the scourge of Europe and was rife in England. In Scotland King Robert the Bruce succumbed to it and was buried in the local abbey. Workmen repairing the floor of the building in 1819 uncovered his body, which was exhumed and a cast was taken of the skull. This showed the distinctive frontal tooth and bone loss so characteristic of the advanced stage of Hansen's disease. You can see the evidence yourself next time you are passing Dumfries Museum.

Matthew Paris – the Benedictine monk (1197–1259), not the differently spelled gay ex-politician journalist – estimated that, at the time he was writing, there were more than 100 leper-houses in England. Outside these 'hospitals', victims were obliged to wear distinctive clothes and warn the public of their approach by sounding a wooden clapper. They were also ordered to pray endlessly and were not allowed into pubs or churches, or to eat with healthy people, wash in streams or walk on narrow footpaths. Rather like smokers today. Although this may all sound a bit harsh, it worked in stopping the spread of the condition, which by the sixteenth century had almost disappeared in England. By the close of the seventeenth century, however, it had begun to spread among the new colonies of America.

Hansen's disease is named after Gerhard Armauer Hansen (1841–1912), a Norwegian physician who in 1873 identified the bacterium which is the cause of the malady, *Mycobacterium leprae* (Hansen's coccus spirally). Apart from the sores, the nerve damage and the progressive debilitation if left untreated, it is deformation of the fingers and the development of large disfiguring nodules on the face – which give some sufferers the look of those wrinkly Sharpay dogs – that characterize the condition. Leprosy can incubate for months or years in an infected person before symptoms appear, making it difficult to find out when the disease was contracted and where. It is transmitted by droplets from the nose and mouth during close frequent contact with untreated sufferers and you can't get it from touching or hugging an infectious person. Luckily, as well as being rather difficult to catch, early diagnosis can now limit the damage and kill off the bacterium.

Hansen's disease comes in two main flavours: tuberculoid and lepromatous, the lepromatous kind being the most severely disfiguring. Because of progressive loss of feeling, people who have had untreated leprosy for a long time may injure their feet or hands repeatedly, without noticing, and consequently lose the use of these organs. It is not really true that leprosy makes your fingers 'fall off', though it can cause deformity (claw hand) and loss of fingers and toes as a result of injury or tissue death.

Today Hansen's disease is still common in many places, favouring temperate, tropical and subtropical climates, and there are about two million sufferers in 119 countries. Roughly 100 cases are diagnosed in the United States each year, mostly in Hawaii and US islands, but also in the south and in California. Various antibiotics are now used to kill the bacterium, along with aspirin and thalidomide (remember that?) to control inflammation. But there are signs that the condition may be waking from its long sleep and the appearance of a new drug-resistant *Mycobacterium leprae* has caused medics to prick up their ears.

2 The Natural World

Humongous fungus: the biggest living thing on the planet

In 1998 Catherine Parks, a scientist at the Pacific Northwest Research Station in La Grande, Oregon, heard that a lot of trees were dying in the ancient Malheur National Forest, in the Blue Mountains of eastern Oregon, and decided to investigate. Using aerial photographs, she identified a large area of dead and moribund trees.

Taking root samples from more than a hundred of the trees from this area, she found they were being killed by a well-recognized fungus. The only evidence of the pesky subterranean fungus visible on the surface was the golden mushrooms that sprout from the trees in little clumps during the autumn, when it's wet. Their caps are yellow-brown, and somewhat sticky when moist. These are edible mushrooms with a strong, distinctively nutty flavour, though opinions differ as to their deliciousness or otherwise. Considered a delicacy by some, others find them rather bland to the palate, and in need of a good dose of garlic butter and salt. The prominent scales on their caps, and the well-developed ring on their stems, identified these mushrooms as the fruiting bodies of *Armillaria solidipes*, the so-called 'honey mushroom', a known tree-killer common to certain hardwood and conifer forests.

Armillaria can be very destructive and is responsible for so-called forest 'white rot' root disease. Unlike most parasites, the honey mushroom can live happily on dead wood and does not need to moderate its growth to avoid killing its host. No, down among the roots and under the bark at the base of the trunk, great white pads of cream-coloured mycelium, with a strong mushroomy perfume, establish themselves, sometimes extending upwards in a network of fine filaments, living off the trees and destroying them by attacking the sapwood and sucking out water and carbohydrates. The fungus spreads to other trees by growing long black rhizomorphs, so-called 'bootlaces', underneath the bark and along the ground, at the rate of about a metre a year.

Parks confirmed the identity of the fungus by doing a bit of DNA testing and compared cultures grown from all her fungus samples. Astonishingly, she found that sixty-one of them came from the same organism. This wasn't just another little outbreak of honey mushroom. What Parks had discovered in, or rather under, the forest was a single fungus that had grown bigger than any living thing anybody had ever seen. This was the biggest organism in the world.

The overwhelming bulk of this mammoth mushroom lives underground, out of sight, and is estimated to occupy some 2,200 acres, or three-and-a-bit square miles (890 hectares). It is 3½ miles (5.6 km) from one side to the other, and goes down 3 feet (1 m) into the ground. Mighty oaks do indeed grow from tiny acorns and this man-size specimen of *Armillaria solidipes* began as a single spore about 2,400 years ago, and possibly longer ago than that, anyway before the calendar that we now use was invented. That's roughly 400 years before the birth of Jesus.

Its huge size is thought to be a possible function of the dry climate in eastern Oregon. Spores in such climates find it hard to grow and new organisms are therefore slow to establish, allowing older specimens to spread. Lacking competition, this humongous fungus has had the ideal conditions for eating trees and growing old, unbothered by young upstarts. Although this particular *Armillaria solidipes* is a tree-killing pest, local scientists are aware that a balance of tree to fungus has been established in this forest for thousands of years, so control, rather than extermination, is likely to be the prescription for this large mushroom factory. But the next thing, surely, is to weigh it.

All about sharks: thirty-three fascinating facts

There are certain subjects on which every gentleman genius ought to be able to discourse with aplomb. Among those you can forget are ironing, how to gossip correctly, Tarot reading made easy and eyeliner. These are girl subjects, and if your girlfriend is having a screaming fit after reading this paragraph, please tell her not to send me complaining letters about my reactionary and sexist character. Can't you keep her under control? Anyway, 'sharks' is a boy subject and here's some information you might not know about those things.

1   Sharks (superorder Selachimorpha) are fish.
2   There are 440 shark species.
3   They are found in all seas.
4   The smallest shark is the dwarf lanternshark (*Etmopterus perryi*), which is about 6½ inches (17 cm) long.
5   The largest shark is the whale shark (*Rhincodon typus*), which can reach a length of 39 feet (12 m). That's longer than a bus.
6   Most sharks live between twenty and thirty years.
7   The spiny dogfish (one type of shark) can live for more than 100 years.
8   Some species of shark give birth to live young; others produce eggs.
9   Out of more than 440 shark species, only four have attacked and killed humans, unprovoked: the bull, great white, oceanic whitetip and tiger sharks.
10 Sharks' skeletons are made not of bone but of cartilage.
11 Because their skeletons are half as dense as bone, sharks are much lighter than they would be otherwise.
12 Sharks cannot swim backwards.
13 Evidence of the existence of sharks goes back more than 420 million years (about the time it takes a second-class letter to arrive).
14 Most sharks must swim to avoid sinking.
15 Some species must swim to avoid 'drowning'.

16 Most sharks will die in fresh water.

17 The shortfin mako shark can swim at more than 30 mph (50 kph).

18 In Australia, shark-meat is used in fish and chips.

19 Some sharks eat practically anything.

20 To eject unwanted items from its gut, a shark will either vomit or evaginate its stomach (turn it inside-out).

21 Many sharks hunt in packs.

22 Some shark species can smell one drop of blood mixed up in a million drops of seawater.

23 A hammerhead shark's funny-looking head, with far-apart eyes and nostrils, is thought to help it smell better (I mean *detect smell better*, not improve its BO problem).

24 Sharkskin is covered in little 'toothlets', which reduce turbulence, allowing the shark to swim faster, working rather as the craters in a golf ball do.

25 Sharkskin was once used as sandpaper.

26 Sharks' teeth are embedded in their gums, not attached to their jaws. They fall out regularly and are replaced by new ones.

27 Some sharks lose 30,000 teeth during their life.

28 A shark's jaw is not attached to its skull but 'floats about'.

29 Unlike other fish, sharks don't have gas-filled swim bladders to keep them buoyant; their huge livers, which make up some 30 per cent of their body mass, keep them up.

30 Most sharks are cold-blooded.

31 Sharks use special receptors, the so-called 'ampullae of Lorenzini', to detect the electromagnetic field produced by their prey.

32 In recent years, the average number of shark attacks in which a human has died has been between four and five a year. Pet dogs kill about thirty people a year in the United States alone, and mosquitoes kill about *three million* worldwide. In twenty years mosquitoes could wipe out the entire population of the UK.

33 Including those killed in fishing, about 100 million sharks are killed by humans every year.

The chimp who learned to speak

As a boy I used to swear (occasionally) and, if my grandma was staying, she would reprove me: 'Using *language*!' she would say, though I never understood how you could swear *without* using language.

It is generally agreed that humans are unique in their ability to use language, profane and otherwise, and though a bear can growl at you if he is cross, he isn't going to be able to ask you to open a window, or hand him his toothbrush. But that is just what Washoe the chimpanzee (1965–2007) learned to do, and this is her story.

Washoe was born somewhere in West Africa in 1965, which is where the US Air Force caught her, for use in space research. In 1967, when she was already two years old, psychologists Allen and Beatrix Gardner started a project at the University of Nevada, Reno, to teach Washoe American Sign Language (ASL).

Chimpanzees communicate in the wild largely by gesture and the Gardners decided to make use of this ability. They began by assembling a team of ASL users, who spoke to her only in sign language, without making any noises. Because they were interested in human language acquisition, the Gardners raised Washoe in the same way as a human child. She sometimes wore clothes and sat at a table for meals in her own trailer, which had a couch, fridge, cooking area and bed. She could play outside in the trees or with toys, including dolls, which she would bathe and talk to.

Washoe seemed to recognize herself clearly when shown her reflection in a mirror, signing, 'Me Washoe'. She was rather disconcerted when first introduced to other chimpanzees, seeming to regard herself as human. But she slowly joined in and enjoyed playing with other chimps.

Washoe learned the signs slowly and made mistakes, which were the same as those made by children learning ASL. But she was also able spontaneously to use signs she had not been taught but had seen being used among the researchers, one day referring to her toothbrush with the appropriate sign, one she hadn't been actively taught. Washoe could also generalize, so that having learned the sign for dog she could apply it to *any* dog. Having acquired the sign for 'open' she could use it for a door, a briefcase or a box, thus revealing that she understood 'open' as a concept.

Very significantly, Washoe could combine words herself, using new constructions of her own that followed grammatical rules and consistent word order (syntax). She signed 'open' and 'hurry' together as a single sign to create a meaningful new idea. She could use prepositions to indicate where something was in relation to something else. When shown an apple in a hat she combined the three words in their proper order, signing 'apple in hat'. She went a step further when shown a doll in a cup, signing 'baby in my drink', spontaneously inserting 'my' in the right place. When seeing a thermos flask in use for the first time, she signed 'metal cup drink', and referred to a swan, a creature she had not seen before, as 'water bird'.

When inexperienced signers met Washoe for the first time, she would slow down her own signing, in sympathy with the beginners. Once, when one of her caretakers, Kat, returned after an absence of weeks, following a miscarriage, Washoe snubbed her, to show what she thought of being abandoned. Kat apologized in ASL and then signed, 'My baby died.' After staring at her for a moment, Washoe looked down, before slowly signing 'cry', and tracing the line of an imaginary tear down her cheek. Chimpanzees themselves do not cry tears and Kat described this single momentary sign as more telling of Washoe's capabilities than all her years of accomplished syntax.

When Washoe was five she was moved to the University of Oklahoma's Institute of Primate Studies in Norman, Oklahoma. Then, in 1980, she went to live at the Chimpanzee and Human Communication Institute at the Central Washington University.

On 30 October 2007 it was announced by the institute that, having learned some 350 words of ASL and carried on goodness knows how many meaningful – if simple – conversations with humans, Washoe had died at the age of forty-two. A few weeks later, dressed in a sober jacket and tie, primate researcher and animal rights campaigner Roger Fouts, who had been one of Washoe's closest and dearest friends since the very earliest days in Nevada, and then in Oklahoma, delivered her eulogy, just as if she had been a human being.

All about the Large Hadron Collider

In case you were wondering, a 'hadron' is a composite particle made of quarks held together by the strong nuclear force. The best-known hadrons are protons and neutrons. Actually, it's more complicated than this, but that should be enough to be going on with. Possibly too much.

The Large Hadron Collider (LHC) is a particle accelerator, and what it does is to accelerate particles. I hope I'm not blinding you with science. But it is not any old particle accelerator, it is the largest and highest-energy particle accelerator in the whole world – the Rolls-Royce of particle accelerators, if you like. Actually, I'm not sure how many particle accelerators there are in the whole world, but if you have one in your garage, you can bet it won't be as good as the LHC.

The Large Hadron Collider is situated in a ring-doughnut-shaped tube, or tunnel, 17 miles (27 km) long, about 574 feet (175 m) under the Franco-Swiss border, near Geneva, Switzerland, where two beams of hadrons – either protons or lead ions or kittens (no, not kittens, I made that up) – are fired in opposite directions, gaining energy with each lap. By smashing the two beams into each other head-on at very high energy, teams of physicists from the four corners of the globe will be able to recreate the conditions that existed a minuscule fraction of a second after the Big Bang. The collisions occur with tremendous force – which is why it's such a long tunnel – and by using special detectors, physicists will be able to analyse the particles created in these deliberate 'traffic accidents'. The LHC promises to be a huge help in advancing human understanding because nobody, yet, fully understands how or why the universe developed in the way it did – especially not my mum.

The Large Hadron Collider was built by the European Organization for Nuclear Research (CERN) and more than 10,000 scientists and engineers from 100 countries, along with hundreds of universities and laboratories, collaborated on its construction.

On 10 September 2008, the proton beams were successfully sent round the doughnut for the first time. But on 19 September 2008, just to show that humans were involved, there was a sudden problem (due to a boring old faulty electrical connection) in about 100 enormous magnets, which got much too hot. Fifty-three magnets were damaged and had to be repaired or replaced during shutdown, but on 20 November 2009 things got going again with the first recorded proton collisions three days later. Nonetheless, because of the problems, the Large Hadron Collider will continue working only at half power for a number of years.

Despite this, a new world record was set for the highest-energy man-made particle collision on 30 March 2010. But they weren't trying to win a gold medal. These collisions are important because they provide a means to test various predictions of high-energy physics, which so far are just guesses. If they can be shown to be false it will disprove the assumptions that underlie them – a very useful step forward. The experiments will never prove them to be *definitely* true, however, only *probably* true – which is good, but not as good as definitely falsifying them. This is no different from any scientific experiment. Scientists are pretty sure about some things, such as that Liberace loved his mum and that water is wet, but they can never be certain of anything. Science is the art of doubt.

One of the most talked about of these predictions is for something that is hypothesized to exist, but which has never been observed in experiments. This something is called the 'Higgs boson', which sounds to me like an animal that inhabits the Great Plains. But it is important because, if it exists, it will resolve various annoying inconsistencies in the way physics is currently explained.

Finally, I thought you might like to know that in one science journal I was reading (I'll spare its blushes), the term 'Large Hadron Collider' was repeatedly misprinted as 'Large Hardon Collider'. I think the journalist responsible must have had a different kind of Big Bang on his mind.

The green anaconda: the largest snake in the world

What is it about snakes that is so interesting to masculine gentlemen of the male persuasion? If we ignore daft psychologists' rationalizations about phalluses, I think we can say that it could well be a mixture of healthy respect for their possible deadliness (snakes', not phalluses', nor psychologists'), an admiration for their beautiful design and a primeval urge to protect one's wife and family by chopping their heads off (the *snakes'* heads – do try to keep up).

Also the names of snakes are good: Sonoran sidewinder, bushmaster, children's python, rhombic night adder, sunbeam snake, water moccasin, reticulated python, longnosed worm snake, rufous beaked snake, Nicobar cat snake, Brahminy blind snake, black rat snake, Brongersma's pitviper, monocled cobra, fierce snake, coachwhip snake, paradise flying snake, tic polonga, rough green snake, giant Malagasy hognose snake, black mamba, cottonmouth, king brown, river jack, South Andaman krait, boomslang, nose-horned viper, inland carpet python, wart snake, beauty rat snake, midget faded rattlesnake, African twig snake, Pope's tree viper, eastern yellowbelly racer.

Why size should be so impressive I do not know, but it is – that and venomosity (is that a word?). The longest snake ever measured is the Asiatic reticulated python (*Python reticulatus*), one of which came in at 33 feet (10 m, longer than a bus). However, length isn't everything, and the green anaconda, a non-venomous boa species from South America, is recognized as the heaviest and fattest snake in the world. Anacondas twirling around the trees in the jungles of South America have a girth of a well-built man, and can swallow whole capybaras. Other foods, while we're about it, include caimans (small crocodiles), iguanas and rabbits (easy).

The green anaconda is also known as the anaconda, common anaconda or water boa, and its Latin name (*Eunectes murinus*) means something like 'good swimmer mouse predator'. South American names include the Spanish *mata-toro*, meaning 'bull killer'.

In the photographs I've seen of captured anacondas it usually takes at least six men to hold them off the ground and they look really heavy. Also, if you got the impression just now that they aren't all that long, that is a mistake: they are very long, just not quite as long as the python I mentioned. The largest anaconda ever measured was almost 28 feet (8.5 m) in length with a waist of 44 inches (1.1 m). They didn't put it on the snake scale but worked out that it must have weighed about thirty-six stone.

Green anacondas are so-named because of their olive-green skin with black splodges. They live in swamps and slow streams in the tropical rainforests of the Amazon and Orinoco basins and, though hopeless movers on land, are stealthy and swift in the water. Their eyes are high up on their heads, so they can lurk invisibly, only their eyes above the waterline, while their lunch (you) swims innocently towards them. When you pass by, the hungry snake will snatch your leg or something with its jaws and then coil around you. Their enormous muscular force is enough to suffocate a man in minutes. Then they swallow you. In 2008, a ten-foot (i.e. small) python, which also constrict their prey, killed a Venezuelan zookeeper while he was on night shift at Caracas Zoo. His colleagues arriving for work in the morning found the snake swallowing his head and beat it away with sticks. Marks on the man's wrist suggested the snake had grabbed him first, before squeezing him to death.

In 1997, Luis Llosa's film *Anaconda* came out. The plot concerns a film crew taken hostage by a mad hunter and dragged along on his improbable quest to capture the world's largest snake. The tagline was: 'You can't scream if you can't breathe.' It might better have been, 'You can't yawn if you left after ten minutes to go to the pub instead.'

Lepus: a constellation you should know

We humans are a pattern-seeking/finding species. If you look at the blobs on your wallpaper for long enough they will soon turn into pictures of things – for some people anyway. Psychiatrists have spent years encouraging patients to see figures and shapes in those inkblot tests, though I can only ever see splodges that look like inkblots. It's worse when I go out and look up into the clear night sky. I agree it's a grand sight but I find it a struggle to see the shapes I'm supposed to see in those constellations. Orion (the hunter) is meant to be an easy one to see, but not to my eyes, and Cassiopeia, supposedly another of the easiest to spot – but surely the trickiest to spell – just looks like a big W to me, not a gorgeous royal babe. Ursa Major and Ursa Minor are just saucepans as far as I'm concerned.

Instead of straining to see the better-known constellations I thought it would be more interesting to discuss one of the also-rans immediately to the south of Orion, which barely gets a look-in. This is a little constellation named Lepus (the hare), not to be confused with Lupus (the wolf), which (Lepus) is best visible during January at round about 9 p.m.

Lepus is one of the eighty-eight modern constellations and was one of the forty-eight listed by the second-century astronomer Ptolemy, who also drew world maps and wrote about music (I bet he didn't see the Rolling Stones coming though). Being a hare, Lepus is sometimes shown being chased by Orion or his hunting dogs. But have a look at the diagram of the constellation below. Can anyone really see a hare in that shape? Carlos Castro, my illustrator, has had a go, but I think Ptolemy was taking liberties. I mean, to me those straight lines make it look more like a tent when you're trying to put it up in the rain and everything goes wrong. The trouble is, I suppose, that 'A tent when you're trying to put it up in the rain and everything goes wrong' lacks the punch of 'Lepus'.

When he wasn't drawing maps or coming up with names for constellations, Ptolemy was an astrologer. All I would say on this point is that I've never understood how astrologers can maintain that the constellations can have any effect on us, because their stars are nothing to do with each other and are nowhere near each other. Some of them are further from each other than they are from Earth. In fact, if you got in a spaceship, drove off round the corner of Lepus, as it were, and had a look, you'd see right through it.

Anyway, where was I? Oh yes, the main stars of Lepus (α, β, γ, δ Lep) make up a quadrilateral and have Arabic names that mean things like 'the Camels Quenching their Thirst', which isn't a lot of use really; it still doesn't look like a bloody rabbit – I mean a hair – I mean a *hare*. And when I read that among the notable features of the constellation is that 'R Leporis is a Mira variable and also known as Hind's Crimson Star', and that 'There is one Messier Object in Lepus, M79 – a faint globular cluster with a magnitude of around 8m.56', I wish I'd become a barber like my friend Mike. Hairs are less trouble than hares.

The golden poison frog

When I was a little shaver, one of the sorts of people I hoped to grow up to be was the lithe and painted man with the blowpipe who intermittently oscillated in 405 lines of black-and-white on my parents' Bakelite telly. Usually he would be hunting monkeys or something up in the arboreal canopy of his Amazonian dwelling place, loincloth swinging in the breeze. As he placed the pipe to his lips, the hushed voice of David Attenborough would murmur, 'The dart's tip is coated not with curare but with a deadly alkaloid batrachotoxin painstakingly extracted from the skin of the golden poison frog . . .' How romantic it all seemed.

Phyllobates terribilis, the golden poison frog, is a very small bright yellow, orange or occasionally green frog from the wet and warm Pacific coastal rainforests on the left-hand side of Colombia. It is an endangered species but doesn't seem to realize this and struts about boldly in its hi-viz jacket, unfazed by humans, monkeys, birds or anything else. Its loud colouring is what is known as 'aposematic' (from *apo*, away, and *sematic*, sign/meaning). It warns predators of its toxicity, and with good reason, for this tiny frog is one of the most lethally toxic creatures in the world.

The skin of the golden poison frog is covered in a powerful alkaloid batrachotoxin, which is just Greek for 'frog poison'. It was named by John Daly and Bernhard Witkop, who discovered that the pure alkaloid consists of this: $C_{31}H_{42}N_2O_6$. If that means nothing to you, it doesn't matter. All you need to know is that the poison prevents nerves from transmitting impulses to muscles, causing arrhythmias of the heart that lead to cardiac arrest and death. The poison is so potent that chickens have died who did no more than peck a paper towel on which a frog had strolled. Golden poison frogs have also killed humans who carelessly touched them. The only animal that seems immune to the poison of the golden poison frog is the frog itself.

One frog contains about one milligram of poison, enough to kill up to twenty men, two elephants or 10,000 mice. A dose of batrachotoxin about the size of a grain of sugar would be lethal for an ordinary-size chap, and just one gram (about the amount of mercury in a thermometer) could kill 15,000. That *'terribilis'* is not there by accident.

The golden poison frog is also known as the golden dart frog and is the source of the poison that indigenous locals put on the darts with which they kill their lunch. Like a bee, the golden poison frog uses its weapon only in self-defence. When agitated or in pain, it secretes the colourless toxin from glands on its back and behind its ears, so, when they want a bit of poison, the natives deliberately upset the frogs by putting them near the fire. They then *carefully* dip the tips of their darts in the poison. I'm guessing they are fastidious with their unused darts, which can still be lethal after two years. You wouldn't want to leave one of those on your mother-in-law's bedside table, would you? How do you mean, 'yes'?

The weird thing is that these frogs are completely harmless if bred in captivity, and can be juggled by children without serious trouble (except from frog-lovers). The poison is thought to come from the food that the frogs eat off the forest floor, including beetles, some of which are themselves known to produce deadly toxins. Feed them on crickets and you'll be OK. But be aware that, unlike homegrown specimens, any of these charming creatures that have been caught in the rainforest and brought back will remain very dangerous for years.

Should all this be making you feel like ordering some golden poison frogs off the internet and putting in a bit of blowpipe practice on that neighbour who gets on your nerves, just be careful where you do it. In the United Kingdom blowpipes are offensive weapons under the 1988 Criminal Justice Act. They are also illegal in California, Massachusetts, the District of Columbia and New York City, but are OK elsewhere in the United States if you are over eighteen years old.

Talking balls: the cricket with the biggest testicles in the world

Not so long ago scientists at Syracuse University in New York discovered a link between big testicles and small brains. Now, before you leap up to tell the world that you are doing OK in both departments, thank you, you should know that these scientists were looking at bats – a 'bats and balls' study, if you like.

What these testicle experts found was that in those species of bat where the females are particularly promiscuous, the males have evolved enormous testicles so as to outdo the competition – other male bats. But since brains and balls both require energy to produce, the so-called 'expensive tissue' hypothesis, bigger balls mean smaller brains. With less promiscuous bats – where the female has only one 'batman' – the boyfriend tends to have a relatively large brain and relatively small bollocks (am I blinding you with science?).

Some seminal research into the testicles of certain bush-crickets has revealed that the male tuberous bush-cricket (*Platycleis affinis*) has the biggest testicles *in the world* – relatively speaking. His testicles make up 14 per cent of his entire body mass. This would be the same as you carrying around a pair of testicles each weighing more than five bags of sugar. Imagine all that extra trouser material required to cart everything about. Shares in the trouser-manufacturing industry would go through the roof, and just think of the size of the bicycle seat you'd need. With all that weight, it would be amazing if it didn't pull your ears down either side of your head.

Dr Karim Vahed, lead researcher on the cricket-ball study, said: 'We couldn't believe the size of these organs. They seemed to fill the entire abdomen.' But the team also found something surprising. Somewhat counter-intuitively the bush-cricket does not necessarily produce more sperm than smaller-balled crickets. Males with bigger testicles actually produce smaller amounts of ejaculate. The traditional (bat-ball) assumption that larger testicles make more sperm – thus giving males an advantage in sperm competition – seems not to be the case with the bollocky bush-cricket. Instead, it may be that in species that mate with more than one partner, big balls have evolved in order to allow repeated mating, using smaller amounts of ejaculate per mating and without the gentleman becoming overdrawn at the sperm bank, as it were. The general principle is that the more partners a female has, the larger the male's testicles are likely to be. 'This very much favours the alternative hypothesis', said Dr Vahed, 'that it's about the number of different females the male can fertilize, rather than getting a greater success per female.'

The team did not investigate how the cricket managed to walk about or jump with that extra baggage, but it seems to manage very well. It has extra-long legs, of course. Neither did the scientists look into the size of the crickets' intellects. But there's one thing you can say: their bollocks are a lot bigger than their brains (the *crickets'*!). Rather like Millwall supporters, I suppose. It's a heavy burden to carry.

3 Little-known Food Facts

The truth about teabags

Here's a useful tip for tea-drinking gardeners: don't throw your used teabags into the compost. 'Why not?' I hear you excitedly ask. Actually, you probably didn't ask why not; you probably thought, 'Who gives a monkey's?!' Well, you should give a monkey's because many teabags are very slow to break down in the soil. That is why you see puzzled granddads bent over their allotments picking bits of white stuff off their onions.

Tea bags are made, usually, of a kind of perforated paper fibre that lets water in and out. The paper is like the sort you get in coffee filters, made of a blend of wood and vegetable fibres. It's bleached abacá hemp pulp, actually. As well as being a word useful in Scrabble, abacá is a plant native to the Philippines. After harvesting, it is pulped and processed, before being used in the manufacture of vacuum-cleaner bags and 'paper' money, as well as in teabags (in case you were wondering). In addition to the more usual wood pulp/abacá mixture, teabags can also be made of silk or plastic – definitely don't put the plastic ones on your roses.

Being quick and easy, teabags were, naturally enough, an American idea. They bobbed to the surface in the early years of the twentieth century. The first patents for teabags – made of hand-sewn silk muslin and containing loose tea – date from 1903. In June 1908, New York tea merchant Thomas Sullivan sent out some tea samples in small silk pouches. He meant you to empty the tea out of the bag first but people, being a bit confused, made their cuppas without doing this, and *hey presto!* an idea was brewed. Sullivan soon swapped silk for gauze, which allowed water to get in and out more easily, but it wasn't until 1930 that William Hermanson of Boston patented the heat-sealed paper-fibre teabag. Heat-sealed teabag paper generally has a thermoplastic such as PVC or polypropylene on its inner surface. This is not very biodegradable but is what makes the teabag resilient enough to withstand being squashed by a spoon while bobbing about in a cup of boiling-hot liquid. Most teabags are now made with about 80 per cent paper fibre, which is fully compostable along with the tea leaves in the bag; it is the heat-resistant polypropylene which gardeners find left over on the compost heap.

The flat teabag with corners first appeared in 1944, and in 1953, after seeing the way tea had kept the British population going through the war, Joseph Tetley and Co. began mass-producing teabags in Britain. Food rationing was still in force and remained so until the following year, so the teabag added a note of cheap cheer to the British diet. In 1964 the finely perforated teabag became available.

The average teabag today contains 2,000 perforations, give or take a few – imagine being the man with the pin who has to put all those in. In today's typical teabag there are 3.125 grams of tea (so-called 'fannings', the leftovers from the larger leaf pieces which are sold as loose tea).

In addition to the traditional square teabag, you can now buy round and pyramidoid bags. The pyramid ones, which contain leaf fragments instead of fannings, or 'tea detritus' as it is rudely called, are supposed to improve the quality of the tea by giving it more room to circulate, but I haven't noticed all that much difference; I think I'll stick to the flat ones.

Naturally enough, research and development continue apace, and, being aware of the biodegradability problem, inventive teabag scientists have now come up with Soilon (who invents these daft names?), a fine mesh made from cornstarch, which, owing to the ease with which it is broken down by microorganisms in the soil, is a distinct improvement over paper and plastic when it comes to throwing it on your rhubarb.

Finally, if you are one of those tea-drinkers who wishes to continue recycling his teabags on his garden, the advice is to sieve out or pick off the surface of the soil any teabags that are still visible after a year, and throw them over the neighbour's fence. You can also speed up the composting process by ripping open the bags (before you discard them, not before you make a cup of tea, *obviously*). And for those too idle even to do this, you may care to know that in 2010, *Which?* magazine found one brand of conventional teabag that is polypropylene-free: Jacksons of Piccadilly.

All about SPAM®

In the 1990s, some early internet users began inundating forums with the word 'spam' in reference to the Monty Python sketch in which two diners, who descend on wires into a café full of Vikings, are offered a surfeit of the precooked canned meat product by Terry Jones in a floral dress, lipstick and an unconvincing brunette wig, while he repeats the word ad nauseam. Anyway, before you could say 'spam', the word had stuck as a term for unwanted and unasked-for commercial emails.

SPAM® (the kind you can eat) is sold on six continents (I'm guessing not Antarctica) and trademarked in more than a hundred countries. It should be noted that the trademarked meat product is differentiated from the unsolicited email type of spam by being fully capitalized: 'SPAM®'. It is produced for the American and Australian markets in Austin, Minnesota, and Fremont, Nebraska. Somewhat strangely, SPAM® destined for British mouths and stomachs is made in Denmark by the Danish Crown Group under licence from Hormel Foods, who own the brand. It is also made in the Philippines and South Korea and more than seven billion cans of the stuff have been so far been sold worldwide. SPAM® even has its own day. Every year in Shady Cove, Oregon, you can witness the SPAM® Parade and Festival. Not quite the Olympic Games, but entertaining enough, I'm sure.

SPAM® contains chopped pork shoulder with ham, salt, water, modified potato starch and sodium nitrite as a preservative. A thin jelly, formed as the stock cools, sits between the meat and the metal of the can. A serving of SPAM® provides a fair amount of salt and fat so you probably want to eat it in sensible amounts.

Now for some history. This is from Hormel's own publicity: 'The first can of SPAM® luncheon meat was produced in 1937 in Austin, Minn. From the beginning, SPAM® was unique – it stood alone in its low price, convenience and delicious taste. It immediately became America's favorite luncheon meat, and by 1941, 40 million pounds of SPAM® had been sold.'

The curious name was introduced, by the way, in 1937 when Hormel Spiced Ham, as it had previously been called, was rebranded. The wonderful Marguerite Patten in one of her cookery books said that Kenneth Daigneau, the brother of a Hormel vice-president, suggested the name. I understand that this was in a naming contest and that he collected a $100 prize. 'SPAM®' is said to be a contraction of 'Shoulder of Pork and Ham' or 'Spiced Meat and Ham', or, in wartime Britain, 'Specially Processed American Meats' or 'Supply Pressed American Meat'. It's all a long time ago now so who knows? There are also a few disgracefully rude and untrue names knocking about, including 'Something Posing As Meat' and 'Spare Parts Animal Meat'.

During the Second World War fresh meat was difficult for frontline soldiers to get hold of and the line on the SPAM®-eating graph shot upwards. In rationed wartime Britain it was gratefully munched by the populace as a convenient and cheerful Lend-Lease food. As a consequence, battered and fried 'SPAM® fritters' became part of the national cuisine, not to say national consciousness. I remember eating SPAM® fritters with relish (the emotional sort, not the condiment) when I was in primary school. Mrs Bentley's SPAM® fritters were the best in the world. Today, SPAM® is also eaten in Japan and China, and a kosher variety, known as 'Loof' (a corruption of 'meatloaf'), was used in field rations by the Israeli armed forces.

Here is my mum's own SPAM® fritter recipe (for about two people).

Ingredients

6 oz (170 g) SPAM®
Olive oil
Thick batter: 2 oz (62 g) plain flour, 1 small egg, 2 fl oz (62 ml) beer or milk, salt and pepper

Method

1 Cut the SPAM® into four slices.
2 Mix the batter in a bowl.
3 Heat one or two tablespoons of olive oil in a frying pan until it is hot but not smoking.
4 Dip the SPAM® slices in the batter a couple of times until thickly coated.
5 Place into the pan and sizzle for three minutes either side, turning occasionally. Golden brown is the colour you are looking for.
6 Pat with some kitchen paper and serve with chips or mashed spuds and a load of frozen peas (cooked, obviously).

Understanding steak

As Benedick says in Shakespeare's *Much Ado About Nothing*, 'A man loves the meat in his youth that he cannot endure in his age.' I tried steak tartare when I was a young blade. It is raw minced steak and I loved it, but now I do not find it to my taste. I know the nomadic Tartars of the Central Asian steppes used to warm and tenderize steak under their saddles during the day's ride, but now that I'm an old dodderer I can't take anything too daring anymore, even after it's been sat on all day by a Tartar's bottom.

My friend 'Jake-the-Steak' likes 'blue' steak, that is to say not rare but *raw*. I don't know why people call it 'rare' because you can get it everywhere. Anyway, I'm not keen on it, because of the red stuff trickling out, which I assumed was blood. Jake explained that red meat has almost no blood in it; nearly all the blood is removed during slaughter. There is practically none in the fat, anyway, and only a small amount remains in the muscle. The stuff trickling out is not blood; it's mainly water, mixed with a protein called myoglobin, which makes it look red.

Myoglobin is related to haemoglobin and its job is to store oxygen in the cells of busy, active muscles, just as haemoglobin stores oxygen in red blood cells. The redder the meat, the more myoglobin it contains and the darker it gets when you cook it, owing to alterations in the iron content. This information didn't help my appetite, but made me wonder what else I didn't know. And it was the following.

If you buy some freshly butchered meat from a man in a straw boater, wearing a striped apron and standing in a tiled shop with sawdust on the floor, you are not only going back in time, you are in the lucky position of being able to conduct an experiment. Leave your meat on the counter for a day next to a plate of meat you've taken out of a supermarket packet. The fresh meat will go brownish while the packet stuff will stay pink. This is because processed meat is preserved using nitrites, which keep it looking pink, even after it has gone off. Vacuum-sealed beef is different again, tending to be purplish under its plastic shroud, but going red within minutes once it's opened and the myoglobin absorbs oxygen from the air. So next time you find yourself wondering why fresh meat looks older than preserved meat, you will know the answer.

By the way, nitrites are not good for you in large amounts. In any case, whether the meat has got nitrites in it or not, its haemoglobin and myoglobin will trigger a process in your insides called nitrosation, which leads to the formation of carcinogenic compounds. *I'm so glad you told me*. This is why boring government advisors issue advice about rationing your sausage and steak intake.

The reason pork looks less pink than beef, and other meats, is that it contains a lot less myoglobin than other red meat, so one pork sausage a year is probably going to be OK, just as two pounds of raw steak a day is not going to be good for your insides.

White meats, such as chicken (and fish, too), are better for you in this respect than red. They are that colour owing not to a lack of blood but to a lack of myoglobin. Fish muscle is white because fish don't have to hold themselves up on muscles like sheep and cows do, they just float there most of the time. Although chicken and turkey are classed as white meat, their legs contain a lot of myoglobin. This is why the leg meat turns dark when you cook it. Other poultry such as peasant and phartride – I mean pheasant and partridge – is darker than chicken, because of all the work done by the muscles. A good way of guessing how much myoglobin there is in any meat is to think about how much that bit of muscle will have been used by the animal in question.

I recently went into a nice restaurant and ordered a huge expensive-looking steak. It arrived accompanied by a scrumptious mountain of onions and a bank-account-emptying bottle of 1787 Chateau Lafite. It was delicious and I rounded things off with a large brandy. But when I went to pay, the waiter said everything was on the house. I asked to compliment the owner and he told me, 'He's upstairs with my wife.' 'What's he doing with your wife?' I asked. 'Probably what I'm doing to his business,' replied the waiter.

The history of tea

Just imagine if, on the last day of your life, all the hair that had been cut off your head and shaved off your chin passed before you on a convoy of trucks along with all the packaging you had discarded over the years, all the old newspapers you'd read and all the food you'd eaten. How much space would it all take up? How many low loaders would it require? What about all the beer you'd drunk – would it fit in a swimming pool and, if so, how big? And what about all the cups of tea?

Of course, some people drink a lot more tea than others and, as a nation, the British, who drink 168 million cups of tea every day, are almost defined by the stuff. The good news for us all is that drinking just one cup a day can reduce your risk of heart attack by about 40 per cent, owing to the presence of 'flavonoids', antioxidants of a kind that neutralize the harmful effects of things called 'free radicals', which sounds to me like a 1970s rock band.

The first tea-drinkers were the Chinese, with tea-drinking being recorded as far back as the tenth century BCE. They also used it as a medicine, and the philosopher Laozi described tea as 'the froth of liquid jade', but whether this was good or bad I don't know. In the mid-thirteenth century the Chinese began processing tea in a new way, roasting the leaves and crumbling them up, thus beginning today's practice of brewing loose tea.

Tea was introduced to Japan by Buddhist monks between 589 and 618 CE but the earliest Western record of tea comes from an Arabian traveller, who remarked that after 879 CE the main source of tax in Canton in southern China, apart from salt, was tea, something Marco Polo, who began the pasta craze by bringing noodles back to Italy from China, also remarked on.

As trading took off in sixteenth-century Europe, news of the Chinese drink *chá* quickly spread. In the early seventeenth century, the Dutch East India Company brought the first tea to Amsterdam and the drink was well known in France by 1636.

Tea first appeared in England during the 1650s, introduced through fashionable coffee houses – the seventeenth-century equivalent of Starbucks – and was soon afterwards brought to the British colonies, including America.

The wholesale importing of tea into Britain began in the 1660s when King Charles II married the Portuguese princess, Catherine of Braganza, a big tea-drinker. Samuel Pepys first tasted it on 25 September 1660: 'To the office, where Sir W. Batten, Colonel Slingsby, and I sat awhile, and Sir R. Ford coming to us about some business, we talked together of the interest of this kingdom to have a peace with Spain and a war with France and Holland; where Sir R. Ford talked like a man of great reason and experience. And afterwards I did send for a cup of tee (a China drink) of which I never had drank before, and went away.'

The East India Company imported China tea and first sold it as a medicinal beverage just as Coca-Cola had been sold as a prophylactic stomach medicine when it first came out. By the end of the seventeenth century it was being drunk only by the aristocracy – in fancy cups – because it was expensive. But by 1750 it had become the national drink, available to many.

The success of tea among the common man in Britain was largely the result of a commercial ploy to fill ships, which were returning empty – and therefore at great cost – from export trips to China. The wily East India Company began a huge PR campaign in England to persuade Joe public to drink the stuff. This is called 'creating demand'. Moreover, they encouraged tea-drinkers to sweeten their drink with sugar, kindly brought back by the East India Company from the West Indies and Africa, thus creating a sort of lucrative 'batteries not included' effect.

Tea had long been cultivated as a medicine in India, but in a small way. When the British East India Company converted swathes of land in India and Ceylon (now Sri Lanka) into tea plantations, large-scale commercial production could begin. In 1824 native tea plants were discovered in the hills between Burma and Assam, and today, India, Ceylon and Assam are names that *mean* 'tea' to many people. For nearly a century India was the biggest tea producer and powerful Indian tea companies acquired some big British tea businesses, including Tetley and Typhoo. India has only recently been overtaken as the world's biggest tea producer by China.

Tea-drinking never took off in the United States to quite the extent that it did in the UK and on 16 December 1773 it became the cause of a huge row between the countries. Colonists in Boston, in the British colony of Massachusetts, took direct action against the British government and the powerful East India Company, which had a monopoly on all tea entering the colonies. The colonists strongly objected to the Tea Act, which had been passed by the British Parliament that year, because they didn't see why they should pay taxes to a remote, unrepresentative government that they couldn't vote out. So they boarded the ships and emptied the crates of tea into the harbour. This rendered it unsuitable for drinking and helped start the American Revolution.

Americans have since preferred coffee.

4 Human Creativity, Endeavour and Folly

The invention of Post-it notes

Post-it notes seem so obvious now that you wonder there was ever a time they didn't exist. But they are youngsters in the world of stationery. This is the story of their invention, which you will be able to use to fascinate people rigid at the next cocktail party you are thrown out of.

The Post-it note is the invention of a 3M engineer named Arthur 'Art' Fry (born 19 August 1931), who spent his student vacations as a door-to-door salesman before becoming an intern at the Minnesota Mining and Manufacturing Company (3M). It must have been a vocation because, according to Fry, he had to work there for five years before he earned what he had done as a part-time salesman.

In 1974, on 3M's private golf course, Fry heard about a strange substance that another 3M employee, Spencer Silver, had made in 1968, while trying to concoct a new adhesive. Mixing some simple organic molecules, he produced 'inherently tacky elastomeric copolymer micro-spheres'. Under a microscope this looked rather like the pimply surface of a basketball. The spaces between the bumps made complete contact impossible between the adhesive and any other surface. It was sticky but not very. Silver had not worked out how to use this strange glue, and to 3M high-ups it was the opposite of a saleable product: an adhesive that didn't adhere.

Fry became interested in this new substance and while in church one day, trying to get his bookmarks to stop sliding out of his hymnal, he was struck by an idea. Sprinting home, he put a bit of Silver's adhesive on to some paper slips. The first one was about a quarter of an inch wide and one-and-a-half inches long, coated with the new adhesive along just one edge. But these reusable bookmarks didn't impress 3M. They liked to make things that people would use up and so would have to order more.

Some time later, Fry wanted to draw his supervisor's attention to a particular section of a report, so he cut out a little sample of the bookmark material, stuck it on the page and drew an arrow beside a question he had jotted down. His supervisor wrote his response on the note, stuck it to a document containing the answer and sent it back to Fry. They had stumbled upon a new way to communicate. Any surface could now be turned instantaneously into a compact, portable, bulletin board. What's more, it was a product that people would definitely use up.

The development process took two years and in 1977 3M decided to test-market the product. But it needed a name. 'Jot and Jerk' was, sensibly, abandoned in favour of 'Press & Peel Pads', which now sound rather like those things with wings that Claire Rayner used to advertise on telly. Anyway, the response was feeble. So they tried again, saturating Boise, Idaho, with canary-yellow pads, now called, 'Post-it Notes', and running stories in the local newspapers. Thousands of free samples were sent to offices, law firms and hospitals, and the town was crammed full of people demonstrating how the sticky pads worked. The response was enormous and 3M decided on a full commercial launch. Post-it notes were released nationally on 6 April 1980, with millions of free Post-its being distributed. Fry explained, 'The digital age generates so many documents, and they all look the same. How do you organize all that material?' One launch ad suggested the answer: 'Take one of these to relieve congestion.'

'We didn't expect to make a profit for five years, but it only took one,' recalled Fry. By 1998 global sales of Post-it items were earning 3M a *billion* dollars a year and the Post-it brand was one of the company's most valuable assets.

In 1992, after nearly forty years with 3M, Art Fry retired. Neither he nor Spencer Silver ever received any special financial reward for their imagination, dogged persistence and billion-dollar idea. This is called, 'not letting staff get too big for their boots'.

All about 'song-poems'

If you've never heard the term 'song-poem', and especially if you've never heard a recording of a song-poem, you have a treat in store. 'Song-poem' is a term dreamed up by somebody in the vanity-music-production business in the 1960s as a stand-in for the word 'lyrics', which was presumably felt to be too esoteric for the wannabe songwriters who were encouraged in ads in pulp magazines to send off their lyrics – song-poems – which would be professionally set to music. A typical ad reads like this: 'Popular, Rock-and-Roll, Country, and Sacred poems needed *at once*! Send your poems today for prompt *free examination and appraisal* . . . Your songs or poems may *earn money for you.*' Naturally enough, your song-poem had to be accompanied by a fee, of up to $400.

Hopeful lyricists could specify the genre – country, pop, soul or whatever – and the studios would hire versatile grafters to force the lyrics into a melody and record the song, in a hurry, over a pre-recorded backing track. One of these musicians was Ramsey Kearney and he is doing a similar job today, judging by his website, which says, 'After years of songwriting as well as being a recording artist, I have decided to do personalized co-writing on select song material. I feel there are amateur writers, who can become tomorrows' [*sic*] perfected songwriter, with the help of an experienced co-writer.' Good for him (we'll come back to discuss his song-poem-singing masterpiece in a minute).

The song-poem recording process was something of a conveyor-belt affair. The singer would cast an eye over the terrible lyrics, learn the tune ('simple' is probably the best word to describe these melodies) and the thing would be recorded over a backing track in double-quick time. Niceties were just trampled upon in the performers' hurry to race on to the next piece, so they could lay down several tunes in a single session.

Although none of the resulting masterpieces was ever going to trouble the charts, the musicians doing the business were all pros, who sang and played well enough. But costs were tightly controlled and corners cut, so to protect their reputations, and camouflage the fact that the same singer was grinding out so many of the songs, the artistes made use of a variety of pseudonyms. One number entitled 'I'm Just the Other Woman' was even sung, in an emasculated eunuchoid falsetto, by a man *pretending* to be a woman.

Philistinism and fascism being two sides of the same coin, the rigid, sometimes right-wing, slant of many of the gormless lyrics is an unsurprising feature. You'll find in the song-poem canon tributes to Richard Nixon, a warning about the dangers of pornography – with the paradoxical benefits of auto-relief – in 'All You Need is a Fertile Mind', along with sentimental tripe such as 'How Can a Man Overcome His Heartbroken Pain?'

Many of the best song-poems have now been released on a thrilling CD, *The American Song-Poem Anthology*, and a cult following has developed. Perhaps the finest song-poem of all time is 'Blind Man's Penis', sung/spoken quite beautifully, in a country style, by, *yes*, Ramsey Kearney. The story of its happening is a curious one.

In 1975 John Trubee was a musically frustrated cashier, working in an unrewarding convenience store in Princeton, New Jersey. One day, when he had become bored to the point of insanity, he noticed an ad in the back of the *Midnight Globe*. 'Co-write on a 50–50 basis, earn $20,000 royalties,' it said. Trubee thought it would be fun 'to send these people the most ridiculous, stupid, vile, obscene, retarded lyrics, to see their response'. So he dashed off a poem called 'Peace & Love', which was of such rhythmically disastrous, non-rhyming, meaningless ineptitude that it made your eyes water. For good measure, he sprinkled the nonsense with rude words, before sending it off to the obscure recording set-up in Tennessee. 'I wanted to get an emotional letter from the jerks in Nashville,' says Trubee.

This jape was his response to what he saw as 'a world that seemed always to have told me I was small and worthless', but instead of rejection he received a letter that said his song-poem was 'very worthy of being recorded with the full Nashville Sound Production', asking him to send a fee of $79.95. Realizing the nature of the deal, he sent off the money and sat back to wait.

Several weeks later he received a seven-inch record with grooves on only one side and a typed label that said, 'Peace & Love (John Trubee–Will Gentry)'. Playing the music, Trubee heard 'some country hack singing the lyrics I wrote' over what he described as 'the lamest, most minimal country track'.

Trubee's lyrics include lines such as 'Warts loved my nipples because they are pink' and 'The zebra spilled its plastinia on bemis, and the gelatin fingers oozed electric marbles', which, though a challenge to sing, are very original and some of the more tasteful bits, too. His best line, however, is undoubtedly the one that has led 'Peace & Love' to become known as 'Blind Man's Penis'. It goes, 'Stevie Wonder's penis is erect because he's blind/It's erect because he's blind'. But the nervous people in Nashville had changed the line, transmogrifying 'Stevie Wonder's penis' into 'A blind man's penis', and repeating it mesmerically on the fade at the end of the record. This small change added extra magic pixie-dust to the song.

After 'Blind Man's Penis' became a cult sensation, John Trubee remarked, 'The obsolete and reactionary machinery of the music industry needs the irreverent pranks of ugly outsiders if it's to survive its rapidly calcifying descent into hermetically sealed greyness,' which I'm sure is true. Anyway, I do hope you get to hear the song; it's out there on the internet, waiting for you.

The unknown map: the Gall–Peters projection

When you look at a map of the world, you know where everything is: Greenland near the top, Antarctica at the bottom, Britain and the rest of Europe in the middle, above Africa, Asia on the right, Australia bottom-right, the Americas on the left there.

The map you are probably thinking about, and the one you normally see on the classroom wall, is called the Mercator projection and it's wrong in several important respects.

The Mercator projection was devised in 1569 by Flemish cartographer

Gerardus Mercator (1512–94), who called it a 'description of Earth corrected for the use of sailors'. It became the standard map for navigation at sea because, with its parallels and meridians straight and perpendicular, navigation was made a bit of a doddle.

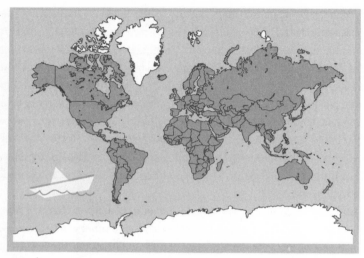

Mercator projection.

But there was a problem. Because maps are flat, and the earth is roughly spherical, all maps distort shape, size or geographical relationships, sometimes dramatically. Unfortunately, Mercator's particular method of distributing the surface of a sphere over a flat rectangle caused east–west and north–south stretching, an effect which increases the further you get from the equator. For example, Greenland looks as big as Africa even though Africa is about fourteen times larger, Alaska looks the same size as Brazil but is actually five times smaller and Antarctica, the biggest continent on the Mercator map, is the fifth in size, in the real world.

These are significant distortions and at the more extreme latitudes the Mercator projection is practically unusable. Indeed, at the poles the map actually becomes infinite. Even old Gerardus realized that his projection was unsuited to general reference and used a different map, called the equal-area sinusoidal projection, when he wanted to show relative areas.

In 1973, aware of these problems, Arno Peters (1916–2002), a German historian, presented a map he'd been working on since 1967, in which areas of equal size on the earth are equally sized on the map.

In fact, the Peters projection was not new, having first been described in 1855 by clergyman James Gall, who presented the idea at a meeting of the British Association for the Advancement of Science. Owing to the similarity of their technique, known as the cylindrical equal-area projection, the maps of these two gentlemen have been effectively combined and are now often known as the Gall–Peters projection.

But Peters was causing quite a stink among cartographers, some of whom were furious with his 'new' projection, not because it didn't work but because Peters had a political point to make. This was that the Mercator map tended to cause poor countries (nearer the equator) to look too small and rich countries to look too big. By using his 'new' projection, poor, less powerful nations were made to look, said Peters, less insignificant.

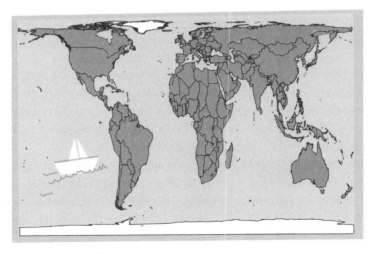

Gall–Peters projection.

One expert, beside himself with indignation at the idea that the Mercator projection was a politically biased map (a tendency of all world maps), was unable to deny that the Peters projection was a more accurate representation of relative geographical size, so he resorted to ridicule, saying that the Peters map looked like clothes hung out to dry on a washing line. He seemed miffed that Peters had spoilt the look of the 'proper' map with which he was familiar.

To the chagrin of some, Peters' analysis did, though, have an effect, and modern atlases no longer use the Mercator projection to show areas that are far from the equator. Some, though not all, North American geographic organizations even rejected rectangular world maps altogether – which would include both the Mercator and the Gall–Peters projection. They said:

> We strongly urge book and map publishers, the media and government agencies to cease using rectangular world maps for general purposes or artistic displays. Such maps promote serious, erroneous conceptions by severely distorting large sections of the world, by showing the round Earth as having straight edges and sharp corners, by representing most distances and direct routes incorrectly, and by portraying the circular coordinate system as a squared grid.

They were certainly right about that. For example, take a look at Alaska, on the far left of the map – Mercator or Gall–Peters, either will do. Now look at the right-hand edge of the Russian Federation, on the far right of the map. Those two areas look thousands and thousands of miles apart, although they are next door to each other in real life.

Even a globe has a top and bottom, and there's not much you can do about all this, except use a variety of maps. Some of the other maps you can get are quite a surprise. Opposite you will find a Pacific-centred map.

If you look at a Pacific-centred map you find Australia in the middle and Britain tucked away up in the corner where Alaska ought to be. There's no doubt that Peters had a point. Look how important Australia

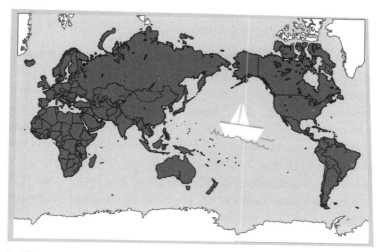

Pacific-centred Mercator projection.

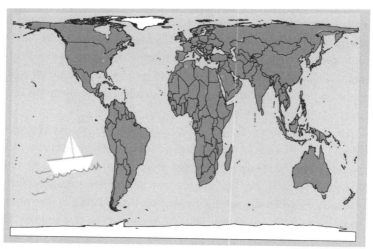

Upside-down world map.

looks when you put it in the middle. You'll also have noticed how much water there is in the world: a lot. But if you think that's a funny map, look at the upside-down one above.

149

The magic of television weather forecasts

In the old days, TV weather forecasts consisted of a man with a pointing stick standing in front of a flip chart. Then came magnetic weather symbols that fell off, followed by lively coloured maps in front of which the weatherman, or by this time, woman, stood, changing the slides with a hand-held gizmo. Nowadays the entire map is liable to go flying all over the place, with winds, isobars and symbols zooming about like dodgems. How do they do all that? Well, let me explain.

The BBC, which has the most experienced and best-resourced TV weather forecasting set-up in the world, gets its weather information from the Meteorological Office, the UK's national weather service. This is part of the Ministry of Defence and trains forecasters from around the world. BBC Weather forecasters, who are Met Office civil servants, are equipped with computer-based weather information displays linked directly to fat computers at the Met Office headquarters that crunch the numbers and predict what is going to happen. The snazzily named 'Weatherscape XT' graphics system allows the forecasters to put together a sequence of dynamic charts and graphics for the forecast and a production team manages the graphics to allow the meteorologists to concentrate on the meteorology.

When the time for the broadcast is coming up, the forecaster goes to the studio, switches on the lights (glamorous I don't think) and puts in an earpiece to hear the programme being transmitted before the weather forecast and to catch any last-minute instructions from the director in the network control room, who is responsible for stitching all the various programmes into a seamless robe. An ingenious device adjusts the automatic camera, lighting set-up and microphone level to suit each particular presenter. All they have to do is press a button. The presenter starts the broadcast on a cue in their ear-hole from the programme director, stopping when the countdown clock reaches zero.

Unlike the systems used by other broadcasters, the background in front of which the BBC forecaster stands is a translucent screen, the back of which is strongly lit with blue light. An electronic 'keying' system, which the BBC calls Colour Separation Overlay or CSO, causes the computer to insert graphics anywhere the camera detects a blue colour. The system eliminates any problem with shadows cast by the presenter, though they must take care with the colour of their clothes to avoid being converted into a floating pink head with a body expunged by graphics.

The great subtlety of the system the BBC uses is that the forecasters can see an image of the graphics projected on to the back of the screen behind them, but too faintly to be detected by the camera, which sees only the blue screen. This enables the presenter to point at exactly the right spot. The difference that this makes is obvious if you compare a BBC TV weather forecast with one broadcast on another channel, where the presenters have to look off to a monitor at their left to see where to point, making the eyelines all wonky.

Using a hand-held switch, the forecaster, who has a degree in meteorology, possibly from Reading University, and knows what image is coming next because he or she has planned it, can progress through the graphics. These are displayed on monitors beside the camera.

Fixed directly in front of the camera lens is a teleprompter, similar to the ones politicians now routinely use when orating at big meetings. This is invisible to the camera but shows the forecaster the complete composite picture that viewers are seeing from their sofas. The countdown clock is superimposed over this picture, so that whenever presenters need to check their position, or find out how long they have left before a nice cup of tea, all they need do is look directly at the camera, adding greatly to the naturalness of the proceedings.

If all this is a bit much for you to take in, just have a look out of the window and see if it's raining.

Why plastic bags are 'greener' than paper bags

Frankly I don't think I would ever have read, or even picked up, a book called *Trimalchio in West Egg*, and it looks as though F. Scott Fitzgerald – or his publisher, more likely – thought it was a bit of a bummer too, because he renamed it *The Great Gatsby*, which is much better. Some titles are just more likely to take off than others: *Jaws*, for example, or *Murder on the Orient Express*, or, for ladies, *Big Cock Sex Stories: My Largest Ever* by somebody calling herself Victoria Anderson. This one, unfortunately, is rather let down by the frightful English in the blurb: 'I have a fetish for well endowed men . . . very well endowed. The bigger one I can find the better.' '*The bigger one I can find the better*'?! That's not English. Back to the creative writing class, Victoria.

Among what Victoria Anderson would probably call 'more worser titles' is a ninety-six-page research paper commissioned by the government, entitled *Life Cycle Assessment of Supermarket Carrier Bags*, by Dr Chris Edwards and Jonna Meyhoff Fry. It doesn't really grab you, that, does it?

Life Cycle Assessment of Supermarket Carrier Bags was supposed to be published in 2007 but is, at the time I write this, still not out, some say because it discovered the wrong facts. Although 6,000 million polythene bags are used in the UK every year (about ten for each man, woman and child in the country), the report found that the sort of plastic bags you get from the shops – the ones that blow into trees and into harbours, killing fish – are actually what Victoria Anderson might call 'more greener' than the purportedly small-carbon-footprint alternatives.

And it's not a minor effect. Plastic bags are about 200 times less harmful to the climate than cotton bags and during their manufacture produce only about 30 per cent of the carbon dioxide of paper bags. *Life Cycle Assessment of Supermarket Carrier Bags* found that even used just once, the plastic bag was 'greener' than cotton or paper bags in nine of the report's ten categories.

You could reverse these numbers if you used your cotton bag every day for more than six months, or reused paper bags four times instead of chucking them away or putting them in the recycling. But, of course, nobody does.

All bags use up energy and produce carbon dioxide when you make them, so the best thing to do is to knit yourself one of those string reticules and use it every day for ninety years, like my grandma. Otherwise, go for the plastic bag, but use it until it dies and don't let it blow into the trees, for this is aesthetically displeasing.

The Harcourt interpolation

Founded on 1 January 1785, the *Daily Universal Register* was the brainchild of printer-publisher-editor John Walter (1738/9–1812). It is better known today as *The Times*. Over the years the 'Thunderer', as it became popularly known, has had, along with its great success, the occasional misfortune. For example in 1789 Walter was convicted of libelling the Duke of York and sent to Newgate prison for a year as well as being fined £50 (getting on for £3,000 in today's money). He also had to stand in the pillory for an hour and was made to give surety for good behaviour for seven years. As sometimes happens in these cases, he was pardoned in 1791 at the request of the Prince of Wales.

Ten years later Walter was convicted again, this time for libelling Lord Cowper, and not long afterwards gave the newspaper to his son to run. But perhaps the most entertaining embarrassment for *The Times* occurred in the 23 January edition, 1882, which included a report of a dull speech made by the Home Secretary of the time, Sir William Harcourt, into which some prankster had introduced a few words of his own. It read:

> I saw in a Tory journal the other day a note of alarm, in which they said 'Why, if a tenant-farmer is elected for the North Riding of Yorkshire the farmers will be a political power who will have to be reckoned with'. The speaker then said he felt inclined for a bit of fucking. I think that is

very likely. (Laughter). But I think it is rather an extraordinary thing that the Tory party have not found that out before.

The paper was on the streets, and gentlemen's breakfast tables, before the heinous interpolation was spotted but as soon as it was, a revised edition was printed for subscribers. No apology appeared in *The Times* until 27 January, four days later, when the restrained fury of the bosses, stunned and affronted by this earth-shattering profanity, was palpable:

> No pains have been spared by the management of this journal to discover the author of a gross outrage committed by the interpolation of a line in the speech by Sir William Harcourt reported in our issue of Monday last. This malicious fabrication was surreptitiously introduced before the paper went to press. The matter is now under legal investigation, and it is to be hoped that the perpetrator will be brought to punishment.

It seems that any witch-hunt that the management set up failed to identify the naughty employee responsible, because a few months later an advertisement for an exciting-sounding book, *Everyday Life in Our Public Schools*, appeared in the 12 June edition of *The Times*, and was similarly adulterated by the introduction of a reference to 'a glossary of some words used by Henry Irving in his disquisitions upon fucking, which is in common use in these schools'.

This witty wordplay doubtless caused further toast and marmalade to be coughed up and spluttered from the lips of red-faced gentlemen in smoking jackets, but this time *The Times* held its tongue, doubtless feeling that drawing attention to this one was not going to help. Nonetheless, it became normal practice at the paper to make quite sure that any disgruntled sacked compositors were immediately paid their notice and were off the premises before you could say 'Hold the front fucking page!'

Great marketing disasters

'A good name is better than precious ointment' (Ecclesiastes 7: 1). As so often with the Bible, there is wisdom in this quote, for a bad name invites a lifetime of ridicule. Take Pleasant Titty, who was baptized in Margate in 1768, her life must have been made miserable by jeering street urchins. Same with Mad Looney, who died in Warwickshire in 1894. What a ghastly time of it he must have had; what can the parents of these unfortunates have been thinking? Product naming presents the same problem. In Poland, for instance, you can buy a soft drink called *Fart*, but it surely can't travel well. Neither is it an easy matter to select the right name for a business, especially nowadays, when large firms operate in many languages across various continents. 'Accenture' was once called 'Andersen Consulting', while 'Diageo' is the name invented for the firm that resulted from the merger of Guinness and Grand Metropolitan. All have international appeal and are pronounceable around the world.

Which brings me to the case of the audit firm PricewaterhouseCoopers, which in 2002 decided to change the name of the consulting bit of its business, previously known as 'PwC Consulting', before 'spinning it off' as a separate entity. The renaming project was supervised by the famous branding consultants Wolff Olins, at the cost of some £75 million ($110 million).

After much expensive 'research' the decision was made to rename the firm 'Monday' to imply fresh thinking and a new start. What immediately struck me when I heard this was that Mondays are traditionally and famously unpopular, with hungover and grouchy staff desperate to do anything rather than come into work. Nonetheless the Wolff Olins people – or *somebody* – came up with the following slogan to launch the new brand: 'Sharpen your pencil, iron your crispy white shirts, set the alarm clock, relish the challenge, listen, be fulfilled, make an impact, take a risk.' How does that strike you? Chief executive of the newly named firm Greg Brenneman described the slogan as 'real-word, concise, recognizable, global, and the right fit for a company that works hard to deliver results', showing, I think, that he knew little of the art of advertising copywriting.

But before you could say 'I wouldn't hire any consultancy firm dim-witted enough to spend £75 million rebranding themselves with an obviously silly new name, likely to make clients and public cast opprobrious sneers in their direction', the firm's new owners IBM immediately decided to drop the idea. This stunning waste of time and money is known as 'big business'.

I suppose a defence could be made that financial businesses are less practised in the black arts of branding and marketing than their commercial counterparts. When I worked in the City, they did, it's true, often seem like chimps trying to make a cake. But the big *commercial* firms, with decades of practice in these fields, know better. Don't they? Well, see what you think of this.

In 1985, the Coca-Cola Company realized that Coke was losing business to its arch-rival Pepsi, whose sweeter taste was preferred in the long-running 'Pepsi Challenge' tests, promoted in huge TV advertising campaigns. These so-called 'sip tests' asked drinkers to sample Coke and Pepsi 'blind' and say which they preferred, but did not account for the possibility of excessive sweetness in a larger portion – say a whole can – of a sweeter drink. In any case, author and wit Dave Barry rudely and accurately described the 'Pepsi Challenge' as 'Pepsi's ongoing misguided attempt to convince the general public that Coke and Pepsi are not the same thing, which of course they are'.

Nevertheless, the Coca-Cola Company did its own blind taste tests with a new, sweeter, concoction and found that it was preferred. It then decided to do something radical – to change the recipe of its well-known and much-loved drink, which had contained the same ingredients since

1903 (when they removed the nine milligrams of cocaine that used to slosh round each glass of the stuff). The new product was put into production and a new name devised: 'New Coke'. God knows how much that cost to come up with. But instead of adding New Coke to their range of drinks, Coca-Cola decided on a quick all-out replacement. Unfortunately they had forgotten that their current (vast) market consisted of drinkers who – for whatever reason – preferred the 'old' Coke to Pepsi and might well prefer it to New Coke too. The idea of 'brand loyalty', a long-understood and very real thing, seems, in the company's excitement, to have been forgotten.

The outcry from Coke fans was immediate and immense and bad publicity sprayed all over the Coca-Cola Company. Coke sales were damaged to the tune of quite a lot while Pepsi executives smirked.

Terrible emergency meetings were held and, as always happens in these disasters, it was a case of 'Quick! Go back to what we were doing before'. Just three months later the old recipe was reintroduced, renamed 'Coca-Cola Classic', just to make it clear that it was something wonderful. Over the next seven years, New Coke was phased out, after abortively being renamed 'Coke II' (that's two, not eleven). After wheezing along for a decade, New Coke was kindly put out of its misery – and everyone else's – in 2002.

But the Coca-Cola Company hadn't finished with marketing disasters, for in 2004 they launched Dasani in the UK – this was their own brand of bottled water. But before you could say 'New Coke' the launch was being called 'a fiasco' and 'a PR catastrophe'.

For starters, the Coca-Cola Company's first online advertisements for their product referred to the drink as 'bottled spunk', with the tagline, 'Can't live without spunk'. Added to this disaster, *The Grocer*, a trade magazine, pointed out that Dasani was actually treated tap water from Sidcup in the London suburbs. Although Dasani was never said to be 'mineral water', its 'purity' had certainly been stressed in publicity.

Then, on 18 March 2004, bromate, an agent produced during water treatment and suspected of causing cancer if swallowed in large quantities, was found in bottles of Dasani. Realizing that marketing and PR had been holed below the waterline, Coca-Cola straight away recalled half a million bottles of the stuff from UK supply, and withdrew it from the UK market.

When asked for their reaction, the company reported that they were 'disappointed' that Dasani hadn't done better.

The 'Blinkenlights' warning

The 'Blinkenlights' warning, which has long appeared in workplaces as a jocular admonishment to people not to interfere with mechanical, technical or computer equipment, is a macaronic composition, meaning that it is written in a mixture of languages, in this case English and a coarse mock-German.

The 'Blinkenlights' warning dates back at least as far as the 1950s and probably further. Pseudo-German parodies of this type were common in Allied machine shops during the Second World War and by the 1960s the 'Blinkenlights' warning had been reported at IBM in the United States and at the Atlas Computer Laboratory in Britain. In the boringly regimented big-business atmosphere of today's workplaces, amusing signs such as 'The typist's reproduction equipment is not to be interfered with without the permission of the office manager' and the 'Blinkenlights' warning are much less common than once they were, frowned on as a dangerous sign of creativity, humour and original thinking. The original wag who composed the piece is today forgotten and there are now several versions knocking about. Here is a typical one, reproduced for your entertainment and approval.

Achtung!

Alles nonteknischen lookenpeepers!

Das komputermaschine ist nicht für gewerken bei dummkopfen mit der gefingerpoken und mittengraben! Experten only switchen onnen muss. Oderwise ist easy to schnappen der springenwerk, blowenfusen und poppencorken mit spitzensparksen. Der rubbernecken sightseeren keepen das cottonpicken händer in das pockets muss. Zo relaxen und watschen der blinkenlights.

Naturally the Germans tried to repay the compliment and translated the 'Blinkenlights' warning into mock-English. It doesn't quite work for the native speaker, but for the sake of completeness I reproduce it below.

This room is fullfilled mit special electronische equipment. Fingergrabbing and pressing the knoeppkes from the computers is allowed for die experts only! So all the 'lefthanders' stay away and do not disturben the brainstorming von here working intelligences. Otherwise you will be outthrown and kicked anderswhere! Also: please keep still and only watchen astaunished the blinkenlights.

The British/Prussian/German/English/American/Canadian/ Hawaiian/Australian national anthem: all about it

Since the 1780s, 'God Save the Queen' ('King' when the monarch is a chap) has been an anthem (official national song) of the United Kingdom and also of a number of Commonwealth realms and British Crown Dependencies. Interestingly, it is also the tune to the American patriotic hymn 'America', better known as 'My Country, 'Tis of Thee'. The lyrics of which were written by Samuel Francis Smith in 1831 after he'd heard 'Heil dir im Siegerkranz', a German version of the song.

Smith finished writing his patriotic words in just thirty minutes, and 'America' was first performed at a children's Independence Day celebration in Boston on 4 July 1831. It was published the following year and became the effective American national anthem until the adoption of 'The Star-spangled Banner' in the 1930s.

'Heil dir im Siegerkranz' – the tune of which Samuel Smith 'borrowed' – was the first German national anthem and was the unofficial national anthem of the German Empire from 1871 to 1918. Before that it had been the anthem of Prussia and several other countries, including Russia (until 1833) and Switzerland (until 1961). The melody was used also for the national anthem of the Kingdom of Hawaii (and the modern Hawaiian anthem sounds like an eerie inversion of the tune). It is Norway's royal anthem, 'Kongesangen', and was the Swedish royal anthem, 'Bevare Gud vår Kung' (between 1805 and 1880). It is also the national anthem of Liechtenstein, 'Oben am jungen Rhein', and therefore has to be performed twice when British soccer teams play Liechtenstein.

'God Save the Queen' – in English – is also the National and Royal Anthem of the Independent States of Antigua and Barbuda (royal), Australia (royal), Bahamas (royal), Barbados (royal), Belize (royal), Canada (royal), Grenada (royal), Jamaica (royal), New Zealand (there's also a Maori version), Saint Kitts and Nevis (royal) and Tuvalu (royal), and the British Crown Dependencies of Guernsey, Jersey and the Isle of Man (royal). It is the official anthem of Northern Ireland and also of England (which doesn't have a proper one of its own), and is used at British sporting events such as Wimbledon and other formal dos with a royal connection. In Canada it has been sung since the late 1700s, being designated the Royal Anthem of Canada in 1967, with 'O Canada' named as the national anthem. There are some French words for the Canadian version.

In Britain, where national anthems are generally regarded with a mixture of sentiment and irreverence, most people can't remember the words after the first verse, and start going, 'Mnm mmn nm mmm nmm mmmnm . . .' In fact, there are several versions in English, including one with a verse that Prince Charles referred to as 'politically incorrect'. Here is that verse:

> O Lord, our God, arise,
> Scatter her enemies,
> And make them fall.
> Confound their politics,
> Frustrate their knavish tricks,
> On Thee our hopes we fix,
> God save us all.

Whether or not that's politically incorrect, it's badly written, don't you think? It's like something from a Hallmark birthday card. Incidentally, the term 'knavish tricks' was an alteration from 'Popish tricks', which had been cleaned up by King George V (1865–1936).

The author, composer and date of publication of the modern tune are unknown, except that it is probably dates from the seventeenth or eighteenth century. The first version of what is nearly-but-not-quite the melody we would recognize (in the key of G major) was published in 1744 and the first performance is thought to have been the following year, when it was sung in support of King George II, after he was thrashed at the Battle of Prestonpans. The first known version of the tune proper is by John Bull, who died in 1628, though it seems to be based on a traditional melody. The compiler of *The Oxford Companion to Music*, Percy Scholes, says it resembles an early plainsong tune, but with the rhythm of a galliard. Henry Purcell used the opening notes as well as the words 'God Save the King' in one of his pieces, and Handel used it in his *Suite No.4 in E minor*, HWV 429, which he composed before 1720.

More than 100 composers have borrowed the tune for their own compositions, including Beethoven (famously), Haydn, Liszt, Debussy, Brahms, Johann Strauss I, Edward Elgar and Charles Ives. In 1970, Jimi Hendrix played it at the Isle of Wight Festival, and there have been two high-altitude performances: the Beatles played it between songs on their rooftop concert in January 1969 and Brian May performed it in 2002 on the roof of Buckingham Palace.

Another interesting thing happened outside Buckingham Palace a couple of days after the attacks on the World Trade Center, in 2001, when crowds of people, including many Americans unable to fly home, gathered at the famous gates to watch the Changing of the Guard. Suddenly, instead of 'God Save the Queen', the Coldstream Guards struck up 'The Star-spangled Banner', reducing several American visitors to tears. The playing of a foreign national anthem instead of 'God Save the Queen' at the Changing of the Guard was unheard of – indeed this was its first occurrence. But it had been ordered by the Queen. So it was done.

Spam names and messages

'Spam', the irritating rubbish that arrives daily on our computers, being snapped up mostly these days by so-called 'spam filters', should not be confused with SPAM®, the precooked canned meat product. If you care, you can read 'All about SPAM®' on page 133. This section is to do with the other kind of spam.

Every morning I go through my spam folder to make sure there isn't anything in there that I want. Usually it is full of offers for fake watches, fake degree certificates, online casinos and pills that they promise will enlarge things. This last one is something I really don't think I need, frankly, but it appears that many men must.

My spam filter is very good but it is sometimes overzealous, quarantining messages from my friends, which I have to retrieve, deleting everything else. One day, as I was chucking out the garbage, I was struck by the singular strangeness of the names attached to messages such as 'Replica have become one of the best complimentary gifts for boyfriends and girlfriends these nowadays' and 'Viagra: Buy Online!!!' For example, 'Jackqueline Bong' and 'Laree Pinkie' don't really sound like real people, and 'Syble Tontarski' is more like an alien from some 1960s science-fiction TV programme. But the uncanny foreign-but-not-quite quality to these names has a unique poetry to it and I wondered who thought them up. I came to the conclusion that a computer program probably does it. In any case I randomly harvested a few and I've grouped them below, with a selection of their messages marshalled underneath. Reading the list through has a kind of soporific effect, rather like chanting a mantra. So don't do this before operating heavy machinery.

Spam names

Cathy Laticia, Yong Cheryl, Fanny Romona, Mrs. Bridget Monica, Jackqueline Bong, Voyage Playing, Dana Argentina, Ronald Oliva, Myrtle Syble, Constance Vena, Dennis Eugenia, Torie Willow, Suzan Ruthann, Giselle Ayana, Valda Celia, Ellis Vertie, Candy Leeann, Cleta Candace, Sheena Risa, Francene Elissa, Hisako Oretha, Cassandra Iris, Marquerite Caitlyn, Emmy Kathlene, Alina Ardith, Freddie Carl, Rina Clemmie, Ehtel Holli, Laquita Yessenia, Cecelia Arnette, Rochell Lenora, France Mertie, Luci Lakeesha, Antonietta Meagan, Sheila Maribeth, Beatris Yoshiko, Holly Leigha, Luis Shanell, Delmy Renae, Salena Delfina, Susan Janine, Remedios Gail, Bebe Edda, Mozell Renate, Brittny Krysten, Johnny Ines, Leanne Enid, Tora Jettie, Karma Melida, Danyell Rena, Simone Queenie, Brittney Mirtha, Bruna Allegra, Darla Wilda, Lera Josefine, Yelena Chloe, Dedra Elanor, Margherita Kyung, Viola Helene,

Lovella Valery, Erma Karolyn, Quinn Dalia, Syble Tontarski, Sherrill Nevada, Laree Pinkie, Magen Virgie.

Spam messages

'Can you imagine about some cheap replica watches?'; 'Make money from home, Works for up to 36 hours'; 'Reward-full Assignment'; 'I was once in your shoes'; 'We were waiting for this'; 'Spice up your regular sexual life'; 'Free money whenever you play'; 'Enhance Your Career Tomorrow'; 'For men, many opt to increase size the natural way'; 'It's your Sale notifier'; 'hzwginpbuxc'; 'If your blood flow has been reduced you will experience problems'; 'Buy the most qualitative replicas'; 'Be a VIP in our City'; 'We are main for Rolex'; 'Erect1Le Dysfunct1on Meds'; 'Masters degree with no efforts'; 'P*entermine 37.5 - 180 pills for $690'; 'Stop premature ejaculations'; 'Best Buy 90000 Satisfied US, UK, Customers!'; 'This could change your life'; 'You Can Enjoy Bigger, Harder, More Intensly Erectoins!'; 'Multiple benefits include FREE shipping'; 'Well, I highly recommend this Pens enlargement pill!'; '12,500USD Bonus treat'; 'VALIUM Online!'; 'I Am So Glad I Did It'; 'Why You Need to Buy Pen1s Pills?'; 'No doctors visit or calls'; 'Save With The Lowest Price'; 'So how to naturally enlarge IT?'; 'Watches explorer, oyster, yachtmaster'; 'I was very insecure about my size'; 'Highly recommended, tadalafil the most popular'; 'Vegas Style Slots'; 'Give your significant other MIND BLOWING orgasms?'; 'Time to move ahead'.

Does anyone ever respond to this pathetic rubbish?

'Strange Fruit'

When I was reading up on this subject in the library, I went into the room where the young sit at computers, next to the room where the old read the papers, and I put 'strange fruit' into a search engine. I was immediately assailed by a lot of disgustingly obscene pictures, including one of a naked man in a sailor's cap, lipstick and clown's boots.

'Strange Fruit' is a song famously performed by Billie Holiday, which she first sang in 1938 and released as a record the following year. The song was written by a Jewish New York teacher, poet and lyricist named Abel Meeropol (1903–86). Meeropol wrote under the pen name 'Lewis Allan', in memory of his two stillborn children, and was the author of the Frank Sinatra and Josh White hit 'The House I Live In'. A member of the American Communist Party, he and his wife Anne would later adopt Michael and Robert, the sons of Julius and Ethel Rosenberg, the American spies who were executed in 1953 for passing information about the atomic bomb to the Soviet Union.

In 1937 Meeropol had seen the now famous photograph of two African-Americans, Thomas Shipp and Abram Smith, dangling by their necks from trees as an excited crowd points and laughs. This picture, he said, 'haunted me for days', and it prompted him to write a poem called 'Bitter Fruit'. The work was published in the *New York Teacher* and later in the Marxist journal *New Masses*, shortly becoming the more creepily titled 'Strange Fruit'. In 1971 Meeropol explained, 'I wrote "Strange Fruit" because I hate lynching, and I hate injustice, and I hate the people who perpetuate it.'

Meeropol set the poem to his own music and took it to Barney Josephson, a leftist shoe salesman, who was owner of Café Society, New York's first integrated nightclub. Josephson said he was 'floored' by the lyrics when first read them, contrasting, as they did, the sweet fragrance of southern magnolia with the smell of burning flesh, and describing the black bodies swinging in the breeze. He quickly introduced the piece to the troubled and brilliant jazz singer Billie Holiday. Meeropol, though, felt she was not very 'comfortable' with the song. 'What do you want me to do with that, man?' she asked in her usual endearing way, along with the question, 'What does "pastoral" mean?' Nonetheless she was to make 'Strange Fruit' famous, and it became her unofficial signature number.

Holiday's ghostwritten autobiography *Lady Sings the Blues* suggests that, with some help, she herself set the poem to music, which was – let's be nice – *incorrect*. When quizzed about this memory lapse, Holiday bluntly said, 'I ain't never read that book.' She could have done with a PR person, that lady. However, it is true that she did vary, and somewhat simplify, the original, rather tricky, melody.

In performances, Josephson specified that it should be Holiday's closing number. Just before she started, waiters were ordered to stop serving and a hush would descend as the lights were lowered except for a single spotlight picking out the singer. 'Strange Fruit' is just three short verses long and took Holiday less than two-and-a-half minutes to sing.

The austere minor-key lament had, and still has, a powerful emotional impact and the reaction was profound. In October 1939, Samuel Grafton of the *New York Post* wrote about hearing the song: 'Even now, as I think of it, the short hair on the back of my neck tightens and I want to hit somebody. I know who, too.' The founder of Atlantic Records, Ahmet Ertegun, claimed that 'Strange Fruit' was 'a declaration of war . . . the beginning of the civil rights movement', and the British-born jazz writer Leonard Feather said it was 'the first unmuted cry against racism'.

Reactions to 'Strange Fruit' were not all positive, though. Holiday was sometimes harassed when she sang it and performances on the road had to be carefully thought about, particularly in the South. *Variety*, rather missing the point, called it 'basically a depressing piece', and *Time*, amazingly, described it as 'a prime piece of musical propaganda'. The song was banned by the BBC and widely elsewhere, and Holiday's label Columbia refused to make a recording of it, likewise fearful of a bad reaction, though they allowed it to be released under an agreement with another company.

Even in Josephson's nightclub audiences seemed unsure whether they should clap or not following Holiday's final quavering fifth, and the owners and proprietors of venues often feared disturbances. Jack Schiffman, whose family owned New York City's Apollo, described the reaction to the song: 'A moment of oppressively heavy silence followed, and then a kind of rustling sound I had never heard before. It was the sound of almost two thousand people sighing.'

When in old age Abel Meeropol developed Alzheimer's disease and finally stopped recognizing people, his elder son played 'Strange Fruit' for him in his nursing home. He appeared to recognize the tune, and perked up when he did. Following his death in 1986, the song was sung at his memorial service.

The very romantic history of concrete

Not so long ago I read about some people in a London suburb who were banned from hanging washing outside their flats in case it fell on other people and hurt them, though a pair of someone's smalls landing on your noggin would surely cause nothing more serious than a pride wound. It reminded me of the contestants in that Shrove Tuesday pancake race in St Albans who were told to walk, not run, for similarly insane safety reasons.

Not all health and safety advice is as nutty as this, of course. I spoke to a nurse once who said that after the compulsory replacement of concrete with spongy matting in children's playgrounds, cases of serious head injury had dropped dramatically in number. This led me to musing about the hard stuff and it's an interesting subject.

Concrete is made of cement (the binding part) and other materials such as ash and aggregate (course material such as gravel, crushed rocks or sand), which is mixed with water, sloshed around and then poured into moulds. Cement comes in two types: in the first (hydraulic cement), chemical reactions harden the cement no matter how wet it is. It will even harden under water or when exposed to gallons of rain. In the other sort (non-hydraulic cement), the mixture must be kept dry for the chemical magic to work. Both kinds of cement bind everything together and dry to form a concrete-hard (obviously) stable material with many of the properties of stone. Just to be clear, by the way, 'cement' is the smooth bonding material, 'concrete' is the lumpy mixture of cement and everything else.

The word 'concrete' has a classical root, coming from the Latin *concretus*, meaning 'compact' or 'condensed'. This is apt, as the ancient

Romans invented an early form of concrete, called *opus caementicium*, which they made from burnt lime, crushed pumice and pozzolana, a volcanic ash from Mount Vesuvius that, in water, reacts with lime to produce cementitious compounds, which will set even under water. Some of the Romans' underwater concrete structures still survive in good nick. Incidentally, 'cementitious' is a word I am now going to introduce at dinner parties, as in, 'Cripes, Rupert, don't think me rude, but your wife's gravy is positively cementitious.' The introduction of concrete allowed the Romans to design and build bigger and more complex structures, with arches, vaults and domes. Hadrian's Pantheon in Rome, built in 126 CE, has a concrete dome; the Colosseum was also made using concrete and many surviving Roman bridges have masonry cladding on a concrete core. But then the Romans got all decadent and their empire fell to bits.

Between the end of the Classical period and the beginning of the Modern period, concrete was more or less forgotten, but in 1678 Joseph Moxon described the 'hidden fire' that he noticed in heated lime when water was added. A shade more than a century later, Bry Higgins (marvellous name) published the most exciting cement bestseller ever: *Experiments and Observations Made with the View of Improving the Art of Composing and Applying Calcereous Cements and of Preparing Quicklime*. Amazon couldn't keep up with the demand.

In 1793 John Smeaton (re-)discovered hydraulic lime, making the first modern concrete by mixing pebbles and powdered brick into his waterproof cement. He used this to rebuild the Eddystone Lighthouse in Cornwall. A new lighthouse now does the job, but 'Smeaton's Tower' has been resurrected on the mainland, right beside the sea. I got claustrophobia *and* vertigo in there one day and had to back out down the narrow stairs, past old ladies and invalids with sticks. Three years later (not three years after my claustrophobia, *in 1796*), James Parker patented a 'natural' hydraulic cement known as Parker's or Roman cement, made with limestone that naturally contains the right amount of clay to make a Smeaton-type concrete.

English inventor Joseph Aspdin patented the first true artificial cement in 1824, which he made by burning finely ground limestone with clay. The burning process changed the chemical properties of the components, making a stronger material. He called his invention Portland Cement because of its similarity in colour to Portland limestone, quarried on the tied island of Portland. This is now the most commonly used cement in the world.

Concrete has been going for thousands of years because it works. Nonetheless, developments continue. For example, it has long been known that although concrete is strong under pressure, it is weak under tension (bending or twisting), which can cause the cement to crack. The answer is a nineteenth-century one: *reinforced* concrete, invented in 1849 by Frenchman Joseph Monier. Reinforced concrete includes metal rods, or nowadays steel, glass or plastic fibres, to carry the tensile loads.

Adding other things to concrete also alters its properties. The Romans used horsehair to reduce cracking and mixed in blood to make it frost-resistant (how on earth did they discover that?). Today, recycled fly ash, a by-product of coal-fired power stations, is commonly used as a cement replacement. In large or complicated concrete pours, where partial setting would spell disaster, sugar, citric acid and tartaric acid are now used to slow down the hardening process.

It sounds absolutely delicious.

Local newspaper headlines

Unlike national newspapers, local papers are often hard pressed to come up with an arresting front-page headline, owing to there being absolutely no news most days beyond the banal toing and froing of the unexciting local population. One of my all-time favourites was reported by James Thurber, who remembered a student journalist who wrote very dull stories. One day, his editor, losing patience, instructed him to make his next piece snappier but, when the story was filed, his headline, which is a classic of its kind, read: 'Who has noticed the sores on the tops of the horses in the animal husbandry building?'

'Man bites dog' is a great headline because it turns the commonplace upside-down, but what is the poor editor to do if there really isn't any news? The answer is obvious: grasp at straws. 'Cycle lane "safe", says council' is non-news of the highest order, being totally boring and devoid of emotion. 'Whitstable mum in custard shortage' is another corker, custard being insanely domestic and possibly the least interesting subject in the world. I suppose that if somebody drowned in a vat of the stuff you might want to read about it, and if there was a global shortage of water – or women – you might be interested, but a shortage of custard? *In Whitstable?* And how was this mum 'in' the shortage? It's a funny word usage. I presume what actually happened was that this mum just went to the shops and found there wasn't any custard. The headline writer, having presumably seen and envied headlines such as 'President in assassination drama', thought that using the same form of words might lend authority and drama to the headline. He, or she, was wrong.

You can't blame journalists for trying. 'Nuns fight strippers' sounds like something you might read in lurid fluorescent signage outside one of those dingy cinemas around Wardour Street, but it was an actual headline I saw in my local newspaper. I guess it was a 'moral outrage'-type piece. 'Fight' is a good, active word and better, no doubt, than 'issue formal objection to', which was probably more true. Another one I have seen, 'Father Christmas arrested', sounds good but you just know it can't have been the real Santa and is unlikely to have lived up to its promise.

Along with the pedestrian headlines, you do get the occasional strikingly surreal announcement. 'Window cleaner killed by giant pencil' conjures up all kinds of crazy pictures and was, sadly, true. One example of that rare thing, a properly newsworthy true story that might go national, is 'Killer in sex change row'. This is pretty good for a local paper, containing murder, 'sexual perversion' and that old favourite, 'waste of public money'. The only local thing it lacks really is a car-parking angle. 'Gun found up man's bum' is almost irresistible, too. But what can it possibly mean? Was the weapon stumbled upon during a medical examination or did somebody suspect it was there and go looking for it? The headline writer seems to have decided to leave that to the reader's imagination. Whatever the case, let us hope that the safety catch was on.

Understanding the Union Jack

The national flag of the United Kingdom of Great Britain and Northern Ireland is the Union Jack. It was formally adopted in 1801 after hundreds of years of fascinating history and numerous versions. The flag is, naturally enough, a wonderful subject for arguments down the pub. For a start, there is disagreement over its proper and correct name. In common parlance it has long been the 'Union Jack', a name coming most probably from 'jack staff', the flagpole on a ship's bow. Members of the British Institute of Hair-Splitters maintain, however, that 'Union Flag' is more proper, even though vexillologists (flag experts) at Britain's Flag Institute point out that 'Union Flag' is a pretty recent development. Since 1902 the Admiralty has officially recognized 'Union Jack' as a correct name for the national flag, and outside Britain the term 'Union Flag' is less well known and therefore more confusing.

The Union Jack comes in two different area ratios. The first is a double square, a ratio of 1:2, but in 2008 the Flag Institute began campaigning for a reversion to the traditional 3:5 ratio, one close to the golden ratio of 1:1.618034.

As if this weren't confusing enough for everybody, the flag is very hard to draw accurately, even with a setsquare and ruler. Much of the difficulty lies in the three overlapping crosses. The red St George's Cross (England) is $\frac{1}{5}$ the flag's width, with a fimbriation – its white border – of $\frac{1}{15}$ the flag's width; the white-on-a-blue-field St Andrew's Saltire (a diagonal cross) (Scotland) is $\frac{1}{5}$ the flag's width – the broader part of the white diagonal is $\frac{1}{10}$ the flag's width; the St Patrick's Saltire (Ireland) is $\frac{1}{15}$ of the flag's width – the narrower part of the white diagonal $\frac{1}{30}$ the flag's width. The centre-lines of the diagonals must

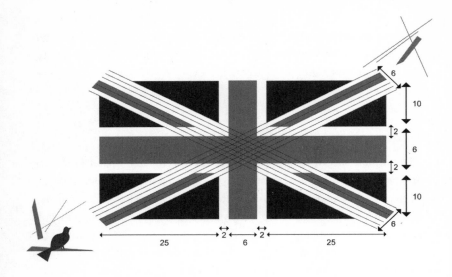

meet in the centre (*see* above). I won't drive you bananas with the colour specifications.

As a matter of interest, Wales – the land of my birth – doesn't feature in the flag, as it has been a part of the Kingdom of England since 1282, so must make do with the St George's Cross.

If you try to draw the St Patrick's Saltire over the St George's Cross it won't join up with itself. This so-called 'counterchange' is the cause of the flag's reflective asymmetry and means that it looks different hoisted in different ways (*see* opposite).

Because it is asymmetrical left-to-right and top-to-bottom, the Union Jack is one of the few national flags to be frequently flown upside-down. I knew an American who lived in London whose hobby it was to look out for Union Jacks incorrectly hoisted on official buildings. He used to cause quite a stir as he announced to officials, in a loud Texan accent, that the hotel or government office was flying its national flag upside-down.

Supposing your flagpole is on the left, as in the pictures, the fat bit of the white diagonal in the top left-hand bit of the flag should be above the red diagonal. There are heraldic or vexillological names for all these

Right way up   Wrong way up

things, which I am avoiding because I know your life is complicated enough at the moment.

Everybody seems to get it wrong sometimes, even the fiercely patriotic British National Party, whose leader Nick Griffin was photographed in 2010 standing proudly beside an upside-down flag, not the first time this had happened to him. He was in excellent company because in February 2009 the UK government sat beside an upside-down Union Jack at the signing of a trade agreement with Chinese premier Wen Jiabao.

Oh, who cares? I hear you cry. Well, an upside-down flag is traditionally a distress signal. Bad luck then for Japan, Italy, Israel, the United Kingdom of Great Britain and Northern Ireland and a few others.

Dirty-minded spam filters and the havoc they cause

In 1996, computer-using residents of the charming town of Scunthorpe in Lincolnshire found themselves forbidden from registering with AOL owing to the zealous 'Mary Whitehouse' tendency of an embryonic spam filter, which had discovered a rude word contained within the name of the town. 'The Scunthorpe problem', as it became known, spread to the Yorkshire town of Penistone and, amusingly, also to Lightwater in Surrey, many of whose bemused residents were aghast when the problem was explained to them.

Although the Scunthorpe problem is said to be a thing of the past, dirty-minded spam filters are still prone to descend like Bowdler on entirely innocent words. In 2008, the American Family Association's website automatically decontaminated an article about athlete Tyson Gay, replacing his surname with what it believed to be a more 'appropriate' word. The resulting article was strikingly headed 'Homosexual eases into 100 m final at Olympic trials'. But much as we might deplore the censoriousness of spam filters, it is undoubtedly true that the internet is crawling with disgusting filth, which is easy to find if you will only go looking for it. Who among us has not received into his inbox unwelcome emails touting pills that promise knobulatory 'enlargement'? When my nine-year-old son read some of these he excitedly thought he was going to be made six inches taller.

Council planning departments have long suffered from building applications containing the word 'erection' going into their trash, and in 2004, the Horniman Museum in London found that its emails were being blocked by spam filters which seemed to believe that instead of being, as they claimed, 'a family friendly museum with exhibits from around the world', they were showing off disgusting horny men. Even harmless emails promoting the Christmas pantomime *Dick Whittington* have been targeted, with one theatre discovering that marketing emails for their admittedly rather carelessly worded 'Big Dick Extravaganza' were ending up in the trash.

One of Canada's oldest magazines, *The Beaver*, was even forced to change its name after going online. Beavers are a national emblem of Canada but the publishers noticed that visitors to their website were staying for less than ten seconds, having been interested not so much in the history of the Canadian fur trade as, well, something else. Beaver College in Pennsylvania changed its name in 2001 for similar reasons.

Perhaps the most amusing case of mistaken identity occurred with a diving club situated on the mouth of the River Foyle in the town of Muff in County Donegal, on the border between the Republic of Ireland and Northern Ireland. The webmaster of the Muff Diving Club website said that on the first day of operation the site had been overwhelmed by hits, and that it was a full-time job to delete the filthy posts which were appearing on their forum page. The club quickly decided to change its name to the Scuba Association of the Town of Muff, hoping against hope that this would lick the problem.

Homeopathy and why it's complete bollocks

Jupiter is the biggest planet in our solar system. Its diameter is 88,736 miles (142,807 km) and if it were a hollow shell you could fit 1,321 Earths inside it, with a bit of room left over for some custard. Now imagine, if you can, a planet with a diameter well over a thousand times bigger than this, reaching from here to the sun – about 93 million miles (150 million km). Suppose that this planet was made of water, and suppose you took one molecule of *allium cepa* – that's red onion to you and me – and stirred it into this gigantic ball of water, the solution would be so dilute that if you gave everybody in the world as much of that water-planet as they could drink during their lifetime, it would be unlikely that anyone would ever get so much as an atom of red onion. As it happens, red onion is, I read, a homeopathic ingredient, used as a remedy for 'belching', 'dreams' and 'offensive flatus', and if you took a homeopathic preparation of it, made in the homeopathic way by diluting one drop of it in 100 drops of water, then diluting one drop of that in 100 drops of water, then diluting one drop of that in 100 drops of water, and so on, thirty or more times, then it would be as dilute as the red onion molecule in the water-planet example.

This is an illustration of a fundamentally incomprehensible paradox of homeopathic medicine, which is that the more you dilute the original substance, the more potent it becomes as a remedy for a condition. It's as if the less you ate the fatter you got.

Homeopathy was invented by Samuel Hahnemann (1755–1843), who believed that the medicine of his time did as much harm as good (could have been right there) and gave up working as a doctor. In 1803 he wrote an essay, 'On the Effects of Coffee from Original Observations', in which he maintained that many diseases are *caused* by coffee. He later abandoned this idea, concentrating increasingly on research into the medicinal properties of highly dilute substances, which he claimed became effective cures when mixed in a special way, by vigorous shaking (succussion).

Hahnemann learned that cinchona, the quinine-containing bark of a Peruvian tree, was effective in treating malaria and reported that it appeared to *induce* malaria-like symptoms in himself. He thought (why?) that it would do the same thing in any healthy person and came up with the idea that 'that which can produce a set of symptoms in a healthy person, can treat a sick person who is manifesting a similar set of symptoms'. This is a beginner's mistake in logic, a bit like suggesting that beer, which makes a sober person drunk, can be used to make a drunk person sober. He ultimately called his idea 'homeopathy', although scientists call it a pretty obvious logical fallacy.

Nonetheless, many people report that homeopathy helps them, and that they feel better and genuinely recover after taking homeopathic remedies. There is certainly no doubt that this is true. Scientific studies of people who take homeopathic remedies do indeed show that a statistically significant number of them report improvement in their condition – whatever it is – when they are treated by a homeopath. The problem is that you get exactly the same results when you give patients a little white pill containing nothing but starch. If you give them two starch pills, they feel better than when you give them only one, and if you give them a red starch pill they feel better than if you give them a white one. If you give them an injection of saline solution, they feel better still. This is called 'the placebo effect' and it shows the power of the human mind to affect the perception of illness and pain. Animals given placebos and homeopathic remedies never get better because of them.

To test how well a new cough medicine or homeopathic remedy is working, and eliminate the influence of the placebo effect, you need to do a 'double-blind randomized controlled trial'. In a typical one of these, a hundred patients with a non-life-threatening medical problem see a homeopath, who prescribes them a remedy. They are then divided into two groups of fifty. One group gets the pills prescribed by the homeopath and the other gets dummy pills. Until the experiment is over, nobody involved, including the experimenters, the patients and the homeopath, knows who is in which group or who has got what pills. The results of these trials are consistent: there is no difference in improvement, or reported improvement, between the two groups. The homeopathic pills work as well, or as badly, as the starch pills.

So the real problem with homeopathy is not that we do not understand *how* it works, it is that though it *doesn't* work people continue to believe that it does. If the evidence of well-designed peer-reviewed trials showed a real effect beyond the placebo effect, the person who discovered this amazing medical fact would become rich and famous overnight and would probably win the Nobel Prize, too.

But people's behaviour shows, I think, that they do not really believe homeopathy works. Nobody uses homoeopathic contraceptives, do they? And no diabetic takes a homeopathically succussed sugar solution instead of insulin. Nobody having his appendix out asks for a homeopathic anaesthetic and nobody with a broken leg swallows a homeopathic pill to mend it – they go to a doctor who puts it in a plaster cast. No, homeopathy is generally used only to treat things that tend to get better on their own: aches and pains, bruises, coughs and colds, runny noses, bad moods and the like.

In fact, when I asked my homeopath if he could give me something for my open-minded scepticism he said no. But, to be on the safe side, I drink a daily glass of water, which contains so many highly diluted substances that I like to think I am curing myself homeopathically of everything, by accident, every time I swallow.

Part Three:

LISTS AND TESTS FOR THE INSTANT GENIUS

Quick information and enquiry for the time-poor gentleman

1 Lightning-quick Lists for the Busy Genius

Business jargon we all hate

Have you ever played buzzword bingo? It's a game that was introduced to me by a colleague (nowadays that would be 'work colleague') when I used to proactively (see below) stack chairs in the office of a global (see below) business consultancy (see below). What happens is that players each have a card covered in the latest buzzwords and discreetly tick them off during meetings each time one is used. The first person to get them all shouts 'Impactful leverage solutions!' and you start again – *forever*. Everybody hates these words, which are transparent efforts to get the banal, pedestrian and unpalatable to sound exciting, fun, important and positive. Here are the best of the worst, with notes, and translations into English.

1 Going forward: 'in future'
2 Seamless: nonsense
3 Global: 'offices in more than one country'
4 Idea showers: 'brainstorms' as were
5 Grow: a horticultural term now meaning to 'increase profits'
6 Roll out: introduce spasmodically
7 Blue-sky thinking: nonsense
8 Change management: sugar-coated mass sackings
9 Pull together: 'put together'
10 Solutions: this has got out of hand. 'Sandwich solutions' just means 'sandwiches'
11 Thought leadership: 'brainwashing'

12 Platform atheist: no flipping idea what this is meant to mean

13 Impactful: nonsense

14 Incentivize: give people money or threaten them with the sack

15 Touch base with you: 'waste your time'

16 Implement: 'do'

17 Team leader: 'upstart'

18 Consultancy: 'money for old rope'

19 Brain dump: rubbish

20 Team player: code for 'lacklustre and useless'

21 Not a team player: code for 'rude, selfish, and unpleasant'

22 Granular: no idea what this means

23 Cutting-edge: commonplace and ordinary

24 Proactive: a made-up word. Whatever happened to 'active'?

25 Heads-up: as a noun, it means a 'tip-off'

26 On my radar: 'I know about that'

27 Big hitter: 'loudmouth'

28 Challenge: 'problem'

29 Low-hanging fruit: 'easy pickings'

30 Take ownership: 'take blame'

31 Pre-prepare, pre-plan, forward-planning: all pleonastic

32 Think outside the box: a cliché revealing the user to be thinking *inside* the box

33 Customer-centric: sycophantic and obsequious

34 The get-go: hideous. Means 'the start'

35 360-degree thinking: 'thinking'

36 Peel the onion: nonsense

37 Product evangelist: beats me what this means – 'salesman'?

38 Strategy: a military term, which generally just means 'plan'

39 Feed through: a transitive phrasal verb meaning 'tell'

40 The big picture: vague term meaning whatever you like it to mean

41 Traction: nonsense

42 Get your ducks in a row: nonsense. Ducks (or ducklings) get *themselves* in a row

43 Core competencies: things you can do

44 Actioning: 'doing', or telling someone else to do

45 110 per cent: meaningless

46 State of the art: 'run of the mill'

47 In the loop: to be 'in the loop' is to be told things other people are told

48 Bespoke: 'the usual'

49 Paradigm shift: something different (often because the previous idea failed)

50 Stakeholders: 'interested parties'

51 Feeding back: responding to something

52 Cascading: sending emails to people, usually

53 Escalate up: take something to the/a boss. The 'up' is redundant

54 Human resources: 'personnel department' as was

55 Come to the party: 'join in'

56 Best of breed: 'best' presumably

57 Go to market: finally sell some service or product

58 Joined-up (thinking/working): left hand knows what right hand is doing

59 Synergy: working together

60 Leveraging: just horrible – verbing nouns weirds language

61 Manage expectations: make sure X knows how useless you are

62 Quick win: loud showing-off about doing your job

63 Scalable: can be reduced or enlarged

64 My door is open on the issue: nonsense

65 Turnkey solution: unutterable nonsense

66 Upskill: 'train'

67 Win–win situation: 'everybody's happy'

68 Singing from the same hymn sheet: 'awake'

69 Flag up: 'warn or tell someone about something'

70 Pushing the envelope: a maths term reduced to nonsense by ignoramuses

71 Bring to the table: nonsense

72 Scoping: finding out what the hell we're supposed to be doing on this job

73 Service user: 'patient' as was

74 Drill down: go from general to particular

75 Multi-tasking: doing two things at once, such as listening to your boss talk balls while swearing under your breath

76 High-altitude view: nonsense

77 Workshopping: talking or working in an informal group

78 Siloed thinking: nonsense

79 Best practice: not putting a live toaster in the bath with you

80 Critical path: from a project modelling technique. Usually misused

81 Deliverables: things you can do by 5 p.m., Monday, next year, etc.

82 Enabler: lazy boss

83 Facetime: hideous nonsense

84 Value-added: 'extra'

85 Monetize: ghastly. Means 'start making money from'

86 Repurpose: hammer in nail with screwdriver

87 Robust: likely to come apart at any moment

88 World-class: about as crappy as everyone else

Ten things to know before meeting the Queen

George W. Bush tended to come a bit of a cropper whenever he met the Queen. During a royal banquet in 1991, before he became President, he told Her Majesty that he was the black sheep of his family, adding, 'Who's yours?' Barbara Bush, seated nearby, is said to have leaned over and told the Queen, 'Don't answer that!' which didn't help really. On his first presidential visit to England, George W. Bush accompanied the Queen along The Mall in an open carriage drawn by six stupendous horses. As they approached Buckingham Palace, one of the animals broke wind with undisguised savagery, rattling the doors and blowing the President sideways. In a valiant attempt to quell his discomfort, the Queen turned to Bush and said, 'I regret, Mr President, that there are some things which even a Queen is unable to control.' 'No worries, your Royal Holiness,' replied Bush. 'Actually, till you owned up I thought it was that there horse.'

Most meetings with the Queen happen on one of her visits or walkabouts and are over before you even have time to ask her what star sign she is. In these cases ordinary politeness will be quite sufficient as she sweeps past, instantly forgetting you and your face. But if you know you are to meet the Queen at, say, a Buckingham Palace or Holyrood garden party, then you need to prepare to avoid some of the pitfalls. Here are a few formal niceties you might like to follow.

1 Stand when the Queen enters a room (only if you are *in* the room, obviously. You don't need to stand up if you see her enter a room on the news).

2 A neck bow (rhymes with cow not low – you aren't expected to wear a bowtie) is acceptable on being introduced (never introduce yourself). Your wife, girlfriend or mistress may do a small curtsy if she can accomplish it without falling over. But for goodness' sake avoid elaborate genuflection. It's so vulgar.

3 If she speaks to you (don't try to get in first) you should address her as 'Your Majesty'. After that, if she's still there, it's 'Ma'am', rhyming with 'spam' not 'farm'. Suitable topics will be general and non-controversial. Don't discuss personal matters, such as the embarrassing behaviour of various members of her family, and avoid saying things like 'Christ, it's hot in here, Your Majesty; I've got a case of "Betty Swallocks" something rotten'.

4 Don't say 'Pleased to meet you', this surely goes without saying.

5 Don't comment on her age, makeup, hair, teeth, dreadful clothes, voice, nose-size, wealth etc. (ordinary politeness).

6 If the Queen extends her hand, don't kiss it. And don't grimly hang on to it while you tell her your life story or, worse, pump it like you were milking a cow. She has to shake hands thousands of times a week, poor woman – hence those long gloves – so a brief touch is plenty and then let go. No high fives, obviously.

7 Don't hug her (ordinary politeness).

8 Don't turn your back on her (ordinary politeness).

9 Don't wear gloves in her presence.

10 If writing to the Queen there's no need to include her full title on the envelope, and anyway you won't have room because it is: Her Majesty Elizabeth the Second, by the Grace of God, of Great Britain, Ireland and the British Dominions beyond the Seas Queen, Defender of the Faith, Duchess of Edinburgh, Countess of Merioneth, Baroness Greenwich, Duke of Lancaster, Lord of Mann, Duke of Normandy, Sovereign of the Most Honourable Order of the Garter, Sovereign of the Most Honourable Order of the Bath, Sovereign of the Most Ancient and Most Noble Order of the Thistle, Sovereign of the Most Illustrious Order of Saint Patrick, Sovereign of the Most Distinguished Order of Saint Michael and Saint George, Sovereign of the Most Excellent Order of the British Empire, Sovereign of the Distinguished Service Order, Sovereign of the Imperial Service Order, Sovereign of the Most Exalted Order of the Star of India, Sovereign of the Most Eminent Order of the Indian Empire, Sovereign of the Order of British India, Sovereign of the Indian Order of Merit, Sovereign of the Order of Burma, Sovereign of the Royal Order of Victoria and Albert, Sovereign of the Royal Family Order of King Edward VII, Sovereign of the Order of Merit, Sovereign of the Order of the Companions of Honour, Sovereign of the Royal Victorian Order, Sovereign of the Most Venerable Order of the Hospital of St John of Jerusalem.

Five-and-a-half conspiracy theories

The *Oxford English Dictionary* defines a conspiracy as 'a secret plan by a group to do something unlawful or harmful', and a conspiracy theory as 'a belief that some covert but influential organization is responsible for an unexplained event'. When conspiracy theories are based on good evidence they stop being conspiracy theories and quietly become accepted as the truth, often after many years. When they aren't based on evidence they can go on growing for decades, causing a good deal of arm waving and shouting down the pub. Here are five-and-a-half of the best.

1 The Roswell 'flying saucer incident'

Some time round about 7 July 1947 residents of Roswell, New Mexico, reported seeing a flaming object in the sky and shortly thereafter scattered debris was discovered at a local ranch. There was general agreement that something interesting had crashed but before you could say 'slow news day', the *Roswell Daily Record* ran the juicy front-page headline 'RAAF captures flying saucer', which is a more exciting one than 'Roswell Army Air Field sweeps up rubbish from crashed weather balloon'. On 9 July the Commanding General of the Eighth Air Force confirmed that a 'radar-tracking balloon', not a 'flying disc', had been recovered, and as soon as bits of the crashed balloon were displayed at a press conference the 'flying saucer' story fizzled out. It was not until the 1970s, when a 'UFO researcher' gave the fairy tale the kiss of life, that an elaborate conspiracy theory took flight, featuring extraterrestrial corpses, secret military operations, a sinister disinformation programme and alien autopsies of the third kind. It was all rather spoiled by a 1995 report by the Office of the Secretary of the Air Force, which declared that the crashed balloon was probably part of Project Mogul, a secret US operation searching out evidence of Soviet atomic bomb tests.

2 Water fluoridation: a Soviet plot for world domination

Adding a controlled amount of fluoride to tap water reduces dental caries (tooth rot) and is otherwise harmless. But since the introduction of fluoridation in the 1950s a conspiracy theory has been going around alleging that it is a communist plot designed to reduce us all to compliant zombies. There is a lovely scene in Stanley Kubrick's *Dr Strangelove* (1964), in which a mad general, Jack D. Ripper, launches a nuclear strike against the Russians because he thinks that, by fluoridating American tap water, the 'international communist conspiracy' is sapping and impurifying his 'precious bodily fluids'. The trouble with the theory is that while our water has been fluoridated the Soviet Union has disappeared and neither does anything else terrible seem to have happened. What's more, those homegrown shopping channels do a better job of reducing people to compliant zombies than a bit of watery Russian fluoride ever could have done.

3 *Shakespeare's plays were written by somebody else, not him*

We know practically nothing about Shakespeare apart from his plays. His childhood goes almost unrecorded although we do know that he went to a 'grammar school'. Imagine how annoying *that* would have been for the English teacher. The authorship of Shakespeare's plays was first queried (unpersuasively) in the improbable sounding *The Romance of Yachting* (1848) by Col. Joseph C. Hart. But Herman Melville, the author of *Moby Dick*, wasn't impressed, describing the book as an 'abortion' that deserved to be 'burnt in a fire of asafetida'. (Asafoetida, as it is spelt in English, also known as devil's dung and stinking gum, is a plant with an especially pungent reek.) Since *The Romance of Yachting* about seventy other authors, including a woman, sometimes supposedly working together, have been suggested as the real authors of Shakespeare's works. Top contenders include Francis Bacon (the hero of the Scientific Revolution, not the painter), Christopher Marlowe and Edward de Vere (seventeenth Earl of Oxford). But not all those theories can be right, can they? Like a lot of these 'theories' they might be true, they might not be true, but there's no evidence for them, or to borrow a term coined by Kingsley Amis, they are inverted pyramids of piss.

4 *The assassination of John F. Kennedy involved several people*

On 22 September 1963 President John Fitzgerald Kennedy (JFK) was shot and killed in an open-top car as he was being driven through sunny Dallas. Kennedy was hit in the back by a bullet, and his head was blasted open by another, which blew the back of his skull off. He also had a bullet wound in the front of his neck. Audrey Parker, a nurse at Parkland Hospital where Kennedy was pronounced dead, described the wound: 'It looked small and round like an entry wound, instead of larger like an exit wound could often look.'

A man was soon arrested on suspicion of the assassination. He was named as Lee Harvey Oswald and it was said he had fired at Kennedy with a high-powered rifle from a position behind him, high up on the sixth floor of the Texas School Book Depository building, which overlooked Dealey Plaza. But Oswald was never tried, because while he was still in police custody he was shot and killed by a local man named Jack Ruby. Nonetheless the idea was quickly established that Oswald was indeed the 'lone gunman'.

But before long, doubts began to emerge about the official story, owing mainly to a large amount of circumstantial evidence that pointed to something funny having gone on. For example, at the time of the killing, many people watching the motorcade had heard loud bangs and seen and smelt smoke coming from under the trees on a hillock beside the road, to the front and right of the presidential car, a long way from the window where Oswald was said to have been shooting.

Over the next five years the assassinations of Malcolm X, Martin Luther King, Jr and JFK's brother Robert generated their own suggestive conspiracy theories and in 1976, after years of resistance, the US government reluctantly ordered an inquiry into the assassinations of King and JFK. The United States House of Representatives Select Committee on Assassinations (HSCA) concluded that more than one person *was* probably involved in the killing of President Kennedy. As one puzzled inquirer put it, 'I never could understand how you could be shot in the front from the back.' Thus representatives of the US government declared themselves to be possibly the most official conspiracy theorists ever, though which people might have been involved in the conspiracy, and for what reasons, remained very interesting but officially unanswered questions.

5 The moon landings were faked to distract people from the Vietnam War

One of the most enjoyable conspiracy theories of the twentieth century, which is still very much with us judging by the internet, is that the National Aeronautics and Space Administration (NASA) faked the Apollo moon landings and that astronauts did not really land on the moon but that the whole thing was shot on an elaborate set with actors dangling from wires being filmed in slow motion. Much is made of supposed anomalies in photographs of astronauts on the lunar surface, which are said to show shadows falling in the wrong places, a flag ruffled by the non-existent wind, clumsy photo-montage, obvious wires holding the actors up and even shots of Roy Disney picking up stuff off the floor. These claims have been so thoroughly discredited and in such detail that it is amazing there is still so much of this stuff out there. I'm all for open-minded scepticism but your argument needs to hang together a bit. I mean, more than 400,000 people worked on the Apollo project for nearly ten years and according to the conspiracy theory none, apparently, has ever told the truth about it, which would make it the most expensive – not to say gossip-free – theatrical production in the history of Broadway. And Roy Disney picking up rubbish? I mean, really!

5½ Elvis Presley faked his own death

The main 'evidence' for the theory that Elve the Pelve faked his own death in 1977 consists of the hundreds of 'sightings' of the King, suitably aged, shopping in Memphis or schlepping his wet wash to the laundromat, if that is the right term. This theory is so feeble that it is only really half a theory and claims – without the slightest believability – to involve members of his family in the cover-up. But it's been a boon to the tabloid press, which has churned out column-miles on the subject, all of it highly dubious, to put it politely. There must be something in these conspiracy theories that appeals to people's desire to make the world appear more exciting than it really is. I suggest they put down the tabloid, turn off the telly and have a look at the night sky. There's enough mystery, wonder and excitement up there for even the most stubbornly bored person. By the way, have you ever wondered why all those Elvis impersonators impersonate him in his fat and puffy years rather than in his young, thrusting and sexually potent years? I have.

Great quotes you don't know

Coming out with an apt quotation has the definite tendency to make you seem a lot cleverer than you are. In fact, people can be so impressed by a quotation that they will assume it is fitting even if it is completely irrelevant and was the only one you could think of at the time. There are a million books of quotations out there but most are full of old favourites threadbare from overuse. Here are some you might not know.

Roses are red, violets are blue, I'm schizophrenic, and so am I.
Oscar Levant

It is a far, far better thing to have a firm anchor in nonsense than to put out on the troubled seas of thought.
J. K. Galbraith

Drawing on my fine command of the English language, I said nothing.
Robert Benchley

The thing with high-tech is that you always end up using scissors.
David Hockney

A wise man proportions his belief to the evidence.
David Hume

79.48% of all statistics are made up on the spot.
John Allen Paulos

Skeptical scrutiny is the means, in both science and religion, by which deep insights can be winnowed from deep nonsense.
Carl Sagan

When I turned two I was really anxious, because I'd doubled my age in a year. I thought, if this keeps up, by the time I'm six I'll be ninety.
Steven Wright

All intellectual improvement arises from leisure.
Samuel Johnson

It is important to keep an open mind, but not so open that your brains fall out.
Stephen A. Kallis, Jr

Shut up, he explained.
Ring Lardner

Politics is the art of looking for trouble, finding it whether it exists or not, diagnosing it incorrectly, and applying the wrong remedy.
Earnest Benn

Someone's boring me. I think it's me.
Dylan Thomas

Education is the ability to listen to almost anything without losing your temper.
Robert Frost

Before you criticize someone, you should walk a mile in their shoes. That way, when you criticize them, you're a mile away and you have their shoes.
Dave Barry

Time is what prevents everything from happening at once.
John Archibald Wheeler

A man's character may be learned from the adjectives which he habitually uses in conversation.
Mark Twain

Men are born ignorant, not stupid; they are made stupid by education.
Bertrand Russell

What contemptible scoundrel has stolen the cork to my lunch?
W. Clement Stone

All successful revolutions are the kicking in of a rotten door.
J. K. Galbraith

Tragedy is when I cut my finger. Comedy is when you fall into an open sewer and die.
Mel Brooks

Incomprehensible police jargon

Did you hear about the policeman who found a penguin wandering in the street? He took it to the police station and asked what he should do with it. 'Take it to the zoo,' said the exasperated senior officer. The following day the policeman turned up at work with the penguin still with him. 'I thought I told you to take it to the zoo,' said his boss. 'I did,' said the policeman, 'but today he wants to go and see a film.'

This penguin might have been described in the reams of paperwork now required from officers as 'MFH'. Here are some more police abbreviations and jargon terms for your entertainment and approval.

- **ABH**: Actual Bodily Harm
- **ARV**: Armed Response Vehicle
- **ASNT**: Area Searched No Trace
- **B&E**: Breaking and Entering
- **BOP**: Breach of the Peace
- **CO19**: Central Operations Specialist Firearms Command
- **Code 99**: Tea-break, in honour of Co-op 99-brand tea
- **D&D**: Drunk and Disorderly
- **DIP**: Drunk in Public
- **DORTC**: Damage Only Road Traffic Collision
- **FATAC**: Fatal Road Traffic Accident
- **GBH**: Grievous Bodily Harm
- **HOLMES**: Home Office Large and Major Enquiry System computer
- **MFH**: Missing from Home
- **MISPER**: Missing Person
- **MOP**: Member of the Public
- **NAI**: Non-Accidental Injury
- **NFA**: No Fixed Abode
- **NFA**: No Further Action
- **NSPIS**: National Strategy for Police Information Systems (computer system)

- **PACE**: Police and Criminal Evidence Act 1984
- **PCSO**: Police Community Support Officer
- **PNC**: Police National Computer
- **POLAC**: Crash Involving Police Officers
- **RTA**: Road Traffic Accident
- **RTC**: Road Traffic Collision
- **Skell**: Unsavoury character (possibly from 'skelder', seventeenth-century term for a beggar)
- **SOCO**: Scenes of Crime Officer
- **TDA**: Taking and Driving Away
- **TFU**: Tactical Firearms Unit
- **TWOC**: Taken Without Owner's Consent
- **VDRS**: Vehicle Defects Rectification Scheme
- **VSS**: Victim Support Scheme
- **WOFF**: Write Off (insurance)
- **WINQ**: Warrant Inquiry

Famous pseudonyms and their real owners

I was reading a book recently that, in passing, mentioned a man whose name was Turd Cox. I'm sorry, but for some reason that made me laugh. If ever there was a name that needed a pseudonym, that was it. Likewise, you can understand why Michael Dumbell-Smith, Spangler Brugh and Diana Fluck decided on the stage names Michael Crawford, Robert Taylor and Diana Dors, cursed as they were with ones that got them off on the wrong foot. Here are some pseudonyms and the actual less-well-known real names of their owners.

- Woody Allen: Allen Stewart Konigsberg
- Jennifer Aniston: Jennifer Anistonapoulos
- Fred Astaire: Frederick Austerlitz
- Lauren Bacall: Betty Joan Perske

- Lucille Ball: Dianne Belmont
- Brigitte Bardot: Camille Javal
- Irving Berlin: Israel Isidore Baline
- David Bowie: David Robert Hayward Stenton Jones
- Elkie Brooks: Elaine Bookbinder
- Mel Brooks: Melvin Kaminsky
- George Burns: Nathan Birnbaum
- Richard Burton: Richard Walter Jenkins
- Michael Caine: Maurice Joseph Micklewhite
- Lewis Carroll: Charles Lutwidge Dodgson
- Eric Clapton: Eric Patrick Clap
- Elvis Costello: Declan Patrick McManus
- Michael Crawford: Michael Dumbell-Smith
- Tom Cruise: Thomas Cruise Mapother IV
- Tony Curtis: Bernie Schwartz
- Doris Day: Doris Mary Ann von Kappelhoff
- Diana Dors: Diana Fluck
- Kirk Douglas: Issur Danielovitch Demsky
- Bob Dylan: Robert Allen Zimmerman
- Judy Garland: Frances Ethel Gumm
- James Garner: James Scott Bumgarner
- Cary Grant: Archibald Alexander Leach
- Rita Hayworth: Margarita Carmen Cansino
- Audrey Hepburn: Edda Kathleen van Heemstra Hepburn-Ruston
- Adolf Hitler: Adolf Schickelgruber
- William Holden: William Franklin Beedle, Jr
- Rock Hudson: Roy Harold Scherer, Jr
- Elton John: Reginald Kenneth Dwight
- Al Jolson: Asa Yoelson
- Boris Karloff: William Henry Pratt
- Deborah Kerr: Deborah Jane Kerr-Trimmer
- Ben Kingsley: Krishna Banji
- Veronica Lake: Constance Frances Marie Ockelman

- Hedy Lamarr: Hedwig Eva Maria Keisler
- Burt Lancaster: Stephen Burton
- Jessica Lange: Mary MacGregor
- Stan Laurel: Arthur Stanley Jefferson
- Peggy Lee: Norma Engstrom
- Janet Leigh: Jeanette Helen Morrison
- Jerry Lewis: Joseph Levitch
- Herbert Lom: C. Angelo Kuchacevich
- Sophia Loren: Sofia Villani Scicolone
- Peter Lorre: Laszlo Lowenstein
- Vera Lynn: Margaret Welsh
- Andie Macdowell: Rosalie Anderson Qualley
- Karl Malden: Malden Sekulovich
- Jayne Mansfield: Vera Jane Palmer
- Frederic March: Frederick Ernest McIntyre Bickel
- Dean Martin: Dino Paul Crocetti
- Hank Marvin: Brian Robson Rankin
- Walter Matthau: Walter Matasschanskayasky
- Freddie Mercury: Farok Pluto Bulsara
- Ray Milland: Reginald Alfred Truscott-Jones
- Marilyn Monroe: Norma Jean Baker
- Demi Moore: Demetria Guynes
- Wolfgang Amadeus Mozart: Johannes Chrysostomus Wolfgangus Theophilus Mozart
- Paul Muni: Friedrich Muni Meyer Weisenfreund
- George Orwell: Eric Arthur Blair
- Ozzy Osbourne: John Osbourne
- Marie Osmond: Olive Osmond
- Jack Palance: Vladimir Palanuik
- Slim Pickens: Louis Bert Lindley, Jr
- Iggy Pop: James Newell Osterberg
- Cliff Richard: Harry Webb
- Joan Rivers: Joan Sandra Molinsky

- Edward G. Robinson: Emmanuel Goldenberg
- Ginger Rogers: Virginia Katherine McMath
- Mickey Rooney: Joe Yule, Jr
- Meg Ryan: Margaret Mary Emily Anne Hyra
- Barbara Stanwyck: Ruby Stevens
- Yves Saint-Laurent: Henri Donat Mathieu
- Jane Seymour: Joyce Penelope Wilhelmina Frankenberg
- Omar Sharif: Michel Demitri Shalhoub
- Martin Sheen: Ramon Estevez
- Elke Sommer: Elke Schletz
- Robert Taylor: Spangler Arlington Brugh
- Mother Teresa: Agnes Gonxha Bojaxhiu
- Mark Twain: Samuel Langhorne Clemens
- Twiggy: Leslie Hornby
- Rudolph Valentino: Rudolfo Pietro Filberto Raffaello Guglielmi di Valentina
- Andy Warhol: Andrew Warhola
- John Wayne: Marion Michael Morrison
- Shelley Winters: Shirley Schrift
- Tom Wolfe: Thomas Kennerley
- Stevie Wonder: Steveland Morris Hardaway
- Natalie Wood: Natasha Nikolaevna Zacharenko-Gurdin
- Jane Wyman: Sarah Jane Fulks

Sporting facts you seldom read about

- The fastest tennis serve belongs to Croatian Ivo Karlovi . It was recorded at 156 mph (251 kph) at the 2011 Davis Cup.
- Michael Edwards, better known as Eddie 'The Eagle' Edwards, was the first competitor to represent Great Britain in Olympic ski jumping. During the 1988 Winter Olympics, the myopic Edwards finished last in the 70 m (230 feet) and 90 m (295 feet) events. His vibrant lack of success endeared him to people around the world, who tuned in to

the Olympics just to see him do badly. And he didn't disappoint. A subsequent pop-star career, with the song 'Fly Eddie Fly', was a failure. Edwards was later declared bankrupt. I like this guy.

- A football is held together with 642 stitches.

- Eric Moussambani, better known (by those who have heard of him) as 'Eric the Eel', is the slowest Olympic swimmer in the history of the Games. In 2000 he took 52.72 seconds to swim 100 m (328 feet) freestyle, longer than it took another Olympian to swim 200 m (656 feet). Hailing from Equatorial Guinea, one of the smallest countries in continental Africa, where 70 per cent of the population live under the United Nations poverty threshold of $2 per day, Eric had never even seen a 50-m (164-foot) pool before, so I think he deserves at least a *crouching* ovation.

- In 1799 Jean Genevieve Garnerin became the first-ever female parachutist, jumping gracefully out of a hot-air balloon.

- The longest Wimbledon tennis match occurred on 22, 23 and 24 June 2010, when John Isner (USA) beat Nicolas Mahut (France) 6–4, 3–6, 6–7 (7–9), 7–6 (7–3), 70–68 (!). The match lasted a silly eleven hours and five minutes, over a three-day period.

- On August Bank Holiday Monday in the Waen Rhydd peat bog on the outskirts of Llanwrtyd Wells (the smallest town in Britain) in Powys, Mid Wales, the annual bog snorkelling world championships take place. Competitors 'swim', as fast as possible, up and down a 60-yard (55-metre) water-filled trench cut through the peat. They wear snorkels, fins (flippers) and a wetsuit, if they have one. No conventional swimming strokes are permitted and there is consequently rather a lot of splashing about in the mud, which has a characteristic brown taint and an odour described by one observer as 'reminiscent of stagnant pants'.

- Fishing is the most popular participation sport in the world.

- On 3 November 2007, Gao Chong of China established the world record for most touches of a football in one minute, using only his head, keeping the ball in the air. He did this 341 times. Silly sausage!

- Lord Freyberg was Governor-General of New Zealand (1946–52) but his hobby was attempting to swim the English Channel, just 21 miles (34 km) at its skinniest bit. On his best go in 1923 Freyberg got within 500 yards (457 m) of the French coast, where he paused for a breather before finishing the feat. Sensing victory, his wife, who was on the support boat, leant over to give him a quick snifter of brandy. Bad decision: Freyberg lost all oomph and had to be dragged back on board, weeping softly into his striped bathing costume.
- The first football World Cup was held in Uruguay in 1930, attracting teams from thirteen countries.
- The World Toe Wrestling Competition, in which competitors lock toes and force their opponent's foot to the ground, started at a Derbyshire pub in 1976. Alan 'Nasty' Nash got his foot in the toe-wrestling door in 1994 by taking the world title and in 1997 was knighted by His Majesty King Leo I of Redonda. (Just to be clear, Redonda is an uninhabited Caribbean island, famous for producing nothing but guano. In 2007, 'Sir' Robert Beech, landlord of the Wellington Arms in Southampton, unilaterally afforded himself 'diplomatic immunity' from the UK smoking ban by declaring his pub an 'embassy' of the country.) Application to have toe wrestling included in the Olympics was turned down.
- Rocky Marciano is the only heavyweight champion to retire unbeaten. He won all of his forty-nine fights.
- The Gloucestershire Cheese Rolling and Wake is held every May in the Cotswolds and is at least 200 years old. At noon, competitors crouch on top of the terrifyingly steep Cooper's Hill until an invited guest, escorted by the Master of Ceremonies, launches down the slope a 7–8 lb (3–3.6 kg) Double Gloucester, decorated with red and blue ribbons. Competitors then race after it. The first over the line at the bottom takes it as a prize. The gradient, in places, is 1:1 and the cheese can reach 70 mph (113 kph). Contestants, some of them women, are often to be observed 'freefalling' rather than running and volunteers from St John Ambulance are kept busy.

- Some 42,000 tennis balls are used during the Wimbledon Tennis Championships.
- The hair-raising World Beard and Moustache Championships are a biennial competition for men with big beards and/or moustaches. Categories include Dalí, imperial and natural moustache, and, for beards, goatee, musketeer and full beard. Some people have too much time on their hands.

Twenty-five amazing Vatican facts

The Vatican, Vatican City or Vatican City State (*Stato della Città del Vaticano* in Italian) is a sovereign city-state ruled by the Pope, whose territory consists of a walled enclave entirely surrounded by the city of Rome. The Vatican is the smallest country in the world, with an area of about three-quarters of a square mile (1.9 sq km; Liverpool is 43 square miles /111 sq km) and a population of just over 800. Here are some vital facts that you should know.

1 Vatican City was established in 1929.
2 It is the sovereign territory of the Holy See, the main see (the area of responsibility) of the Bishop of Rome (the Pope).
3 The Pope is an elected non-hereditary absolute monarch.
4 Vatican City issues its own passports.
5 The Holy See is not a country and issues diplomatic and service passports only.
6 The Vatican has the world's only exclusively Catholic population.
7 The Vatican has Latin cashpoints.
8 There is no capital city.
9 There is no national economy apart from tourism.
10 One third of the Vatican is gardens.
11 The Vatican has no coast.
12 The biggest export is postage stamps.
13 The Vatican has no birthrate, no maternity hospital and no children.

14 The Vatican's post office issues its own stamps. Its postal system is very efficient and is widely used by Romans, whose own system is sluggish by comparison.

15 Vatican Radio broadcasts in twenty languages around the world.

16 The Vatican has its own railway station.

17 The Vatican has its own helipad.

18 Italians are allowed to donate 8 per cent of their annual taxes to the Vatican.

19 The Vatican has no official language.

20 Per capita, the Vatican is the most crime-ridden place in the entire world. Its crime rate is twenty times that of surrounding Italy. Crimes include theft, embezzlement, fraud and insulting the police and civil servants. This is twenty times the rate in surrounding Italy.

21 The Vatican has the most police per head of any nation, but no prisons.

22 The Vatican financed the construction of the Watergate complex, one of Washington, DC's most desirable living spaces and the site of the notorious break-in at the Democratic National Committee head-quarters that led to the downfall of President Nixon.

23 The Vatican was the first carbon-neutral state, offsetting its carbon footprint against a Hungarian forest it had established.

24 The Pontifical Swiss Guard (Vatican guard) serves as the Vatican's only military force. They are all Swiss.

25 In 1996, Dr Marten's made a pair of white brogues especially for the Pope.

Seventy-two famous left-handers

A fascinating hypothesis called the 'vanishing-twin theory' says that left-handed people are the remaining half of a pair of identical twins, of which the right-handed foetus failed to develop. Regrettably, Australian scientists debunked this delightful conjecture years ago and shortly thereafter researchers discovered that specific alleles of at least one of three single-nucleotide polymorphisms upstream of the LRRTM1 gene were linked to left-handedness. Frankly I prefer the vanishing-twin thing.

On 13 August every year lefthanders everywhere celebrate Left-handers' Day. Here are 72 famous southpaws.

1	Aristotle	26	Don and Phil Everly (The Everly Brothers)
2	Neil Armstrong	27	W. C. Fields
3	Carl Philipp Emanuel Bach	28	Bela Fleck
4	Lord Baden-Powell (ambidextrous)	29	Gerald Ford
5	Peter Benchley	30	Henry Ford
6	Napoleon Bonaparte	31	Errol Garner
7	Alan Border	32	Bob Geldof
8	David Bowie	33	Jean Genet
9	Kenneth Branagh	34	King George II
10	Benjamin Britten	35	King George VI
11	Pierce Brosnan	36	Cary Grant
12	Bill Bryson	37	Rex Harrison
13	George Bush, Sr	38	Jimi Hendrix
14	Julius Caesar	39	Hans Holbein
15	Lewis Carroll	40	Rock Hudson
16	Fidel Castro	41	Danny Kaye
17	Charlie Chaplin	42	Diane Keaton
18	Prince Charles	43	Helen Keller
19	Winston Churchill	44	Paul Klee
20	Phil Collins	45	Judy Garland
21	Denis Compton (left-arm bowler, right-hand batter)	46	David Gower (right-arm bowler, left-handed batter)
22	Bill Clinton	47	Nicole Kidman
23	Tom Cruise	48	Leonardo da Vinci
24	Albrecht Dürer	49	Marcel Marceau
25	M. C. Escher	50	Harpo Marx

51	Paul McCartney	63	Bart Simpson
52	Michelangelo	64	Gary Sobers (left-arm bowler, left-handed batter)
53	Marilyn Monroe		
54	Benjamin Netanyahu	65	Terence Stamp
55	Kim Novak	66	Rod Steiger
56	Barack Obama	67	Terry-Thomas
57	Raphael	68	Emma Thompson
58	Ronald Reagan	69	Henri de Toulouse Lautrec
59	Robert Redford	70	Queen Victoria
60	Peter Paul Rubens	71	H. G. Wells
61	Albert Schweitzer	72	Prince William
62	Paul Simon		

Twenty TV facts you won't believe

According to researchers, the average person will spend nine years of his life watching television. Nonetheless he may well remain unacquainted with these slightly obscure TV-show facts. See how many of them you believe, then drop one or two into conversation to be thought omniscient (not *omnipotent*, that's God).

1 It takes between six and eight months to make an episode of *The Simpsons*.
2 Other titles considered for *Friends* were *Across the Hall*, *Six of One* and *Insomnia Café*.
3 Simon Cowell used to own eighteen hamsters and taught them tricks.
4 An alternative juror for the 1996 Whitewater trial (involving the Clintons) wore a *Star Trek* uniform (with 'phaser'). She was dismissed for talking to a journalist.
5 *Sesame Street* is so popular in Pago Pago, the capital of American Samoa, that they were going to name the island's main street after it.
6 *Cosby* (not to be confused with *The Cosby Show* or *The Bill Cosby Show*) was loosely based on British comedy *One Foot in the Grave*.

7 American sitcom *Sanford and Son* was based on the British comedy *Steptoe and Son.*

8 John Cleese and Connie Booth's *Fawlty Towers* spawned three US versions: *Chateau Snavely* (pilot only), *Amanda's* (thirteen episodes) and *Payne* – the story of Royal Payne and his wife Constance Payne (nine episodes).

9 *Bonanza* was aired in eighty-five countries and is one of the most widely syndicated TV series ever, with a weekly audience of some 250 million.

10 Jet Propulsion Laboratory scientists wore 'Spock ears' while monitoring the 1967 Mariner V Venus fly-by.

11 The first commercial shown on British TV was for the *Daily Mail*, transmitted on 26 September 1928 during a demonstration of his invention (television) by John Logie Baird at the National Radio Exhibition in Olympia. It was watched on twelve television sets by fifty people.

12 The first commercial on American television was transmitted in 1941. It was for Bulova watches and cost the company the grand sum of $9.

13 The world's most expensive TV commercials today are those played during the Super Bowl. In 2008, the cost for putting a thirty-second commercial in this slot was $2.7 million.

14 Until *The Simpsons* broke the record, the longest-running primetime cartoon series was *The Flintstones.*

15 Voice-actor Mel Blanc, who did Bugs Bunny as well as many of *The Flintstones* voices, had a near-fatal car crash in 1961. While he lay in a full body-cast recovering from the accident, sixteen people had to squeeze into his bedroom to record *The Flintstones* show.

16 *The Simpsons'* JFK-esque Mayor Quimby shares his unusual surname with *Tom and Jerry* producer Fred Quimby.

17 *Tom and Jerry* was created for MGM by William Hanna and Joseph Barbera. There are more than 200 classic films in the series, and seven of them won Oscars.

18 Hanna and Barbera also produced (stand by): *The Huckleberry Hound Show*, *Yogi Bear*, *Hokey Wolf*, *Pixie and Dixie and Mr Jinks*, *The Quick Draw McGraw Show*, *The Flintstones*, *The Yogi Bear Show*, *Snagglepuss*, *Top Cat*, *Wally Gator*, *Touché Turtle and Dum Dum*, *Lippy the Lion & Hardy Har Har*, *The Jetsons*, *The Magilla Gorilla Show*, *Atom Ant*, *Secret Squirrel*, *Squiddly Diddly*, *The Hillbilly Bears*, *Winsome Witch*, *The Banana Splits Adventure Hour*, *Wacky Races* (co-production), *The Perils of Penelope Pitstop*, *It's The Wolf*, *Motormouse and Autocat*, *Scooby-Doo, Where Are You!*, *Help! . . . It's the Hair Bear Bunch!*, *Wait till Your Father Gets Home*, *Inch High, Private Eye*, *The Addams Family* (first animated version), *Hong Kong Phooey*, *The Smurfs* and a lot more, too.

19 'Master of disaster' Irwin Allen (1916–91), who produced such creaky but wonderful TV classics as *Voyage to the Bottom of the Sea*, *Lost in Space*, *The Time Tunnel* and *Land of the Giants*, was so incredibly mean with money that knocked-about props such as guns and 'computers' were often recognizable from one show to another.

20 Each member of the *Monty Python's Flying Circus* team has had an asteroid named after him. Could have been worse – could have been a haemorrhoid.

Top ten Hollywood sex symbols of yesteryear (ladies, obviously)

Stand back: here they are.

1 Betty Boop (1930–)

Originally drawn as a French poodle, Betty Boop is a cartoon character created by Max Fleischer and modelled on the sexy actress, 'It-girl' and flapper Clara Bow. When she was turned into a human character in 1932, her big poodle ears became earrings. The winking, short-skirted Boop was a big hit, but her sexuality was toned down by the prudes in the mid-1930s. Shame!

2 Ursula Andress (1936-)

The best word for this blonde babe is 'Phwoar!' In the film *Dr No*, the gorgeous Swiss creature emerges from the Caribbean in a white bikini. This bikini was sold in 2001 for 35,000 euros. When Andress posed nude for *Playboy* in 1965, sales went up enormously – along with other things.

3 Mae West (1893-1980)

Sexy but not 'pretty', Mae West was a successful vaudeville performer before moving to Hollywood to become a comedienne, writer and actress. Known for her double entendres, she gave the censors white hair with quips such as, 'Is that a gun in your pocket, or are you just glad to see me?' A wartime lifejacket was named the 'Mae West' in honour of her bathykolpian pulchritude (you should look those up, they are very useful words).

4 Marilyn Monroe (1926-62)

The callipygous (another fine word) Marilyn Monroe has got to be top of the list really. (I don't mean top of *this* list, of course, which is arranged entirely according to my own whimsy: I mean top of an imaginary, overarching, metaphorical list of all-time gorgeousness.) Anyway where was I? Oh yes, Marilyn had it all: a great face – pretty, vulnerable-looking, yet naughty – and a sort of magnetic sexuality. Her figure was nothing like that of many current sex-symbols, that is to say skeletal – it was normal-looking, only more so. She was chosen to appear on the front cover of the first *Playboy* magazine. Unbeatable choice!

5 Rita Hayworth (1918-87)

During the Second World War Rita Hayworth was the serviceman's ideal pin-up. In the film *Gilda* the censors got their knickers in a twist over her sultry one-glove striptease. She had five husbands – at different times – including Orson Welles (the only actor ever to have to go on a diet to play Falstaff). It didn't last, she said, because she couldn't 'take his genius any more', which was a kind way of putting it.

6 Marlene Dietrich (1901-92)

Dark, mysterious and haughty, Marlene Dietrich was glamorous, yet haunted, with a soft German accent, often drawled through a cigarette, which added to her exotic allure. The antidote to Mae West, she was the thinking man's (or maybe the S&M man's) crumpet. Fantastic legs, slender fingers and world-beating cheekbones.

7 Jayne Mansfield (1933-67)

Sometimes rudely referred to as the poor man's Marilyn Monroe, to whom she bore a mild resemblance, the platinum-blonde Mansfield had an hourglass figure and was well known for two outstanding attributes, which she wiggled at every camera pointed in her direction (46DD in case you're wondering). She was once introduced on TV with the words, 'Here they are . . . Jayne Mansfield'. She died in a car crash, in which her 'airbags' failed to save her.

8 Brigitte Bardot (1934-)

Another European lovely, this time French. At her sex-symbol height, the ultimate 'sex kitten' Bardot was blonde, pretty and curvaceous. In 1974, she appeared nude in an Italian edition of *Playboy* magazine, celebrating her fortieth birthday. Quite a bit of retouching required by that time, I'd guess. Nice work if you can get it.

9 Scarlett Johansson (1984-)

Scarlett Johansson is a modern sex symbol in the classic style of yesteryear, an American actress and singer whose pretty face is blessed with the most seductive lips in the history of osculation. Rather petite herself, her hooters are nonetheless handsomely proportioned. So, well done her. *Esquire* magazine has called Johansson the 'Sexiest Woman Alive' and *GQ* magazine named her its Babe of the Year in 2010. Woody Allen described Johansson as 'sexually overwhelming', but he's in his late seventies, don't forget, and would be overwhelmed by a spinster librarian's toasted teacake. She has a twin – unfortunately he is a chap called Hunter.

10 Sophia Loren (1934-)

About the same age as Woody Allen, Italian sex symbol Sophia Loren looks a thousand times lovelier than him. As well as being beautiful and sexy, Sophia Loren has a working brain – not a requirement in a sex symbol but it does help. On being complimented on her figure she is claimed to have said, 'Everything you see, I owe to spaghetti.' One of those dark-haired Latin babes, she has managed to age superbly well, having posed scantily clad at the age of seventy-two, and still has a most striking face. Her boobs could do with a bit of an iron though.

Famous last words

On 14 January 1957, Humphrey Bogart popped his clogs, but before he died he said, 'I should never have switched from Scotch to Martinis', which was very witty. Unfortunately, his wife Lauren Bacall claims that what he really said was, 'Hurry back,' as she left the house briefly to get something. This is much more believable but lacks zing.

The reported deathbed utterances of the famous are obviously largely apocryphal, but since the people alleged to have said them are dead, no one has ever sued. Indeed, they might well have been grateful for having a dull or humourless groan turned into a quotable one-liner. Even with an eye on posterity it's hard to be witty or pithy unless you've practised a bit beforehand. As the Mexican revolutionary leader Pancho Villa said before being slaughtered, 'Don't let it end like this. Tell them I said something . . .'

Anyway, here are a few of the more entertaining last words purportedly uttered by the great and the good.

- 'Go away . . . I'm all right.' H. G. Wells (1866–1946)
- 'This is it. I'm going. I'm going.' Al Jolson (1886–1950)
- 'Doctor, do you think it could have been the sausage?' Paul Claudel (1868–1955)

- 'I am about to – or I am going to – die; either expression is used.' Dominique Bouhours (1628–1702), grammarian
- 'I have a terrific pain in the back of my head.' Franklin D. Roosevelt (1882–1945)
- 'If this is dying, I don't think much of it.' Lytton Strachey (1880–1932)
- 'On the contrary!' Henrik Ibsen (1828–1906), on being asked if he was better
- 'I've had eighteen straight whiskies. I think that is a record.' Dylan Thomas (1914–53)
- 'Is it the Fourth?' Thomas Jefferson (1743–4 July 1826)
- 'Too late for fruit, too soon for flowers.' Walter de la Mare (1873–1956)
- 'I'd hate to die twice. It's so boring.' Richard Feynman (1918–88)
- 'Am I dying or is this my birthday?' Lady Nancy Astor (1879–1964) on waking to find herself surrounded by her family
- 'I feel faint.' Adlai Stevenson (1900–65)
- 'Bugger Bognor!' King George V (1865–1936) when it was suggested that visiting Bognor Regis might improve his condition
- 'I knew it. I knew it. Born in a hotel room – and God damn it – died in a hotel room.' Eugene O'Neill (1888–1953)
- 'I don't feel good.' Luther Burbank (1849–1926)
- 'Die, my dear doctor? That is the last thing I shall do.' 3rd Viscount Palmerston (1784–1865), apocryphal. What he really said was, 'That's Article 98; now go on to the next.'
- 'Dying is a very dull and dreary affair. And my advice to you is to have nothing whatever to do with it.' W. Somerset Maugham (1874–1965)
- 'I wish I'd drunk more champagne.' John Maynard Keynes (1883–1946)
- 'This isn't *Hamlet*, you know, it's not meant to go into the bloody ear.' Laurence Olivier (1907–1989), to his nurse, who had spilt water on him
- 'Either that wallpaper goes, or I do.' Oscar Wilde (1854–1900)
- 'Nonsense, they couldn't hit an elephant at this distance.' John Sedgwick (1813–64), in response to a suggestion that he should not

stick his head above the parapet during the Battle of the Wilderness

- 'Put that bloody cigarette out.' Saki (Hector Hugh Munro) (1870–1916), just before being shot dead by a sniper
- 'I'm bored with it all.' Winston Churchill (1874–1965)
- 'That was a great game of golf, fellas.' 'Bing' Crosby (1903–77), before collapsing on a Spanish golf course
- 'I've never felt better.' Douglas Fairbanks, Sr (1883–1939)
- 'Nothing matters. Nothing matters.' Louis B. Mayer (1884–1957)
- 'I told you I was ill.' Spike Milligan (1918–2002), epitaph

Twenty things you might not know about The Beatles

Think you know everything about The Beatles? Check out these interesting facts.

1 The Beatles were initially a five-piece line-up: Lennon, McCartney, Harrison, Stuart Sutcliffe (bass) and Pete Best (drums).
2 The Beatles honed their act in Hamburg clubs over a period of three years.
3 Paul McCartney's father was a cotton salesman.
4 The left-handed McCartney briefly played Stuart Sutcliffe's bass. Sutcliffe asked him not to change the strings, so McCartney played it upside down.
5 In December 1960, George Harrison was sent back to England from Hamburg for being under-age (seventeen).
6 At the same time Paul McCartney and Pete Best were deported for attempted arson.
7 Stuart Sutcliffe suggested that the band should be called the 'Beetles' in tribute to Buddy Holly and the Crickets.
8 Before becoming The Beatles, the band tried calling themselves Johnny and the Moondogs, Long John and the Beetles, and the Silver Beatles.

9   Sutcliffe left the group in 1961 and Pete Best was replaced as drummer by Ringo Starr the following year.

10 Ringo Starr was born Richard Starkey.

11 After leaving The Beatles, Stuart Sutcliffe enrolled at Hamburg Art College, studying under pop artist Eduardo Paolozzi.

12 After being fired from the band, Pete Best worked for a time at Garston Jobcentre in Liverpool.

13 In 1960, Starr belonged to another band, Rory Storm and the Hurricanes.

14 Stuart Sutcliffe collapsed in Hamburg and died on 10 April 1962, aged twenty-one.

15 There have been more than 3,000 cover versions of 'Yesterday', making it the most covered pop song ever.

16 The Beatles copied their 'moptop' haircuts from one worn by a German friend and fan, photographer Jürgen Vollmer.

17 Ringo Starr spent three years in hospital as a child.

18 John Lennon returned his MBE in 1969 in protest against the Vietnam War.

19 Pete Best married a lady called Kathy, who worked at the biscuit counter in Woolworth's.

20 In 1995, *Anthology 1* was released, including tracks with Best as drummer. He received estimated royalties of between £1 million and £4 million.

Alfred Hitchcock's cameo appearances

Alfred Hitchcock (1899–1980) was one of the most commercially, critically and artistically successful Hollywood directors of all time. He started in the black-white-and-silent days, went on to make *Blackmail*, the first British talkie, and later moved to Hollywood, where he directed a string of stylish hits, including *Psycho*, one of the most nerve-jangling thrillers of all time.

Hitch was an unusual tmixture of businessman and artist. His profitable films, which are often regarded as cinematic masterpieces, are simultaneously popular with audiences, a hard trick to pull off. As a director, he had a natural authority on set, always wearing a grey suit, even under the hot lights, but once, when his birthday coincided with a shooting day in the studio, an assistant director took the opportunity to relax the formality and dared to open a bottle of champagne, asking everybody please to help themselves to 'a piece of Mr Hitchcake's cock'. Nerves, probably.

Hitch would have enjoyed this, being of a humorous disposition himself. One of his own touches was to include himself in a cameo appearance in some of his early films and, from *Rebecca* onwards, in all thirty of his American films. He learned to get this over with near the beginning so that audiences, who recognized him easily from his popular TV show, would not be distracted by waiting for him to appear.

Here is an alphabetical list of Hitchcock's thirty-eight cameos in the fifty-two of his films that survive (one of his earliest films has perished). They are listed alphabetically by film title. The year of release is also there for you, along with a rough timing for the walk-on, in case you want to check them out for yourself.

1 *The Birds*, 1963, 0.02: Hitch passes Tippi Hedren as she leaves the pet shop. He has two white Sealyham terriers on leads. These dogs were Hitchcock's own pets, Geoffrey and Stanley. When he directed *Marnie* the production company credit read 'Geoffrey-Stanley productions'. I seem to recall that Hitchcock reversed his car over Geoffrey, or maybe it was Stanley, killing him. But I can't be sure.

2 *Blackmail*, 1929, 0.10.25: A boy annoys Hitch as he tries to read a book on a tube train.

3 *Dial M for Murder*, 1954, 0.13.13: As Ray Milland displays a photograph of his class reunion, Hitchcock can be seen in the picture, on the left of a large circular table of revellers, leaning towards the camera.

4 *Easy Virtue*, 1928, 0.21.15: He's walking past a tennis court with a walking stick in his hand, one of a series of props he used in these cameos.

5 *Family Plot*, 1976, 0.40: A dramatic and unmistakable shadow of a finger-wagging Hitchcock can be seen on the frosted-glass window on the door of the Registrar of Births and Deaths.

6 *Foreign Correspondent*, 1940, 0.12.44: As Joel McCrea leaves the hotel, a hatted and coated Hitchcock walks along reading a newspaper.

7 *Frenzy*, 1972, 0.03: Hitch is visible wearing a bowler hat and looking bored as a speaker addresses a crowd on the South Bank of the Thames. He makes a second appearance in a high-angle shot a moment later.

8 *I Confess*, 1953, 0.01.33: One of the long-shot cameos. Hitchcock can be seen after the opening titles, dramatically silhouetted against the Quebec sky, walking from the shadow into the light in a low-angle long shot up a very tall flight of steps.

9 *The Lady Vanishes*, 1938, 1.33: Another walking shot, which he favoured. Dressed in a dark coat on a platform at Victoria Station in London, Hitchcock whizzes past, smoking a cigarette, and seems to

hunch his shoulders while Michael Redgrave and Margaret Lockwood are acting away like gooduns.

10 *Lifeboat*, 1944, 0.25: How is Hitch going to include himself in a film that takes place on board a lifeboat in the middle of the sea? Easy, he's visible in hilarious 'before' and 'after' pictures in an advertisement for Reduco Obesity Slayer, on the back of a newspaper being read by one of the characters.

11 *The Lodger*, 1927 (two appearances). First, 0.03: Visible, on his own for once, back to camera, at a desk, with a busy newsroom on the other side of the window. Second, 1.32: In a flat cap in the crowd behind a railing, watching an arrest.

12 *The Man Who Knew Too Much*, 1956, 0.25: This is Hitchcock's remake of his own 1934 film. He is clearly visible in the crowd watching Moroccan acrobats in the square. As usual he has on his grey suit even under the hot North African sun.

13 *Marnie*, 1964, 0.05: He somewhat furtively exits a hotel bedroom shortly after Tippi Hedren passes by.

14 *Mr & Mrs Smith*, 1941, 0.42.57: A boring one. He walks under the awning in front of Robert Montgomery's building.

15 *Murder!*, 1930, 1.00: Hatted, Hitch walks past the murder-house with a lady on his arm.

16 *North by Northwest*, 1959, 0.02.09: This is Hitch on top form. Just as his title credit rolls off to the right, he follows it to catch the bus, the doors of which shut in his face.

17 *Notorious*, 1946, 1.04.44: Hitch, standing in a monkey suit at Claude Rains's fancy party, gulps champagne and moves off.

18 *The Paradine Case*, 1947, 0.36: A musical cameo, of which there were several. This time he is leaving a train, carrying a cello in its case.

19 *Psycho*, 1960, 0.06.35: Hitch stands on the pavement in a cowboy hat visible through the window of the office in which Janet Leigh plays one of two secretaries. The other is played by Pat Hitchcock, his daughter, so they are in the same scene. Note: Hitch is *not* on the zebra crossing a little later, as many people think.

20 *Rear Window*, 1954, 0.25: Seen winding a clock in one of the apartments. He turns to look at the pianist whose room it is.

21 *Rebecca*, 1940, 2.01: Easy to miss, he walks in the background after George Sanders uses the telephone booth.

22 *Rope*, 1948, 0.02: Visible during the titles, in the only exterior shot in the film, walking down the street with a folded newspaper in his hand. His silhouette is also said to be visible (0.55) through the window, in a flashing neon ad for Reduco, though I can't see it.

23 *Saboteur*, 1942, 1.04: Hard to see in this low-light shot, standing in the street as the saboteur's car stops.

24 *Secret Agent*, 1936, 0.08: Hitch is said to appear descending the gangplank but I'm not sure.

25 *Shadow of a Doubt*, 1943, 0.17: Another amusing one. He is on the train, back to the camera, playing cards with an elderly couple. His hand contains an entire suit of spades.

26 *Spellbound*, 1945, 0.35: Musical again. He comes out of the lift at the Empire Hotel, carrying a violin case and – once more – smoking a cigarette.

27 *Stage Fright*, 1950, 0:39:49: He turns to look back at Jane Wyman in the street. One of the obvious ones.

28 *Strangers on a Train*, 1951, 0.10.34: Another musical one. String section again. Costumed in a light suit for once, Hitch lifts a double bass on to the train as Farley Granger gets off.

29 *Suspicion*, 1941, 0.46.54: He is seen in long shot, posting a letter in the village. At 0:04, he leads a horse during the hunt.

30 *The 39 Steps*, 1935, 0.06.56: Hitchcock is the huge-looking man in a hat and overcoat who throws a piece of litter on the ground as a bus pulls up for Robert Donat.

31 *To Catch a Thief*, 1955, 0.10: Looking old and careworn he sits at the back of the bus next to Cary Grant, who looks at him, but he continues to stare ahead.

32 *Topaz*, 1969, 0.33: One of Hitchcock's wittiest cameos. Seemingly infirm, being pushed by a nurse in a wheelchair in the airport, he

suddenly gets up out of it, shakes hands with a man and walks off.

33 *Torn Curtain*, 1966, 0:08: Sitting in the lobby of the Hotel d'Angleterre(!) dandling a baby on his knee. He doesn't look a natural nanny in that suit.

34 *The Trouble with Harry*, 1955, 0.22.14: Another hard one to spot, Hitch walks behind the parked car of an old man who is examining paintings displayed outside.

35 *Under Capricorn*, 1949, 0.03: Two appearances again. He's in the square during the parade, in a dark coat and brown hat, and, at 0:13, he is one of the men on the steps of Government House.

36 *Vertigo*, 1958, 0.11: Musical once more. He walks past dressed in a grey suit and carrying what might be a trumpet in a case.

37 *The Wrong Man*, 1956, 0.0.18: An interesting one, this. *The Wrong Man* is a documentary-like true story. Hitchcock introduces the film as himself, in silhouette, dramatically backlit.

38 *Young and Innocent*, 1937, 0.15: He's one of two men outside the court, wearing a flat cap. He is holding a camera and, though it's a silent film, seems from his body language to be objecting to being moved on by a policeman.

Twenty-nine football facts you might not know

This list of fascinating football facts relates to so-called 'association football' or soccer. Most of this information is unknown to your typical football fan, so you'll sound like the world expert soccer genius if you drop a few of these golden knowledge nuggets next time you're in the stands.

1 The term 'association football' was coined to distinguish the game from other forms of football, in particular rugby football.

2 The word 'soccer' first appeared in the 1880s as an abbreviation of the word 'association' or the 'soc' bit of it anyway.

3 First reports of the game appear in a Chinese military manual, dating from around 476 BCE. It was known as *cuju*.

4 Early football involved players kicking a leather ball through a hole in a piece of cloth.

5 The rules of football were formally established by the Football Association in 1863.

6 Only three teams have ever won the FA Cup without letting in any goals. Their illustrious names: The Wanderers (1873), Preston North End (1889) and Bury (1903).

7 There are seventeen laws in the official 'Laws of the Game', published by FIFA.

8 The international governing body of association football, futsal (indoor football) and beach football is FIFA, Fédération Internationale de Football Association (International Federation of Association Football).

9 The Arsenal changed their name to Arsenal so as to appear at the top of alphabetical lists.

10 For years Blackburn had no official ground and were consequently dubbed the 'Rovers'.

11 Jean Langenus of Belgium wore a jacket, plus-fours and a striped tie to referee the 1930 World Cup final. Good show!

12 In the 1938 World Cup semi-final, Italian Giuseppe Meazza's shorts fell down as he was taking a penalty, revealing his shortcomings. Holding them up with his hand, he then scored.

13 Albert Camus was a goalkeeper before tuberculosis dashed his hopes and turned him into a philosopher.

14 In 1950 India withdrew from the World Cup because FIFA refused to allow the team to play barefoot.

15 Sir Stanley Matthews had such good manners that he never received a booking in his thirty-three-year career.

16 In 1954 Turkey knocked out Spain in a World Cup qualifier by drawing straws blindfold.

17 In 1957, the Salisbury and District Football Association of Rhodesia hired a witch doctor to improve the performance of Salisbury, who had lost every match the season before.

18 Ryan Giggs's real surname is Wilson. He took his mother's maiden name when his parents split up.

19 In 1973 Italian referee Marcello Donadini was bitten in the back by a player who disagreed with a decision he'd made.

20 Football manager, journalist and captain of Spurs Danny Blanchflower stormed off in fury when he was surprised by Eamonn Andrews on an edition of *This is Your Life*. 'I consider this programme to be an invasion of privacy,' he explained.

21 Bristol City put on a chimps' tea-party before their 1976 game with West Ham in a desperate attempt to attract paying fans.

22 Singer Julio Iglesias played for a Real Madrid youth team but gave up after a car crash.

23 At a 'friendly' match in Brazil a referee shot dead a player who had queried one of his decisions, subsequently fleeing the scene on a horse.

24 In 1996, Gillingham fans had to undergo 'vegetable searches' after they started a craze for waving sticks of celery while singing a very rude song.

25 In 1998 referee Martin Sylvester sent himself off after he punched a player during a game in the exciting Andover and District Sunday League.

26 TV chef Gordon Ramsay almost ended up playing for Rangers but took up cooking instead after a knee injury.

27 In 1980, Liberian Head of State Samuel Doe threatened to jail his team if they lost to Gambia. He let them off.

28 In 2002, in protest at a refereeing decision, Malagasy team Stade Olympique L'Emryne scored 149 deliberate own goals against opponents AS Adema.

29 Football is the world's most popular spectator sport.

Abraham Lincoln and John Fitzgerald Kennedy: twenty-five weird coincidences

The occurrence of an event in conjunction with another event is known in everyday-speak as a 'coincidence', from the Latin *co-*, meaning 'together', and *incidere*, meaning 'to happen'. Although coincidences can seem suggestive, not to say uncanny, you've got to be a bit careful. After all, as Plutarch said, 'It is no great wonder if in the long process of time, while fortune takes her course here and there, numerous coincidences should spontaneously occur.'

Nonetheless, have a look at this list of twenty-five coincidences concerning presidents Abraham Lincoln and John Fitzgerald Kennedy and see what you reckon.

1   Each president had seven letters in his last name.
2   Both presidents were named after their grandfathers.
3   Both were second children.
4   Both men were lawyers by training.
5   Abraham Lincoln was elected president in 1860. John F. Kennedy was elected president in 1960.
6   Abraham Lincoln was elected to Congress in 1846. John F. Kennedy was elected to Congress in 1946.
7   Lincoln's secretary was named Kennedy. Kennedy's secretary was named Lincoln.
8   Both presidents had four children, two of whom died young.
9   Both were abnormally tall – more than six feet (1.85 m).
10 Both had serious genetic diseases. Lincoln had Marfan's syndrome (or something like it) and Kennedy had Addison's disease.
11 Both were assassinated.
12 Both were shot in the head.
13 Both died on a Friday.
14 Both were killed beside their wives.

15 Lincoln was killed at a Ford Theatre. Kennedy was killed in a Ford Lincoln.

16 Both alleged assassins were shot before they could be tried. (Since neither putative assassin was ever tried, and in the case of Oswald significant doubt about his role still lurks, I have referred to both as 'alleged' assassins, which is only fair.)

17 There are fifteen letters in each 'assassin's' name.

18 John Wilkes Booth (allegedly) shot Lincoln at a theatre and fled to a warehouse. Lee Harvey Oswald (allegedly) shot Kennedy from a warehouse and fled to a theatre.

19 Both 'assassins' were killed with a Colt revolver.

20 Both Lincoln and Kennedy were succeeded by Southern Democrats named Johnson.

21 Andrew Johnson was born in 1808. Lyndon Johnson was born in 1908.

22 There are six letters in each Johnson's first name.

23 Andrew Johnson declined to run for re-election in 1868. Lyndon Johnson declined to run for re-election in 1968.

24 Both Johnsons suffered from urethral stones. No other president has had them.

I leave you to make up your mind what to do with this collection of information – especially the thing about urethral stones, which frankly made my eyes water.

Nobel Peace Prize winners: a list

In 1867, Swedish chemist and engineer Alfred Nobel (1833–1896) patented his new invention – dynamite. As owner of Bofors, a major armaments manufacturer, Nobel must have found his new explosive rather handy. But somewhat to everyone's amazement he left instructions in his will that an international prize for *peace* was to be awarded in his name, to the person who 'shall have done the most or the best work for fraternity between nations, for the abolition or reduction of standing armies and for the holding and promotion of peace congresses'. This was rather amusing, coming from Mr Dynamite.

The Nobel Peace Prize sometimes goes to an organization, or is divided equally between two or more people, or between an organization and a person, or, if not awarded, goes into a special fund. It was first given out in 1901 and along with a medal and a certificate to hang on your wall you get a cash sum. In 2010 this amounted to ten million Swedish kronor (about £980,000 or $1.6 million).

In 2009, President Barack Obama won the prize, 'for his extraordinary efforts to strengthen international diplomacy and cooperation between peoples'. Now, this was an odd choice, because the fellow had only been in the job for a few months and wasn't exactly short of cash either. But the recipients of the Nobel Peace Prize have sometimes been even more surprising. In 1973 it was won by Henry Kissinger. This immediately alerted talent-spotters from the world of international comedy to the dark, not to say 'gallows', humour of the Peace Prize Committee, clearly a promising troupe of wickedly funny pranksters who could be relied on for farcical japes of great surrealism and originality. Anyway, here's a brief selection of my favourites from the long list of winners.

- 1901: Jean Henry Dunant, Switzerland, Founder of the Red Cross, *and* Frédéric Passy, France, one of the founders of the Inter-Parliamentary Union.
- 1906: Theodore Roosevelt, USA. Won partly for his successful mediation to end the Russo-Japanese war. Plus he looked good on a horse.
- 1911: Alfred Hermann Fried, Austria, Founder of Die Friedenswarte. Fantastic handlebar moustache.
- 1914–16: The first time the prize was not awarded. The money went into the Special Fund.
- 1917: International Committee of the Red Cross, Switzerland.
- 1918: Not awarded. The prize money went into the Special Fund.

- 1919: Woodrow Wilson, USA, founder of the League of Nations. Good top hat wearer.
- 1922: Fridtjof Nansen, Norway, initiator of 'Nansen [refugee] passports'
- 1923–24: Not awarded. The prize money went into the Special Fund again.
- 1925: Austen Chamberlain, United Kingdom, negotiator of the Locarno Treaty and a statesmanlike monocle-wearer, *and* Charles Gates Dawes, USA, originator of the 'Dawes Plan'. A pipe smoker.
- 1928: Not awarded. The prize money went into the Special Fund. Once again.
- 1929: Frank B. Kellogg, USA, part-originator of Briand–Kellogg Pact. Looked like an old lady.
- 1932: Not awarded. The prize money went into the Special Fund. Once more.
- 1933: Sir Norman Angell (Ralph Lane), UK, writer; on the Executive Committee of the National Peace Council. Very high forehead indeed.
- 1934: Arthur Henderson, UK, President, Disarmament Conference, 1932. Soft, almost invisible moustache.
- 1935: Carl von Ossietzky, Germany. The German government refused him a passport to attend the ceremony.
- 1936: Carlos Saavedra Lamas, Argentina, President, League of Nations; mediator between Paraguay and Bolivia. Pointy-tipped swarthy moustache.
- 1937: Viscount Cecil of Chelwood, UK, founder, International Peace Campaign. Bald as you like and always looked terribly ill.
- 1939–43: Not awarded. A third of the prize money went into the Main Fund and two-thirds into the Special Fund, now ticking over nicely.
- 1945: Cordell Hull, USA, participant in setting up the United Nations. Always looked like he was hiding something in his mouth.
- 1946: Emily Greene Balch, USA, Honorary International President, Women's International League for Peace and Freedom. Very spinsterish-looking Quaker.

John Raleigh Mott, USA, President, World Alliance of Young Men's Christian Associations. Humourless-looking man. Should have married Miss Greene Balch, they'd have made a good pair.

- 1947: Friends Service Council (the Quakers), UK, *and* American Friends Service Committee (the Quakers), USA.
- 1948: Not awarded. A third of the prize money went into the Main Fund and two-thirds into the Special Fund. They could have had a really good party with those funds.
- 1949: Lord Boyd-Orr, UK, President, National Peace Council and World Union of Peace Organizations. Eyebrows like white boats.
- 1950: Ralph Bunche, USA, Acting Mediator in Palestine, 1948. Looked good in a hat.
- 1952: Albert Schweitzer, Alsatian (not the dog, the place), patronizing missionary surgeon and general nuisance. Big white moustache.
- 1953: George Catlett Marshall, USA, General President American Red Cross; Originator of the 'Marshall Plan'. Looked good in a uniform.
- 1955–6: Not awarded. A third of the prize money went into the Main Fund and two-thirds into the Special Fund. Surely Mahatma Gandhi could have done with it. He never won the prize.
- 1960: Albert Lutuli, South Africa, President, African National Congress. Striped-tie wearer.
- 1962: Linus Pauling, USA, campaigner against nuclear weapons and *for* vitamin C. World's only beret-wearing chemist.
- 1964: Martin Luther King, Jr, USA, civil rights campaigner, plagiarist and 'ladies' man'.
- 1966–7: Not awarded. A third of the prize money went into the Main Fund and two-thirds into the Special Fund.
- 1970: Norman E. Borlaug, USA, agronomist and humanitarian. Saved thousands of millions of people from starvation by engineering a new kind of wheat. Marvellous man.
- 1971: Willy Brandt, Federal Republic of Germany. Ladies' man who liked a drink.
- 1972–3 Not awarded. The prize money went into the Main Fund.

What, again?

- 1973: Henry Kissinger, USA. A somewhat fleshy glasses-wearer who was once photographed apparently picking his nose, *and* Lê Ðức Thọ (Phan Ðình Khai). Declined the prize on the grounds that his country – Vietnam – was still not at peace.
- 1975: Andrei Dmitrievich Sakharov, Soviet Union. Nuclear physicist and human rights activist. Bald.
- 1976: Betty Williams *and* Mairead Corrigan, UK, joint founders of the Northern Ireland Peace Movement.
- 1977: Amnesty International, UK.
- 1978: Mohamed Anwar Al-Sadat, Egypt. Moustache and medals, *and* Menachem Begin, Israel. Huge glasses. For jointly negotiating the Camp David Agreement.
- 1979: Mother Teresa, India, founder of Missionaries of Charity. Human prune.
- 1983: Lech Wałęsa, Poland, campaigner for human rights, and serious moustache wearer.
- 1984: Desmond Tutu, South Africa, former Secretary General, South African Council of Churches. Bishop and something of a giggler.
- 1986: Elie Wiesel, USA, Chairman of the President's Commission on the Holocaust. Straggly hair.
- 1988: United Nations Peace-Keeping Forces, United Nations. They have guns, these people.
- 1989: Tenzin Gyatso, 14th Dalai Lama, Tibet. Wears a blanket.
- 1990: Mikhail Sergeyevich Gorbachev, Soviet Union. Looks good in a fur hat.
- 1991: Aung San Suu Kyi, Burma. Couldn't go to the ceremony because she was a prisoner of the government.
- 1993: Nelson Mandela, South Africa, *and* Frederik Willem de Klerk, South Africa. The odd couple.
- 1994: Yasser Arafat, Palestine. Scratchy beard, *and* Yitzhak Rabin, Israel. Bald, *and* Shimon Peres, Israel. Cousin, weirdly, of Lauren Bacall.

- 1995: Joseph Rotblat, UK, *and* Pugwash Conference on Science and World Affairs, UK. What marvellous names, Rotblat and Pugwash. Sounds like a firm of lawyers.
- 1998: John Hume, Ireland. Looks like the human form of a pint of Guinness, *and* David Trimble, UK. Glasses.
- 2001: United Nations, *and* Kofi Annan, Ghana, for their work for a better-organized world. Whatever that means.
- 2002: Jimmy Carter, USA. Remember him?
- 2005: International Atomic Energy Agency, Austria, *and* Mohamed ElBaradei, Egypt. Prize awarded for their efforts to prevent nuclear energy being used for military purposes. Yes, I'm glad they stopped that.
- 2007, Intergovernmental Panel on Climate Change, Switzerland. Sorry, is this about climate change or peace, this prize?
- 2009: Barack Obama, USA. The only Hawaiian-born recipient as far as I know.
- 2010: Liu Xiaobo, China. A fondness for leather jackets. He couldn't make the ceremony, though, as he was a prisoner in the People's Republic.

The best advertising slogans money can buy

For well over a hundred years people have been paid good money to come up with advertising slogans that are memorable, concise, tell you something about the product and provoke an emotional response in the 'target' customer. In the early days, they sometimes got it a bit wrong. For example, Brooke Bond's tea was advertised with 'Good tea unites good company, exhilarates the spirits, banishes restraint from conversation and promotes the happiest purposes of social intercourse', which is rather on the long side. In any case, nobody these days would use the word 'intercourse' in an ad unless they were trying to provoke a smile.

Sometimes the slogan is blunt, for example, Ronseal's 'Does exactly what it says on the tin' or Listerine's 'Stops halitosis!' But advertisers often sell the 'sizzle' not the sausage, as with AT&T's 'Reach out and touch someone', and Grape-Nuts's lovely 'Makes red blood!' Some slogans are attached to brands so well known that advertisers needn't say anything meaningful. 'Coke is it' is one of these. Here are a few of the best slogans, going back to the nineteenth century.

- 'It floats': Ivory soap (1891)
- 'The greatest show on earth': Barnum & Bailey circus
- 'All the news that's fit to print': *New York Times* (1897)
- 'Good till the last drop': Coca-Cola (1908)
- 'Good to the last drop': Maxwell House coffee (1917)
- 'It beats . . . as it sweeps . . . as it cleans': Hoover vacuum cleaner (1919)
- 'You'll wonder where the yellow went when you brush your teeth with Pepsodent': Pepsodent
- 'Screw yourself': IKEA
- 'More doctors smoke Camels than any other cigarette': Camel cigarettes
- 'Stops halitosis!': Listerine mouthwash
- 'I ♥ New York': New York State Department of Commerce
- 'Crowdstopper': Durex condoms
- 'Think outside the bun': Taco Bell
- 'Use matches sparingly': Swan Vestas
- 'Relieves gas pains': Volkswagen
- 'Put the freshness back': Shake 'n' Vac
- 'If you don't get it, you don't get it': *Washington Post*
- 'Beanz meanz Heinz': Heinz baked beans
- 'Quick, Henry, the Flit!': Flit insecticide
- 'A little dab'll do ya!': Brylcreem
- 'Finger lickin' good': Kentucky Fried Chicken
- 'I'm lovin' it': McDonald's
- 'Raid kills bugs dead': Raid insecticide
- 'Domestos kills all known germs. Dead!': Domestos bleach

- 'You're never alone with a Strand': Strand cigarettes
- 'Lipsmackin' thirstquenchin' acetastin' motivatin' goodbuzzin' cooltalkin' highwalkin' fastlivin' evergivin' coolfizzin' Pepsi': Pepsi-Cola
- 'Sometimes you feel like a nut, sometimes you don't': Peter Paul Mounds
- *'Vorsprung durch Technik'*: Audi
- 'Come to Marlboro Country': Marlboro cigarettes
- 'Isn't that a lot for a bottle of Scotch? Yes': Chivas Regal
- 'Reassuringly expensive': Stella Artois
- 'Connecting people': Nokia
- 'Where's the beef?': Wendy's
- 'Lifts and separates': Playtex Cross-Your-Heart bra
- 'Once you pop, you can't stop': Pringles
- 'I liked it so much I bought the company': Remington shavers
- 'We're number two; we try harder': Avis Rental Cars
- 'Full of Eastern Promise': Fry's Turkish Delight
- 'Don't leave home without it': American Express
- 'Guinness is good for you': Guinness
- 'They're gr-r-reat!': Kellogg's Frosted Flakes (Kellogg's Sugar
- Frosted Flakes of Corn/Frosties)
- 'Where the rubber meets the road': Firestone Tyres
- 'Horlicks guards against night starvation': Horlicks
- 'Tastes so good cats ask for it by name': Meow Mix cat food
- 'I never knew you had dandruff': Head & Shoulders shampoo
- 'I can't believe I ate the whole thing': Alka Seltzer
- 'The sweet you can eat between meals without ruining your appetite': Milky Way
- 'FCUK': French Connection UK
- 'Fresh squeezed glaciers': Adelma mineral water
- 'Let your fingers do the walking': Yellow Pages
- 'Snap, Crackle and Pop': Kellogg's Rice Krispies
- 'Makes red blood!': Grape-Nuts breakfast cereal

- 'Made in Scotland from girders': Irn Bru
- 'Probably the best lager in the world': Carlsberg
- 'Refreshes the parts other beers cannot reach': Heineken lager
- 'Made to make your mouth water': Opal Fruits
- 'The world's local bank': HSBC
- 'Shot from guns': Quaker Puffed Wheat/Rice
- 'Hello boys': Wonderbra
- 'Fair and balanced': Fox News

The first word of thirty-one famous books

There are some celebrated opening sentences to books and some of them, such as the strange fragment that begins James Joyce's *Finnegan's Wake*, are unarguably original. Nonetheless, authors often and unaccountably choose a dull word as their book-starter. In the following list I had to leave out quite a few owing to the preponderance of yawn-worthy pronouns and articles, though I left in Truman Capote's and Henry James's opening word even though it is one of the most clichéd and boring. I suppose James Joyce's *Finnegan's Wake* and Colleen McCullough's *Antony and Cleopatra* kick off with the most novel.

1	All	*Slaughterhouse 5*, Kurt Vonnegut, 1969
2	Call	*Moby Dick*, Herman Melville, 1850
3	'Christmas	*Little Women*, Louisa May Alcott, 1868
4	Granted	*The Tin Drum*, Gunter Grass, 1959
5	Happy	*Anna Karenina*, Leo Tolstoy, 1877
6	He	*The Old Man and the Sea*, Ernest Hemingway, 1952
7	Here	*Winnie-the-Pooh*, A. A. Milne, 1926
8	I	*Invasion of the Body Snatchers*, Jack Finney, 1955
9	It	*Fahrenheit 451*, Ray Bradbury, 1953
10	It	*Raffles*, E. W. Hornung, 1899
11	Last	*Rebecca*, Daphne du Maurier, 1938
12	Lolita	*Lolita*, Vladimir Nabokov, 1955
13	Marley	*A Christmas Carol*, Charles Dickens, 1843

14	Miss	*Middlemarch*, George Eliot, 1872
15	Mrs.	*Mrs. Dalloway*, Virginia Woolf, 1925
16	No	*War of the Worlds*, H. G. Wells 1898
17	Once	*The Tale of Peter Rabbit*, Beatrix Potter, 1902
18	Ours	*Lady Chatterley's Lover*, D. H. Lawrence, 1928
19	People	*The Lady with the Dog*, Anton Chekhov, 1899
20	Quintus	*Antony and Cleopatra*, Colleen McCullough, 2007
21	Riverrun	*Finnegan's Wake*, James Joyce, 1939
22	Running	*Rabbit is Rich*, John Updike, 1981
23	Scarlett	*Gone With the Wind*, Margaret Mitchell, 1936
24	Stately	*Ulysses*, James Joyce, 1922
25	The	*In Cold Blood*, Truman Capote, 1966
26	The	*The Turn of the Screw*, Henry James, 1898
27	Through	*The Sound and the Fury*, William Faulkner, 1929
28	'To	*The Satanic Verses*, Salman Rushdie, 1988
29	'Tom!'	*The Adventures of Tom Sawyer*, Mark Twain, 1876
30	Unable	*The Adolescent*, Fyodor Dostoevsky, 1875
31	'Where's	*Charlotte's Web*, E. B. White, 1952

125 slang terms for the penis

Of all the people, places, things, actions and everything else that there is in the world, surely the male pudendum must be the one with the largest number of slang terms attaching to it – if you'll pardon the disgusting imagery. My research for this selection has been utterly draining and, while the following is not an exhaustive list, it does contain some of the most poetic, elegiac and ingenious slang terms. If your favourite isn't here, I'm sorry, but I could have filled this book three times over and I had to stop somewhere.

1 Chopper
2 Willy
3 One-eyed burping trouser gecko
4 Skin flute
5 Turkey neck
6 Shooting stick
7 Weapon

8	Custard wand	40	Thing
9	Ankle spanker	41	Bishop
10	Beef stick	42	Jimber (erection)
11	John Thomas	43	Widow-consoler
12	Kennel raker	44	Knob
13	Schmeckel	45	Bone
14	Fiddlestick	46	Giggling-pin
15	Shaft	47	Brat-getter
16	Tonsil tickler (large)	48	Summer sausage
17	Liver disturber (large)	49	Pink oboe
18	Dibber	50	Beer can
19	Baby maker	51	Meat
20	Dong	52	Kick stand
21	Beef thermometer	53	Person
22	Tallywhacker	54	Cock
23	Hampton (Cockney rhyming slang: Hampton Wick = dick)	55	Pocket rocket
		56	Cornholer
24	Baby arm	57	Veiny bang stick
25	Milkman	58	Dick
26	Fanny ferret	59	Ding-a-ling
27	Yoghurt rifle	60	Pole
28	Bald-headed yogurt slinger	61	Shlong
29	Blue-veined custard chucker	62	Whang
30	Splat gun	63	Pecker
31	Pork sword	64	Pud
32	Meatloaf	65	Trouser trout
33	Gravy pipe	66	Rod
34	Captain Standish	67	Todger/Tadger
35	Fanny spanner	68	Kidney wiper (large)
36	Cream horn	69	Tool
37	Johnson	70	Honey pump
38	Baby rifle	71	Chew toy
39	Crab ladder	72	Gristle stick

73	Doinker	100	Plonker
74	Prick	101	Cherry popper
75	Domepiece	102	Eleventh finger
76	Dork	103	Smile rifle
77	Gut wrench	104	Pillicock
78	Jimmy	105	Love pump
79	Bush beater	106	Noodle
80	Fanny rat	107	Tube steak
81	Percy	108	Organ
82	Whore-pipe	109	Girl-catcher
83	Meat	110	Porridge gun
84	Chromosome snake	111	Choad
85	Vein sausage	112	Big foot Joe
86	Member	113	Happy lamp
87	Crack-haunter	114	Package
88	Love muscle	115	Pile driver
89	Middle leg	116	Portuguese round stick
90	Nudger	117	Ramrod
91	One-eyed trouser snake	118	Twanger
92	Piece	119	Roger
93	Equipment	120	Donger
94	Fuck stick	121	Diddlestick
95	Flagpole	122	Winkle
96	Garden hose	123	Spritz pipe
97	Happy pole	124	Old chap
98	Hammer	125	Comrade Wobbly
99	Lance		

2 Genius Tests:
Test Yourself to Destruction

Are you a genius? Take the test

On the afternoon of Tuesday, 28 January 1986, the *Challenger* space shuttle came apart with a bang and crashed into the sea. In due course a commission was formed to look into the reasons for the disaster. One of its members was Richard Feynman, an internationally renowned Physics professor. Feynman couldn't stand Washington politics and was a reluctant commission member. Brushing aside the political niceties, he homed straight in on the problem, famously performing an impromptu experiment during the televised hearing, in which he put a piece of the shuttle's O-ring gasket into his cup of iced water and showed that the O-ring was much less bendy when he took it out again.

The simplicity of this experiment was typical of Feynman, who was described by one of his teachers as 'a magician' – a genius so clever that even other geniuses couldn't work out how he did it. But just in case he was getting big-headed, his mother, seeing him referred to in print as 'the smartest man in the world', remarked, 'If that's the world's smartest man, God help us.'

Of course, the idea that you can decide from a test exactly how smart a person is and then give this quality a number is rather debatable anyway. Feynman's IQ had, in fact, been measured at only 124 – above average, but nothing special, and I've met many people with high IQs who are a thousand miles from being geniuses. As Einstein, who was probably what most people regard as a genius, said, 'Imagination is more important than knowledge.' Genius indicates more than the ability to solve number and space problems: it takes in profound creativity, originality and insight, too. Here's a test to find out where you come on the genius scale. Good luck, and remember, think creatively.

1　Decipher the following inscription, which was found around the rim of an ancient Roman vessel dug up in London: 'ITI SAPIS POTANDA BIGO NE.'

2　Is it legal for a Norwegian to marry his widow's sister?

3　Divide 30 by half and add 10. What is the answer?

4　Who wrote Handel's *Messiah*?

5　When was the *1812 Overture* written?

6　Which independent, sovereign island nation comprises the four states of Yap, Chuuk, Pohnpei and Kosrae?

7　A farmer has 211 sheep, all but 9 of which die in an outbreak of sheep-measles. How many are left?

8　What is the verb in this sentence?

9　How many animals, of both sexes, did Moses take on the Ark?

10　Which animal are the Canary Islands named after?

11　You are running a marathon and are in third place. If you overtake the person in second place what position will you be in?

12　How many birthdays does the average man have?

13　Take 1,000 and add 40. Add 1,000. Now add 30. Add another 1,000. Now add 20. Add a further 1,000. Now add 10. What is the answer?

14　How many 67p stamps are there in a dozen?

15　Amy's father has five daughters: the first four are Baba, Bebe, Bibi and Bobo. What is the name of his fifth daughter: Biba, Amy, Babo, Colin or Bubu?

Answers

1　IT IS A PIS POT AND A BIG ONE.

2　No. He's dead.

3　70. 30 divided by half, .5, or 50% equals 60. Try it on a calculator.

4　George Frideric Handel.

5　1880.

6 Micronesia.

7 9.

8 The verb is *is*. Its infinitive is *to be*.

9 Moses took no animals on the Ark, it was Noah.

10 Dogs. From the Latin *Insula Canaria*, meaning 'Dog Island'.

11 Second. If you overtake the second person you take his place, so you are second.

12 Just the one.

13 4,100. Try it on a calculator, then.

14 12. There are always twelve of anything in a dozen.

15 Amy. Read the question carefully.

Results

Score one point for each correct answer. 1–5: Dullard; 6–10: Mid-ranking intellectual drone; 11–14: On the ball; 15: Genius, no doubt about it.

Which sports car suits your personality?

Experts say that your house or flat represents your true personality whereas your car is an index of the way you want people to see you. Who are these 'experts'? You hear them referred to all the time on the news in such phrases as 'Experts say "big" is the new "small"'. How can you be an expert in bigness or smallness? But maybe they are right about this one. How many times have you walked down a street of dingy houses only to see vast, smart and shockingly expensive cars parked ostentatiously by the wheelie-bins? Seldom is it the other way round – you never see film stars sputtering up to a premiere in a Reliant Robin or a Citroën 2CV do you? No, they come in Rolls-Royces, Bentleys and, of course, sports cars.

I suppose the exemplar of the theory that your car represents the image you wish to present to the world is my sometime German teacher Mr Price. (He wasn't a teacher who was German, he was an English teacher – who didn't teach English, but *was* English – who taught

German. Clear?) Mr Price looked rather like an unmade bed that somebody had encouraged to go into teaching, much against its will. His grey suits hung off him like sacking blown against a scarecrow, his shoes seemed to belong to somebody else and he appeared permanently in need of a proper shave, especially in the nooks around his wattle. I don't know what his house was like but I can tell you about his car, which was entirely unexpected, being, as it was, a silver MG Roadster, a very sporty-looking sports car. The trouble was that Mr Price didn't look after it and it would only start after he heaved a battery from the boot and plugged it in with jump leads. A better example of what you want things to look like and what things are really like it would be hard to imagine.

According to experts – here we go again – the term 'sports car' was coined after the First World War, though embryonic sports cars had been around since the first decade of the twentieth century. Designed by people with names like Ferdinand Porsche, these early sports cars are the sort you can imagine Toad of Toad Hall driving. Although large, with big lamps and spoked wheels, they already have that hungry look that all sports cars must have.

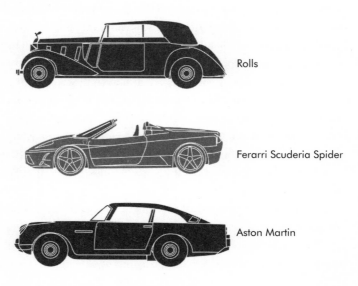

Rolls

Ferarri Scuderia Spider

Aston Martin

As they developed, of course, sports cars became smaller, lighter, lower and more powerful. Nowadays, most are rear-wheel drive, with two seats, two doors, tight handling, a fantastic growl, lots of shiny bits, terrible fuel economy, little passenger-, leg- or luggage-space and a magnetic BAQ (Babe Attraction Quotient).

Just like a lady, a really corking sports car will be fast as well as bright, with top-notch performance and plenty of go. French models with sleek bodies and excellent handling are particularly attractive. All of them require regular servicing.

Anyway, to find out which sort of sports car would best suit your personality, why not take the following test? Tick one box per question.

Which sort of car best represents the one you now drive?

1	Rolls-Royce	☐	4 Sensible Honda	☐
2	Mercedes	☐	5 Bicycle	☐
3	Aston Martin	☐	6 Don't/can't drive	☐

Which dwelling best represents the one you now live in?

1 Stately home with land, rivers, woods etc. ☐
2 Country house/medium-size mansion ☐
3 City loft apartment/eighteenth-century townhouse ☐
4 Suburban family home ☐
5 Temporary/student rented accommodation ☐
6 Tent/friends' floors/cardboard box/etc. ☐

Which sports do you most enjoy watching and/or playing?

1 I own a football team ☐
2 Polo ☐
3 Cricket/chess ☐
4 Football/family swimming ☐
5 Female mud wrestling ☐
6 Where's my other shoe gone? ☐

Which of the following women do you find most attractive?

1	Camilla Parker Bowles	☐	4	Elizabeth Taylor	☐
2	Sarah Palin	☐	5	Marilyn Monroe	☐
3	Sophia Loren	☐	6	Andrea Dworkin	☐

Which car best represents the one you would like to drive?

1 Red Ferrari Scuderia Spider 16M ☐

2 Black Jaguar XK ☐

3 Royal Blue BMW Z4 sDrive35is ☐

4 Grey Aston Martin Cygnet ☐

5 Yellow second-hand Triumph TR6 ☐

6 Pink recumbent tricycle (with card in spokes to make the right noise) ☐

Results

Total your scores by adding together the numbers beside the boxes you have ticked. A score between 5 and 10 marks you out as a sucker for the *big* car, one you can zoom along in on the motorway. This is an 'Everybody pay attention to me!' car. Ferraris, Jaguars and the like are the car for you. A score between 11 and 16 is an index of well-balanced good taste – self aware without ostentation. You can comfortably accommodate your backside to the leather seating of a sporty BMW or a stylish Aston Martin. A score between 17 and 23 puts you possibly at the beginners' end of the spectrum, or else a bit less interested in all that coolosity and stylation. A score of between 24 and 30 shows that you couldn't care less about this stuff and are a geography teacher with a beard or, possibly, a nun. Good for you!

Work out your deathday

All of us walk around knowing our birthday, yet all of us have another day of the year that our descendents will associate with us but which most of us will never know. This is our 'deathday', the day on which we will finally shuffle off this mortal coil. At the time of writing, the average life expectancy for men in this country is about seventy-five years, and about eighty for women. But this number is creeping up and it is predicted that many of today's youngsters will live to be 100. The poor old Queen is going to be signing telegrams all day long.

Below you will find a simple test that you can take to calculate your own deathday. Actually, to be honest, unless you commit suicide on the day or someone murders you to order, there's no way to do this, so it's more of a *death-age* calculator. According to your answers to the questions (be honest, for goodness' sake) you will be instructed to add or subtract from your starting number, which is an average life expectancy in years.

First you must work out your body mass index (BMI). This is the single most reliable indicator of life expectancy in this country. In fact, my doctor told me that he has no fat patients over seventy. When I asked why he said, 'Because they're all dead.' Some unexpected things, such as being the oldest child, can add a year or so to your life, and bear in mind that if you never wear your seatbelt or you work in bomb disposal, that can skew the figures a bit, too.

Along with the BMI business, there is another annoying question in the calculation: how many units of alcohol do you drink? If you're unsure of this, as many people are, you might care to know the following typical alcohol unit totals: bottle of wine: 7 units; pint of beer: 2 units (depending on strength); alcopop (if you drink those things): 1.2 units; single measure of spirits: 1.1 unit. Anyway, here's the test, and the best of luck to you.

Calculate your body mass index (BMI)

I   Multiply your height in metres by itself.
II   Divide your weight in kilograms by your height (see I above).
III A BMI of 18.5 to 25 is healthy, 25 to 30 is overweight, and over 30 is obese.

Your starting number

- If you are male, your starting number is 75 (the average male life expectancy in years).
- If you are female (look, your wife or girlfriend might want to take this test, too), your starting number is 80 (the average female life expectancy in years).

1

- If your BMI is the same as it was when you were 21, add 10 years.
- If your BMI is not the same as it was when you were 21 but is between 18.5 and 25, do nothing.
- If your BMI is between 25 to 30, take off 2 years.
- If your BMI is more than 30, take off 10 years.

2

- For each grandparent who is, or who lived to be, 80 or older, add one year.
- For each grandparent who is, or who lived to be, 70 or older, add half a year.

3

- If your mother is, or lived to be 80 or older, add 4 years. If your father is, or lived to be 80 or older, add 2 years.
  If your parents are still alive but have not reached this age, do nothing.

4

- If a sibling, parent or grandparent died of a heart attack, stroke or arteriosclerosis before the age of 50, take off 4 years.
- If any of the above family members died between 50 and 60, take off 2 years.

5

- If a sibling, parent or grandparent died of diabetes or a peptic ulcer before the age of 60, take off 3 years.
- If they died of stomach cancer before the age of 60, take off 2 years.

- If any of the above family members died of an illness before the age of 60, take off 1 year.

6

- If you are an only child or the oldest child, add one year.

7

- If you smoke more than 40 cigarettes a day, take off 12 years.
- If you smoke 20 to 40 cigarettes a day, take off 7 years.
- If you smoke, but it's less than 20 a day, take off 2 years.

8

- If you regularly drink more than 21 units of alcohol a week, take off 8 years.
- If you drink less than 21 units of alcohol a week, add 3 years.
- If you drink alcohol but not much and not regularly, add 1.5 years.
- If you never drink alcohol, don't add or subtract anything.

9

- If you exercise five times a week (including brisk walking), add 5 years.

10

- If you have a high fat diet, take off 5 years.
- If you eat mostly grilled food, if you have 5 portions of fruit or vegetables a day and don't stuff yourself, add 5 years.

11

- If you are often ill take off 5 years.

Now do the sums. I hope your result is good but don't forget that nobody wants to live like a monk (except monks I suppose), and any of us might die tomorrow from a falling piano. Anyway, fingers crossed.

The 'do you hate your job?' test

In his superb pot-boiling essay 'In Praise of Idleness' (1932), Bertrand Russell said, 'Work is of two kinds: first, altering the position of matter at or near the earth's surface relatively to other such matter; second, telling other people to do so. The first kind is unpleasant and ill paid; the second is pleasant and highly paid.' I agreed with this penetrating analysis so I thought I would look up the most popular jobs to see what they were. I imagined I'd find things such as beer tasting, being the mystery shopper at high-class restaurants, driving racing cars, being a test pilot, starring in action films with beautiful actresses or teaching tennis in Swiss finishing schools for young ladies. Instead, to my surprise, I found the following:

1   Retail sales
2   Office administration
3   Food preparation and service
4   Nursing
5   Teaching
6   Waiting (not hanging around, but taking orders)
7   Customer service, including call centres
8   Material moving (see Russell's quote above)
9   Cleaning
10 Secretarial

After thinking about it for about ten seconds I realized that these jobs are popular only in the sense that they account for the employment of large numbers of people. I'm sure many, if not most, people who work in call centres do not regard it as a wonderfully rewarding vocation.

You might love your work but many people don't. (Love *their* work, I mean, not yours.) Here's a quiz to find out how highly you regard your job. Put a tick in boxes I, II or III, to indicate which statement best reflects your own feelings about your job.

1 Attitude

I   I love my work so much that I'm the first in and the last out. ☐

II   I don't mind going to work in the morning, but I love to come home. ☐

III   I dread waking up on weekdays, and my weekends are ruined by the terrible thought of Monday. ☐

2 My mood

I   At work I always have a smile on my face (you can ignore this if you're a funeral director). ☐

II   I do my work cheerfully and well but it's not the be-all and end-all of my life. ☐

III   I sit with a snarl of hate on my lips watching the seconds ticking interminably by. ☐

3 The boss

I   My boss is supportive, encouraging, helpful and sticks up for me. S/he is a wonderful human being and a warm friend. ☐

II   The boss is OK, but I sometimes have to manage him/her a bit. ☐

III   Dear God, help me not to strangle this unforgivable shit of a human being. ☐

4 Pay

I   I can't believe they actually pay me to do something I love so much. ☐

II   The pay is acceptable, but I could do with an increase now and again to match the rising cost-of-living. ☐

III   A hermit couldn't live on this slave wage. I cannot afford luxuries such as food and toilet paper, and have to bathe under a tap in the street. ☐

5 Environment

I   From my desk, I can see the sea lapping on the shore and smell the sage blowing up from the sun-drenched beach. □

II My workspace is warm, dry and comfortable, but the coffee
    machine and photocopiers are on their last legs. □

III They keep telling me to think outside the box, while making
    me work in a cubicle. The smell of the fungus on the wall,
    the damp carpets, the stench from the fishmonger's next
    door, the creaking of the rusty fire escape, blocked by a
    washing machine, the screaming of the boss, the crying of
    unpaid illegal Chinese and Ukrainian workers, the dripping
    rain through the cracked roof, the failing 1997 computer, the
    unpredictable ice-cold and boiling-hot heating system and
    the desk like an ironing board make me wish I was doing
    something nice like rowing a Phoenician galley, with the
    crack of the whip ringing in my ears. □

Score yourself out of a maximum 15 points by adding them all to make a
total. It's 1 point for box I, 2 points for box II and 3 points for box III. If
you score between 5 and 8 you are happy in your job, particularly at the
lower end. If you score between 9 and 11, you are less happy, particularly
at the upper end. If you score between 12 and 15, you are fairly unhappy.
If you scored the maximum of 15, you need to get out of there, mate – it's
going to do you in.

Are you innumerate? Take the test

I recently saw a commercial on television for a shampoo that was alleged
to make your hair 'up to nine times shinier'. This struck me as daft
because degrees of 'shininess' must be a very hard thing for which to
award numbers. You don't see some girl on the train and think, 'Wow! Her
hair is four-and-a-half times shinier.' It was also meaningless in the sense
that 'up to nine times' includes 'no times', so if your hair was just as dull
– or duller, even – compared with before you used this shampoo you could
hardly complain, because the claim was still true. Neither did the

commercial say what it was that your hair was going to become nine times shinier than – silk? Last time? Everyone else's? It's always worth asking 'More than who?', 'Bigger than what?' or 'Cheaper than which?'when you hear a claim of this sort. I was, incidentally, suspicious of that 'nine times', which sounded as if it might have been chosen because it was more persuasive than the overused 'ten times'. The man doing the voiceover didn't explain which Nobel-Prize-winning biologist had done the study on which this 'statistic' had been based. The people around me didn't seem to find this commercial odd, which, I think, revealed that they were suffering from a common form of innumeracy.

The three Rs – reading, 'riting and 'rithmetic – are still held to be the foundation of a basic education and most people do emerge from school able to read a bit and write a note for the milkman. But not so many come out able to do much more than add up, take away (sometimes on their fingers) and multiply the smaller counting numbers, let alone do trigonometry or cube roots. If you are shaking your head and saying 'Well, I can' or 'Some people do', then you are making one of those easy-to-make mistakes: confusing 'not so many people' with 'no people'. This is part of the problem I'm on about.

Quite a few otherwise intelligent people suffer from the kind of innumeracy that, amongst other things, enables shysters to take advantage of them, as in the commercial I mentioned. This lack of a basic understanding of numbers can be a nuisance because if you are unused to, say, averaging or using percentages and fractions properly, everyday life is going to be more difficult to manage.

Doing percentages is one of those useful calculations that can be a problem if you don't really understand what you are up to. My auntie Alice told me that the weatherman had said there was a 50 per cent chance of rain on Saturday and a 50 per cent chance of rain on Sunday, so there was a 100 per cent chance of rain over the weekend.

Another error is to be impressed by a headline that screams something like 'Half of brain surgeons worse than average'. Sounds terrible, except that half of *any* class of people are going to fall below the average, by definition – even geniuses, Olympic athletes and rocket scientists.

You've got to be careful with averages. There are three main kinds: the *mean*, where you add up all the numbers and then divide by the number of numbers; the *median*, which is the number in the middle of your sample; and the *mode*, the number that occurs most often. Suppose 100 people take a numeracy test with the following results: 44 score 80 per cent, 5 score 100 per cent, 12 score 20 per cent, 16 score 13 per cent, 9 score 66 per cent, 4 score 3 per cent and 10 score 17 per cent. The mean would be 42.7 per cent, the median would be 20 per cent and the mode would be 80 per cent. To show the results in the best light you would mention the mode: 80 per cent. If you wanted to do the opposite you would quote the median: 20 per cent. Because the mean averages everything out, including the extremes, you get 42.7 per cent, in this case not really an accurate reflection of the typical intelligence level of the group, which is higher. You have to be on your guard with these averages – after all, the average adult in this country has one breast and one testicle.

John Allen Paulos has written entertainingly about the problem of innumeracy, and I have used one or two examples quoted in his book, cunningly entitled *Innumeracy*, in which he notes that the Bible (Genesis 7: 19–20) says on the subject of the Flood: 'And the waters prevailed exceedingly upon the earth; and all the high hills, that were under the whole heaven, were covered. Fifteen cubits upward did the waters prevail; and the mountains were covered.'

Fifteen Biblical cubits equals 22.5 feet (6.858 m), so one can't help wondering whether the mountains were smaller in those days, but the main problem with this is that if, as it implies, something between 10,000 and 20,000 feet (3,000–6,100 m) of rain – that is about half a billion cubic miles (two billion cubic km) of water – fell on the earth in forty days and forty nights (just 960 hours), it must have been coming down at 15 feet (4.5 m) an hour, which would be enough to sink anything on the surface, especially a home-made boat full of elephants and things. Even if you are kind, and take forty days and nights to mean 'a long time', that is still going to be enough rain to ruin your yacht varnish. Unless you are on the alert, this kind of thing can pass you by.

So innumeracy is not so much a question of your not having learnt your times tables, it's more a case of not understanding what's going on 'underneath'. Here's a little quiz to test your own numerical sophistication. See how you get on.

1   If the price of a pair of shoes goes up 50 per cent before Christmas and is then slashed by 50 per cent in the New Year sales, what is the net reduction over the period?

   100 per cent   ☐
   75 per cent   ☐
   50 per cent   ☐
   25 per cent   ☐

2   Mr Brown and Mr Smith are teachers. They work in adjacent classrooms in the same school, and the children they teach come from the same village, eat the same food and do the same amount of exercise as each other. But every year, when the school nurse examines the arms of the children in Mr Brown's class they are found to be an average of two inches (5 cm) longer than those of the children in Mr Smith's class. How come?

3   How likely is it that last week's lottery numbers will come up exactly the same this week?

It is less likely that they will come up the same this week as last week.   ☐

It is more likely that they will come up the same this week as last week.   ☐

The same numbers are just as likely to come up this week as they were last week.   ☐

4   What is 13 per cent of £1,000,000?
5   What is 3/4 of 150?
6   What is 3/4 as a decimal?
7   What is 6/8 as a decimal?
8   Finally, suppose a man in the pub offers you the choice of two envelopes – one red and one green. He tells you that one of them (you do not know which) contains twice as much money as the other. You choose the green envelope, as it matches the colour of your teeth, and upon opening it discover a £100 note. The man now offers you the chance to exchange envelopes. (Who is this fellow and what's he up to?) You realize that the other envelope (red) must contain either £200 (a £100 gain) or £50 (only a £50 loss). Do you change envelopes?

Answers

Question 1: 25 per cent
Question 2: Mr Brown's children are 17-year-olds and Mr Smith's are 13-year-olds.
Question 3: The same numbers are just as likely to come up this week as they were last week.
Question 4: £130,000
Question 5: 112.5
Question 6: 0.75
Question 7: 0.75
Question 8: No matter how much is in the envelope you open you will always have to change your mind and switch envelopes. The problem here is that, unless you know how likely the envelope is to contain a certain amount of money, you're stuck. Did you work that out? If so, you are less innumerate than many (though I don't know how many).

Are you a worrier? (And, if so, how to conquer worry)

Winston Churchill seemed to have a quote for every occasion. He produced so many memorable ones that you can't help wondering where he got the time to be Prime Minister and do all the other things he did. Oh, yes, I forgot, his wife picked up after him and he had a house full of servants who filled his bath, cooked his dinner, laid out his clothes and manicured his estate. He didn't need anyone to comb his hair, though, because he had so little of it. Anyway, he did have a good way of putting things and one of his best quotes is this: 'When I look back on all these worries, I remember the story of the old man who said on his deathbed that he had a lot of trouble in his life, most of which had never happened.'

All of us worry a bit, and some of us worry a lot, about things that either never happen or, if they do, turn out to be easily manageable and much less trouble in reality than in our dreams. Health, work and money, and our personal relationships, including affairs of the heart, probably constitute the bulk of the worries that we waste time on. So I thought it would be a good idea to come up with a remedy for worry and explain how to banish it.

First go down this list and tick any question to which you would answer 'yes' or 'probably'.

1	Do people regard you as a right old worrier?	☐
2	Have you always been a worrier?	☐
3	Do you find it hard to take a compliment?	☐
4	Are you anxious when you are on your own at home?	☐
5	Do you keep putting things off?	☐
6	Are you shy?	☐
7	Are you bothered what people might think?	☐
8	Do you fail to live up to your own high standards?	☐
9	Do you feel that your true self is hidden inside?	☐
10	Are you obsessively worried about your health?	☐
11	Does the idea of death alarm you more than other people?	☐
12	Do you worry even when things are fine?	☐
13	Do people say you worry too much?	☐
14	Do you quickly find fault with restaurants and hotels?	☐
15	Do you hate confrontation?	☐

16 Do you brood over things rather than do something about it? ☐
17 When you go through your post do you dread what you might find? ☐
18 Would people describe you as creative? ☐
19 Do you self-medicate with alcohol or 'substances' when you are worried? ☐
20 Have you ever set fire to libraries or public buildings, or gone on a shooting spree in a shopping centre? ☐

Now count the ticks. A score of between 0 and 6 means you worry either not at all (0), in which case you are a psychopath, or about as much as most people. Scores of between 7 and 12 mean you are a bit of a worrier and need to take a few deep breaths, while a score of between 13 and 19 means you are a card-carrying worrier, and if you are at the top end you might want to go and see someone about it. If you ticked no. 20, and have indeed set fire to buildings and let off guns down the shops, you are at the upper end of the worrier scale and need locking up, frankly.

Worry is a function of personality, and reserved, creative, perfectionist, critical and sensitive people tend to worry more than others. Conquering worry is therefore harder for people like this. While everyone, worriers included, ought to remember that worry is a normal part of life, you should have a chat with your doctor if it is affecting your life to the extent that you can't manage properly. For most worriers, though, a bit of exercise and fresh air, or a good laugh with a friend, can do wonders to lift mood and reduce anxiety. Here's a worry joke to get you started up the gentle slope of recovery.

A young accountant was being interviewed by his prospective employer, the boss of a two-man grass-cutting business. 'I want you to take my money worries off me,' said the employer. 'Your salary will be £120,000.' 'How on earth can this tiny business afford that?' asked the accountant. 'That', said the employer, 'is your first, very pressing, worry.'

A genius's first aid test

If I was king of schools I would make certain lessons compulsory. Among these would be how to start a car on a cold morning and how to do basic first aid. Studying these two subjects would save a lot of time, tears and lives in later life. Here's a multiple choice test for you to do to find out whether you would be able to give first aid in an accident or whether you'd be likely to be giving the kiss of death.

Imagine this scenario: you are walking down the road when the cradle holding two window cleaners falls two storeys on to a man juggling knives on the pavement. All three are injured but now what?

Question A: What should you do first?

1 Assess the casualties to find out who needs help first ☐
2 Interview the casualties to see if they like Rod Stewart ☐
3 Call 999 for an ambulance ☐
4 Check the area for hazards to avoid being injured yourself ☐
5 Do a bit of flower arranging ☐

Question B: What should you do next?

1 Assess the casualties to find out who needs help first ☐
2 Call 999 for an ambulance ☐
3 Text your girlfriend ☐
4 Check whether anyone is bleeding heavily ☐
5 Do a special dance ☐

Question C: You have checked that the area is safe. Who should you deal with first?

1 The window cleaner who is in agony and is moaning obscenities ☐
2 The lady at a window who keeps shouting, 'Take his shoes off!' ☐
3 The man passing out leaflets for Dianetics ☐
4 The other cleaner who is quiet, has no visible wounds and seems to be napping ☐

249

5   The juggler who has a knife in his arm and is bleeding heavily
    and untidily ☐

Question D: You attend to the quiet man but his head comes off
in your hand so you move on to the juggler who has a knife in
his arm and is bleeding heavily. What should you do first?

1   Comb his hair ☐
2   Comb *your* hair ☐
3   Take the knife out of his arm as quick as you can ☐
4   Stop the bleeding ☐
5   Get him to hospital right away ☐

Question E: The knife has fallen out but he's still bleeding
like a goodun. How should you stop it?

1   Put a tourniquet – like a belt or strap – tightly around his arm
    to stop the bleeding ☐
2   Push firmly on either side of the wound to squish the edges
    together ☐
3   See if you can guess his age ☐
4   Lay him down with his legs higher than his head ☐
5   Give him a stiff brandy ☐

Question F: He has stopped bleeding and is calm and you have
dialled 999. The other man (the one with his head still on) has
stopped moaning because he was lying on his keys and is
reading the paper. What complication might your knife casualty
now typically suffer?

1   Shock ☐
2   Obsessive-compulsive disorder ☐
3   Knitting ☐
4   Extreme thirst ☐
5   Pregnancy ☐

Question G: How should you treat your casualty's shock?

1 Lay him down with his legs higher than his head ☐
2 Tell him to pull himself together ☐
3 Say 'Oh, you do look ill' ☐
4 Put him in the recovery position ☐
5 Give him a cup of sweet tea ☐

Answers

Question A: 4. Check the area for hazards. If you are injured, you can't help others. You can wait to call 999 until you've checked that the area is safe.

Question B: 1. Assess the casualties to find out who needs help first. If you ticked answer 5 you are probably not a natural at this first-aid business.

Question C: 4. A quiet casualty should be attended to first. Bleeding and moaning are more noticeable but a quiet casualty might be unconscious and most seriously injured.

Question D: 4. Reduce the bleeding first.

Question E: 2. Push firmly on either side of the wound to squish the edges and reduce blood flow. Don't put a tourniquet on his arm. Cutting off blood flow to a limb can cause serious harm.

Question F: 1. Shock can be a serious clinical condition and is not the same thing as amazement, surprise or becoming upset. In shock the body diverts blood to the vital organs and away from the skin, causing pallor, sweating, nausea, low blood pressure and a rapid pulse.

Question G: 1. Lay him down with his legs higher than his head. This will help the blood flow to his brain and make him feel better, too. Don't forget to be nice at the same time.

Test your sex drive

There's nothing I need to say about this quiz, except tick the answer that most closely resembles your own sexual position. Sorry, that came out wrong. And neither did that sound too good. Anyway, good luck.

How would you rate your sex drive?

1 I could have sex ten times a day ☐
2 I could have sex 4–5 times a week ☐
3 I could have only have sex once or twice a year ☐
4 Not interested, love ☐

Do you believe in sex before marriage?

1 Yes ☐
2 No ☐
3 Not if it delays the ceremony ☐

How often do you think about sex?

1 All day long ☐
2 A couple of times a minute ☐
3 A couple of times a day ☐
4 Never ☐

Which of the following most makes your mouth water?

1 A huge ice cream covered in chocolate ☐
2 A huge naked woman covered in chocolate ☐
3 A small naked woman covered in chocolate ☐
4 A pork pie ☐
5 A plate of mashed yeast and a few nuts ☐

Would you consider cheating on your partner?

1 Yes, of course ☐
2 Only if she wasn't looking ☐
3 No, much as I'd love to, I think it would be a disaster ☐
4 Not enough energy, mate ☐

What do a banana, a cucumber and a salami say to you?

1 Sounds like we're having a picnic ☐
2 They are all like willies ☐
3 Look out – the Martians have landed ☐

What do melons, coconuts, peaches and fried eggs say to you?

1 They are all like bosoms (descending in order of size) ☐
2 They can't talk – what a stupid question ☐
3 This fruit salad has got eggs in it ☐

When you're trying to impress, you wear:

1 Skin-tight Lurex ☐
2 Split-crotch panties ☐
3 A gentleman's abdominal support ☐
4 A blanket with a hole cut in the middle ☐

When you wake in the morning, you feel:

1 Hard ☐
2 Horny ☐
3 Corny ☐
4 Ready to go ☐
5 Already been ☐

When you sight likely sexual prey you usually:

1 Turn on the sexual aggression ☐
2 Turn on the schmooze ☐
3 Turn on the radio ☐
4 Wait and see if she will come over and ask for your number ☐

Does rejection decrease your sex drive?

1 Are you kidding? It makes me worse ☐
2 No. It's their loss ☐
3 It *does* decrease my sex drive ☐
4 I wear a hair shirt for a month, me ☐

Do you sleep naked?

1 Yes ☐
2 No ☐
3 Don't know ☐
4 I am naked under my pyjamas ☐

How long can you keep it up?

1 Hours ☐
2 A few minutes ☐
3 A few seconds ☐
4 Can't. Not even with a crane ☐
5 Can't remember, love ☐

How often do you have sex on your own?

1 All the time ☐
2 Every now and again ☐
3 Thursdays only ☐
4 Christmas ☐
5 Never ☐

Do you find onanism offensive?

1 Yes ☐
2 No ☐
3 Only if the waiter does it while he's taking the order ☐

You believe that oral sex is:

1 Better than intercourse ☐
2 Louder than intercourse ☐
3 Foreign-sounding ☐
4 Ridiculous – I don't want it in my ear ☐

How often do you use pornography?

1 Every day ☐
2 Once in a blue moon ☐
3 Once in a blue film ☐
4 What – with *my* eyes? ☐

How often do you have sex?

1 Less than I want   ☐
2 About enough, thanks   ☐
3 Much more than I want   ☐
4 Don't be so sodding nosy   ☐

How often would you have sex if you could wave a magic wand?

1 All day long   ☐
2 More than I do   ☐
3 About as often as I do   ☐
4 Less often   ☐
5 Do you mean have sex and wave a magic wand *at the same time*?   ☐

To score your result, just add the numbers. The highest total you can get is 79 and the lowest 19. The higher your total the stronger your sex drive. So, well done you if you got big numbers. Anything between 19 and 25 marks you out as either a bit past it or just not all that interested. You'd probably prefer a nice sit down with your hot water bottle and a cup of tea. Make me one while you're about it.

Part Four:

THE DICTIONARY
OF UNNATURAL
BIOGRAPHY

*Movers and shakers every gentleman
should know about*

The real 'Crocodile' Dundee

In 1986 the Australian comedy film *'Crocodile' Dundee* became an unexpected worldwide hit. The plot concerns a hunky Australian adventurer and crocodile killer, Michael J. 'Crocodile' Dundee, played by Paul Hogan, who is tracked down in the outback by a tasty female journalist, Sue Charlton, and brought to New York, where, though mystified by escalators and bidets, he manages to terrify some local ne'er-do-wells by producing a gigantic knife, before finally winning Sue away from her unsympathetic boyfriend.

What you might not know is that 'Crocodile' Dundee was based on a real person, a man by the name of Rodney Ansell (1953–99), who was just as interesting as the fictional character he inspired. Paul Hogan, who not only starred in the film but came up with the original story, said he got the idea after watching Michael Parkinson interview Ansell, who told how he had run away from home at the age of fifteen to catch wild buffalo and had become an accidental national hero when he emerged from the bush bristling with exciting tales of his barefoot adventures.

Ansell's most famous story concerned a terrifying ordeal in which a giant crocodile capsized and sank a boat in which he was travelling with his two cattle dogs near the mouth of the Victoria River in Australia's remote Northern Territory. The three were thrown into the water but managed to swim ashore unbitten, only to find themselves trapped in the not very friendly outback.

A small dinghy had survived the crocodile's attack and with only a single oar, a rifle and a couple of knives – but no water – Ansell and his dogs travelled up the salty Fitzmaurice River for several days and nights, becoming severely dehydrated, before finding fresh water in the nick of time. He told how for nearly two months he survived by eating, and drinking the blood of, wild animals, including sharks, that he had shot. One day some locals stumbled upon Ansell, and he was finally able to return to civilization.

The media were not slow to descend on the blond, good-looking adventurer, but were disappointed to find him report that the lack of female companionship had been his only problem. The time he spent in Australian cities talking to the press proved to be just as much of an adventure. Staying on one occasion at a smart Sydney hotel, Ansell slept on the floor and was intrigued and bemused by the novelty of the bidet, providing wonderful source material for Hogan's film.

As well as starring in *'Crocodile' Dundee*, Hogan wrote the story and was co-writer of the screenplay. Not bad for a man who had started his career very modestly as a painter on the Sydney Harbour Bridge. During the early 1980s, he moved away from turps and undercoat to star in a series of US TV commercials for the Australian Tourism Commission, popularizing the phrase 'extra shrimp on the barbie', and on British TV in advertisements for Foster's lager, in which he played an unsophisticated stereotypical Aussie who at the ballet announces in amazement, 'Strewth, there's a bloke down there with no strides on'. The character Hogan went on to play in *'Crocodile' Dundee* is much the same kind of person.

'Crocodile' Dundee grossed well over $47 million in Australia alone but Rodney Ansell made no money from the film and became a bitterly angry man. Let's face it, though, he was a bit odd already. His life started to unravel, he became addicted to drugs and lost his home. Then, in 1999, his existence came to an unromantic and abrupt end, near Darwin, when, barefoot as usual, he ambushed and killed a police sergeant. Picking up his gun, the policeman's partner shot Ansell dead. He was just forty-four years old.

The truth about Sherlock Holmes

Sherlock Holmes is famous around the globe for his curved pipe, his deerstalker cap and his 'catchphrase', 'Elementary, my dear Watson'. Surprisingly, perhaps, none of these is described by Arthur Conan Doyle in any of the Sherlock Holmes stories. Holmes is also famous for his brainy brilliance, yet in *A Study in Scarlet*, Dr Watson lists a few areas in which he would not win *Who Wants to Be a Millionaire?*: 'Knowledge of Literature – nil; Knowledge of Philosophy – nil; Knowledge of Astronomy – nil; Knowledge of Politics – Feeble.' Here is the truth.

1. Sherlock Holmes appeared in a total of fifty-six short stories and four novels.

2. The first Holmes story, *A Study in Scarlet*, was not a big hit, and neither was the second, *The Sign of the Four*, both of which were serialized novels. Only a letter from Lawson Tait, a well-known surgeon, saying that he and the Lord Chief Justice, John Duke, were Sherlock Holmes fans led Conan Doyle to continue with the series.

3. The Sherlock Holmes stories cover a period from around 1880 to 1914.

4. 'A Study in Scarlet' appeared in *Beeton's Christmas Annual* 1887 and 'The Sign of the Four' in *Lippincott's Monthly Magazine* in 1890. The first series of short stories appeared in *Strand Magazine* in 1891. Further short stories and two novels were published in serial form, until 1927.

5. The phrase 'Elementary, my dear Watson' appears in none of the sixty Sherlock Holmes tales.

6. Holmes's deductive method was modelled on that of the Scottish physician Joseph Bell, who taught Conan Doyle medicine.

7. Conan Doyle began writing after setting up as a young doctor. The very long gaps between patients left him with little else to do.

8. Sherlock Holmes regularly took cocaine, injecting it in a 'seven-per-cent solution'.

9. The Sherlock Holmes pub in Northumberland Street, London, was previously the Northumberland Arms, which, little changed, appears as the Northumberland Hotel, in which Sir Henry Baskerville stays in *The Hound of the Baskervilles*. (Old) Scotland Yard is on the other side of Northumberland Avenue, and the Turkish baths used by Holmes and Watson were slap-bang next to the hotel. The entrance is still visible in Craven Passage.

10 The beer in the Sherlock Holmes pub is expensive.

11 Artist Sidney Paget created the 537 Holmes illustrations that appeared in *Strand Magazine*. The editor thought he was commissioning Sidney's more famous brother Walter, who had illustrated *Treasure Island*. Sidney used Walter's thin face as a model for that of Holmes.

12 Conan Doyle sometimes got a bit confused with details. Watson's painful bullet wound moves from his shoulder in an early story to his leg in a later one.

13 Holmes was unaware that the planets revolve around the sun until told so by Watson.

14 Holmes's famous deerstalker cap was referred to by Conan Doyle just as an 'ear-flapped travelling cap'. Illustrator Sidney Paget did the rest.

15 Paget never showed Sherlock Holmes smoking a curved pipe.

16 Sherlock Holmes retired to Sussex to keep bees.

17 On 8 July 1989, Leslie Bricusse's *Sherlock Holmes, The Musical* opened at the Cambridge Theatre in London. So dire was it that it closed after just one performance.

18 In 2002 Sherlock Holmes received an Honorary Fellowship from the Royal Society of Chemistry.

19 Unlike Sherlock Holmes, who was a sceptic, Conan Doyle enthusiastically believed in spiritualism despite having been educated at the Catholic Stonyhurst College.

20 So far, an estimated seventy-five actors have played Holmes in something like 211, mainly bad, films.

The man under the bridge: the murder of Roberto Calvi

At or about 7.30, on the morning of Friday, 18 June 1982, a postman passing under Blackfriars Bridge, on the banks of the Thames in London, noticed the body of a man hanging by the neck from some scaffolding. On taking him down, the police found that bricks had been stuffed into his pockets and through the open fly of his trousers. Along with the bricks they found some $15,000, in three different currencies, and an Italian passport.

The body was that of Roberto Calvi, who had gone missing from his Rome apartment a week earlier. Calvi was chairman of the large privately owned bank Banco Ambrosiano (named after St Ambrose, Bishop of Milan), which had just collapsed with gigantic debts, causing a political scandal as much of the missing money belonged to the Mafia and a lot of the rest belonged to Banco Ambrosiano's main shareholder, the Istituto per le Opere Religiose (in English, the Institute of Religious Works or, in plain words, the Vatican Bank). Quite what this shareholder knew of the Mafia money in its vaults is an interesting question. Calvi, who was known as 'God's Banker' because of the Holy See's close association with him and his bank, had then fled to London on a false passport in the name of Gian Roberto Calvini, having taken the precaution of first shaving off his distinctive moustache.

But there were some funny things about this apparent suicide. For example, the dusty bricks found in Calvi's pockets had left no marks on his fingers, and rumours began to spread that this was not suicide, but murder.

Attention turned to the Masons, because Calvi had been a member of the exclusive and shady Masonic lodge Propaganda Due, or P2, which was run by Italian financier Licio Gelli. Propaganda Due was seen by some as a 'state within a state' and had among its members the heads of the Italian intelligence services, senior military leaders, journalists with clout, parliamentarians and businessmen, including Silvio Berlusconi, now famous for being Prime Minister of Italy and having purple hair.

When police searched Gelli's villa, they found the 'Plan for Democratic Rebirth', an interesting document calling for consolidation of the media, suppression of trade unions and the rewriting of the Italian Constitution. Sounds like what's been going on for a while, in more than one country.

Members of P2 were known as *'frati neri'* or 'black friars', leading some to suggest that Blackfriars Bridge was a significant location for Calvi's murder. On the other hand, the bridge is only five minutes from the Bank of England, but nobody was suggesting the bank's governor had anything to do with it.

The machinery of justice grinds slowly but in 1991 a Mafia informer named Francesco Marino Mannoia claimed that Calvi had indeed been killed, over the loss of Mafia funds when Banco Ambrosiano collapsed. According to Mannoia the order to kill Calvi had come from Mafia boss Giuseppe Calò. He claimed that the killer was Francesco Di Carlo, a gentleman who was living in London at the time. Di Carlo denied this, but admitted that he had been asked. According to him, the killers were Vincenzo Casillo and Sergio Vaccari. Neither denied it, both being a bit dead.

In 1997, Italian prosecutors also alleged the involvement of Flavio Carboni, a Sardinian businessman, Ernesto Diotallevi (supposedly one of the leaders of the criminal Banda della Magliana) and Mafia informer Francesco Di Carlo. The following year, Calvi's body was exhumed and an independent forensic report decided that he had been murdered, owing to his neck injuries being 'inconsistent with hanging', and the absence of any rust or flaking paint on his shoes, which ought to have come off the scaffolding over which he was supposed to have clambered.

In 2005, Licio Gelli was investigated on charges of ordering the murder of Calvi, along with Giuseppe Calò, Ernesto Diotallevi, Flavio Carboni, Carboni's ex-girlfriend Manuela Kleinszig and Calvi's former driver and bodyguard Silvano Vittor. The charges alleged that Calvi's murder was ordered to prevent him from blackmailing P2, the Vatican Bank and the Mafia. Gelli acknowledged that Calvi had been murdered but denied involvement and was not tried. In June 2007, the court ruled Calvi's death a murder, not suicide, but all the accused were acquitted owing to insufficient evidence. On 7 May 2010, the Court of Appeals confirmed the acquittal of Calò, Carboni and Diotallevi.

The dead Democrat

Among the crew of relatively unknown candidates in the 1998 Oklahoma Democratic Senate primary, a sixty-nine-year-old housewife from the town of Norman, Jacquelyn Morrow Lewis Ledgerwood, was the only woman on the ballot. But she did well, coming in second, with 21 per cent of the vote, prompting a two-person runoff against the first-place candidate, Don E. Carroll, a forty-year-old air-conditioning repairman. The only problem was that Jacquelyn Ledgerwood had been dead for a good six weeks before the election, having succumbed to a heart attack on 15 July.

According to Oklahoma's attorney general, a candidate's name might be removed from a *runoff* ballot only if a replacement candidate was named within five days of the death of a party's nominee. But since Ledgerwood was not the nominee when she died this did not apply. In any case, the five-day limit had been missed. The attorney general also took pains to point out that Oklahoma voters were perfectly entitled to vote for a cadaver if they wished, as a form of 'none-of-the-above' nose-thumbing. People's voting decisions are notoriously capricious in any case. The executive director of the state Democratic Party, Pat Hall, reported hearing one man say he was going to vote for Ledgerwood because she had the longest name, which was no sillier a reason than many.

It was now beginning to look as if a dead person might for the very first time be elected to the Senate – though how anybody would spot the difference between a dead and a living senator was a moot point. Whatever the case, Democratic Party officials saw no reason not to take advantage of the situation, pointing out that, because of all the publicity, Mrs Ledgerwood had an excellent chance of winning the runoff. Pat Hall remarked, 'She has not taken out one bit of advertising, but her name is now known in all seventy-seven Oklahoma counties, and around the world for that matter.'

Three-term Republican senator Don Nickles was now beginning to see the horribly real possibility that, as the wind came sweepin' down the plain, he would be running in the November elections against a very popular corpse, who might actually win. A statement from the dead lady's family added fuel to the fire of speculation: 'Perhaps the achievement of Jacquelyn Morrow Ledgerwood's purpose of spiritual renewal in running for the US Senate is not dead and can still be attained with a win in the runoff, and a miracle victory in the general election November 3,' it said.

A politician to his fingertips, air-conditioning man Don Carroll, who had beaten the dead Ledgerwood in the primary, described the situation as 'sad' and 'rather strange', but remained sanguine about the possibility of losing to a stiff. 'You just have to take it as it comes,' he said. Mark Nichols, Republican senator Don Nickles's confusingly named campaign manager, hedged his bets: 'We're putting our trust in the Oklahoma voters,' he said – possibly with his fingers crossed behind his back.

In the end, everyone – except Jacquelyn Ledgerwood, of course – was able to breathe a great sigh of relief. The runoff ended with Don Carroll picking up a very healthy 75.2 per cent of the vote, and the mouldering Jacquelyn Ledgerwood winning only 24.8 per cent. Nickles beat Carroll, in the end, winning the Senate election with some ease. But none of it might have mattered anyway, because, as Gore Vidal pointed out, 'It makes no difference who you vote for; the two parties are really one party representing four per cent of the people.' Nonetheless, Jacquelyn Ledgerwood had done even better in percentage terms than she had the first time round. And, let's face it, capturing nearly a quarter of the vote isn't at all bad for a dead lady.

The mystery of Kaspar Hauser

When I was a gobstopper-sucking young urchin I heard about a fellow called Kaspar Hauser who had been kept for years in a dark dungeon before being released on to the streets of Germany, only to be killed by a stranger who had handed him a mysterious message in back-to-front writing. This story is true and is so weird that I thought I should tell you about it.

On 26 May 1828, people going about their business in Nuremberg, Bavaria, noticed a confused and anxious teenage boy wandering the streets, utterly disoriented. He could barely walk and was almost mute. He kept repeating that he wanted to be a cavalryman, but was otherwise not much help to mystified onlookers.

The boy had with him an anonymous letter in which the writer explained that he had taken the boy in as a foundling sixteen years previously and had brought him up, teaching him to read and write but never letting him out of the house. The letter went on to say that the boy wished to become a cavalryman, 'as his father was'.

Along with the first letter there was another, supposedly written by the boy's mother years before when he was an infant. It was addressed to the writer of the first one (are you keeping up with all this?) and explained that the baby was named Kaspar, that his birthday was 30 April 1812 and that his father was dead. The trouble was that, as anyone could see, the two letters were written in the same handwriting. Something funny was going on.

Young Kaspar was taken to the house of Captain von Wessenig, to whom the first letter had been addressed, requesting that he either take the boy under his wing or get rid of him – the 1828 equivalent, presumably, of 'tough love'. When Kaspar was kindly questioned so as to discover what on earth was going on and who he was, he would only say he didn't know and or burst into tears, or say 'I want to be a cavalryman, as my father was', or 'Horse. Horse'.

Frankly bemused, Captain von Wessenig had him escorted to the police station, where he signed his name, 'Kaspar Hauser'. He was in good physical shape and was able to climb more than ninety steps to his room, where he received many curious visitors. Although he appeared healthy and otherwise normal, he would eat nothing but bread and water and it was suggested that he had been raised as a wolf-child in the forest. However, he was not slow or stupid and was, in fact, able to give his own version of events.

For as long as he could recall, he said, he had been kept totally alone in a dark, bathroom-size cell containing only a straw bed and a wooden horse. He awoke each day to find bread and water beside him, which sometimes tasted bitter. After drinking the bitter water, he would fall into a deep sleep and when he awoke his hair and fingernails would have been cut.

He said he never saw or heard another human being until, one day, a mysterious man with a concealed face taught him how to walk and how to write his name. The stranger had instructed him to repeat the sentence 'I want to be a cavalryman, as my father was', but the boy explained that he did not understand what this meant. It was at this point, he said, that he was released on to the streets of Nuremberg. This story caused an international sensation. Unsurprisingly – it sounded crazy, with a capital K.

Kaspar Hauser was put into the care of a teacher, Friedrich Daumer, who looked after him at his house, where he made huge strides in all subjects, impressing his teacher with his love of drawing. But on 17 October 1829 he failed to come to lunch and was discovered in the cellar, bleeding from an incision in his forehead. He said he had been attacked by a hooded man while on the toilet and recognized his voice as that of the stranger who had kept him in the darkened cell. Following the trail of blood, Daumer saw that, after the attack, Kaspar had fled to his room and then climbed through the trap door into the cellar.

The police were called and he was transferred into the care of Johann Biberbach who looked after him with his wife. On 3 April 1830, a pistol shot was heard from Hauser's room and he was found bleeding from a minor wound to the right side of his head. He explained that he had got on to a chair to reach some books but had accidentally taken hold of a pistol that was hanging on the wall, causing it go off.

The following year, he was transferred into the care of Johann Meyer of Ansbach. This relationship was not a good one, and on 9 December 1833, the two had a row after Meyer objected to Hauser telling lies. Five days later, on 14 December, the youth came home with a deep wound to the left side of his chest. He said that a stranger had lured him into the Ansbach Court Garden and had been handing over a small bag when he suddenly stabbed him. The police searched the garden and found a purse containing a note written in mirror writing sprinkled with dashes. In translation it reads:

Hauser can tell you exactly what I look like and where I am from. To

save Hauser the effort, I want to tell you myself where I am from – – –.
I come from – – – the Bavarian – – On the river – – – – – I even want to
tell you the name: M. L. Ö.

What the point of this note was supposed to be was anyone's guess, but
it was academic. Kaspar Hauser died of his wound on 17 December 1833.
His headstone was inscribed, in Latin, 'Here lies Kaspar Hauser, riddle
of his time. His birth unknown, his death a mystery.'

But suspicions about all the mysterious events surrounding Kaspar
Hauser had been aroused. The police were unimpressed that, after
encouraging them to go in search of the bag in the Ansbach Court Garden,
he seemed indifferent to its contents once it had been discovered.
Moreover, the note not only contained spelling and grammatical errors
typical of Hauser himself, it was folded with strange, characteristic
diagonal folds just as he always folded his own letters. This all led the
court of enquiry to conclude that his story about being attacked was
fantasy and that he had stabbed himself.

Indeed, all of Kaspar Hauser's tales seem very unlikely in their
particulars. There were never any witnesses to his misfortunes, and
many of those trying to care for him found him unattractively self-
obsessed and habitually untruthful. The purported razor attack must be
the only case in history where the victim has been set upon – pretty
harmlessly – while on the bog. And he doesn't cry out but, for some
reason, leaves a trail of blood to his room, before going to the cellar,
where he is discovered.

His account of accidentally shooting himself following an argument in
which he was humiliatingly reproached for lying – a very touchy subject,
you might think – beggars belief. Mrs Biberbach, in whose house this
event happened, remarked on Kaspar Hauser's 'horrid mendacity' and
'deception', and said he was 'full of vanity and spite'. Others reported
that he was extravagantly vain and untruthful.

Kaspar Hauser, whoever he really was, seems to have wanted
everybody to pay attention to him. His tragic and mysterious upbringing

and the strange men who attacked him – for unspecified reasons – were bound to cause a stir, and they did, as did the various (benign) wounds he received. Self-inflicted wounds tend to be made on the upper extremities including forearms, wrists and arms opposite the dominant hand. This was the position of the wounds received by Kaspar Hauser. The final knife wound was probably just too enthusiastic. Moderate self-mutilation is frequently seen in people with personality disorders. A recent American study reported that imaginary 'alleged assaults following scuffles were the most common cause of [forensic] referrals, and most of those were males'.

German Psychiatrist Karl Leonhard (1904–88) took an interest in the Kaspar Hauser case and, applying a twentieth-century analysis, said, 'From many reports on his behaviour one can recognize the hysterical as well as the paranoid trend of his personality.' It has also been pointed out that any boy raised in a darkened room for most of his life with almost no contact with other human beings would be a very different kind of person from the articulate, subtle hysteric that Kaspar Hauser was.

Whatever the truth, the mystery is irresistible and in 1975 *The Enigma of Kaspar Hauser*, a film written and directed by Werner Herzog, won the Grand Prize of the Jury at the 1975 Cannes Film Festival.

W. C. Fields: a man and his nose

Charles Bogle, Otis Criblecoblis and Mahatma Kane Jeeves were all pseudonyms of the juggler, writer and comedian William Claude Dukenfield (1880–1946), better known as W. C. Fields.

As a youth Claude Dukenfield worked in an oyster house but in his spare time he began to juggle, developing an act which he performed at church shows. Leaving home at eighteen, Dukenfield performed as a 'tramp juggler' in vaudeville, under the name W. C. Fields, topping the bill with his marvellous comedy-juggling act, in which he silently juggled cigar boxes, sticks, hats and whatever else seemed to come to hand.

Fields made his Broadway debut in a musical comedy in 1906 and toured the world with his unique act, which stands up extremely well today. His 1934 film, *The Old Fashioned Way*, features large chunks of this highly entertaining, funny and original display, and many small juggling tricks appear fleetingly in other films, too, in which he always plays a world-weary drunken misogynist and child-hater. The drunkenness was an accurate reflection of the bibulous performer, but the actress Gloria Jean described him as kindly and gentle in real life, a man who enjoyed playing with his grandchildren.

Fields was one of the few performers who managed to make his obvious alcoholism an advantage. He had been a good-looking young man but the booze gave him a huge nose, which he turned into a kind of trademark. He reportedly kept to hand a flask of martinis that he called his 'pineapple juice'. When a joker one day replaced the contents with real pineapple juice he is supposed to have said, 'Who put pineapple juice in my pineapple juice?'

After a successful film career, and a lifetime's habit of depositing small sums in bank accounts all over the country and then forgetting about them, Fields spent his last weeks in hospital, where he was one day caught reading the Bible. His atheism was well known but he remarked that he was 'checking for loopholes'. In an irony that he might have enjoyed, W. C. Fields died on Christmas Day 1946, from the effects of drink. Here are a few of his (reported) quotations.

- I like children – but I couldn't eat a whole one.
- I must have a drink of breakfast.
- I am free of all prejudices. I hate everyone equally.
- A rich man is nothing but a poor man with money.
- I was in love with a beautiful blonde once, dear. She drove me to drink. That's the one thing I am indebted to her for.
- Horse sense is the thing a horse has which keeps it from betting on people.
- All the men in my family were bearded, and most of the women.
- Never try to impress a woman, because if you do she'll expect you to

keep up the standard for the rest of your life.

- Once, in the wilds of Afghanistan, I lost my corkscrew and we were forced to live on nothing but food and water for days!
- The best thing for a case of nerves is a case of Scotch.
- Start every day off with a smile and get it over with.
- Marry an outdoors woman. Then if you throw her out into the yard on a cold night, she can still survive.
- Never cry over spilt milk – it might have been poisoned.
- Never give a sucker an even break.
- The best cure for insomnia is to get a lot of sleep.
- I never drink water. I'm afraid it will become habit-forming.
- On the whole, I'd rather be in Philadelphia.
- I once spent a year in Philadelphia. I think it was on a Sunday.
- Last week, I went to Philadelphia, but it was closed.
- Don't worry about your heart, it will last you as long as you live.
- I always keep a supply of stimulant handy in case I see a snake, which I also keep handy.
- My father occupied the chair of applied electricity at the state prison.
- I cook with wine. Sometimes I even add it to the food.
- If at first you don't succeed, try, try again. Then quit. There's no point in being a damn fool about it.
- Women are like elephants. I like to look at 'em, but I wouldn't want to own one.

The man who shot an iron bar through his head and survived

The next time someone says to you 'Not tonight dear, I've got a headache', tell them about Phineas P. Gage (1823–60).

On 13 September 1848, twenty-five-year-old Phineas Gage, the foreman of a gang of men clearing rubble so tracks could be laid for the Rutland & Burlington Railroad near Cavendish, Vermont, had drilled a hole into the rock. It was his responsibility to put in blasting powder, a

fuse and sand, and tamp the charge into the hole with a 3 foot 7 inch- (1 m-) long iron rod, an inch-and-a-quarter (3 cm) in diameter. This rod, which was to become as famous as its owner, was unusual, having been made by a neighbouring blacksmith 'to please the fancy of its owner', as it was put at the time.

Once Gage had prepared the charge, he was supposed to light the fuse and the gang would then watch from a safe distance as the thing went bang. On this occasion, however, he had left out the sand, and at about half-past-four in the afternoon, perhaps as his tamping rod caused a spark against the rock, the powder exploded prematurely, shooting the metal pole, which was tapered at the top end, up through his head. It entered under his left cheek bone, passed behind the left eye, and exited from the top of his skull in the middle of his head and slightly to the right. Weighing 13 lb 4 oz (6 kg), the rod was nonetheless said to have landed about 80 feet (25 m) away 'smeared with blood and brain'.

But Gage wasn't dead, and after a brief period of unconsciousness he was able to speak and could walk with little or no assistance. He then sat upright while driven in a cart three-quarters of a mile (1.2 km) to his lodgings in Cavendish, where Dr Edward H. Williams was soon on the scene. He described what he found.

I first noticed the wound upon the head before I alighted from my carriage, the pulsations of the brain being very distinct. Mr Gage, during the time I was examining this wound, was relating the manner in which he was injured to the bystanders. I did not believe Mr Gage's statement

Above: An illustration based on a daguerreotype portrait of a handsome Gage, with his iron bar, discovered in 2010.

at that time, but thought he was deceived. Mr Gage persisted in saying that the bar went through his head.

After an hour Dr John Harlow took over. This is what he recorded:

> You will excuse me for remarking here, that the picture presented was, to one unaccustomed to military surgery, truly terrific; but the patient bore his sufferings with the most heroic firmness. He recognized me at once, and said he hoped he was not much hurt. He seemed to be perfectly conscious, but was getting exhausted from the hemorrhage. Pulse 60, and regular. His person, and the bed on which he was laid, were literally one gore of blood.

Dr Harlow now took charge of Gage's treatment and slow recovery. As the brain began to swell as a result of its injury he became semi-conscious and was able to speak only in grunts, but on 7 October he took a step to his chair. Somewhat amazingly, just a month later, he was walking up and down stairs and by the middle of November reported that he no longer had any pain in his head.

After a visit to his family in New Hampshire, Gage returned to Cavendish in April. Dr Harlow noted that his patient had partial paralysis of the left side of his face, a loss of vision in his left eye and a drooping of the upper eyelid on the same side. He was sporting a large scar on his forehead, and had what Harlow called, 'a deep depression' on the top of the head, two inches by one-and-a-half inches wide, 'beneath which the pulsations of the brain can be perceived . . . I am inclined to say he has recovered,' he reported. 'Has no pain in head, but says it has a queer feeling which he is not able to describe.' This must have been the understatement of 1849.

But Phineas Gage had not survived intact; he was behaving so strangely that his friends and family didn't recognize him as the same person. He had become unreliable and was prone to swearing at inappropriate times and making uninhibited remarks. 'Disinhibition' is a classic symptom of damage to the front part of the brain, the 'frontal

273

lobes'. People with this condition can suffer emotional 'blunting' along with their loss of touch with the norms of social behaviour, and all-round can be rather hard work for their friends.

Gage, perhaps sensibly, gave up his railroad job and appeared for a time at Barnum's American Museum in New York City, then spent a few years as a long-distance stagecoach driver between Valparaiso and Santiago in Chile. According to Dr Harlow, he made what he called 'my iron bar' his constant companion during the rest of his life.

But in 1859 his health began to give out and he moved to San Francisco to live with his mother, brother-in-law and sister. In February of the following year, he suffered the first in a series of increasingly severe epileptic seizures; typical late-term effects of a traumatic brain injury of the kind that Gage suffered include the formation of scar tissue, which leads to the development of epilepsy. On 21 May 1860, just under twelve years after his accident, Phineas P. Gage died, aged thirty-six, and was buried in San Francisco's Lone Mountain Cemetery.

Seven years later, Dr Harlow arranged for his exhumation and his skull and tamping iron are now displayed at the Harvard Medical School.

The 'Geordie Pantsman'

When I left home my mother told me, 'Make sure you put on a new pair of underpants every day', so I did and by the end of July I was wearing 212 pairs and couldn't sit down. This may be an old joke but fifty-one-year-old architect Gary Craig actually did exactly that, except he accomplished it in one fell swoop, on Thursday, 1 April 2010. At the time of writing, Gary, from Tyneside in the north-east of England, holds the record for wearing more underpants at the same time than anyone else in the world, having donned 211 pairs in just twenty-five minutes.

Gary's feat was officially confirmed by the Guinness World Records organization after some 150 people – mainly excited women, by the looks of things on his website – gathered at a South Shields nightclub to watch incredulously as he completed the task, slipping on the last few pairs, each emblazoned with the name of a sponsor, including BP, which, as everyone knows, stands for 'Big Pants'.

But Craig's effort nearly came a cropper because, unbeknownst to him, in November 2009 an Australian TV presenter named Steve Jacobs had established a new record of 200 pairs but, not knowing Gary, didn't tell him so. As a result Gary only learned shortly before his attempt that he was going to have to beat the 200-pair tightie-whitie record rather than the previous record of 190-something. It was quite an emotional climax, therefore, with the self-styled Geordie Pantsman announcing that he wanted 'to give the Australians something to think about'.

All this got me thinking about underpants. The world's first briefs were sold in Chicago on 19 January 1935 by Coopers Inc. The so-called 'Jockey' briefs sold more than 30,000 pairs in three months and when they were introduced into the UK they sold at the rate of 3,000 a week. By 2008 the men's underwear market in the UK was worth £674 million, with sales of men's undies unaccountably rising by nearly a quarter between 2000 and 2005. Anyway, they are never difficult to get hold of.

But Geordie Pantsman had a unique problem. For a start, he had to buy 211 pairs of pants, ranging in size from the smaller 40-inchers (102 cm) right up to the most enormous 60-inch (153 cm). XXXXL size. Then he had to get the sponsors' logos on the briefs. Most of all, he had to prepare the garments in a special way, by putting one pair carefully inside another to make small groups of 'stacked-pants'. These stacks were then laid out on the floor in order of size so that he could proceed in a systematic way, by taking the first stack and putting them on as far as his ankles, one inside the other like Russian dolls, and pulling them up one at a time from inside the stack. The last-minute addition of eleven pairs, required to outdo the Australian 200-pair record, needed some thinking about, too. Gary pointed out that he couldn't get any more big pants on so he had to introduce smaller ones, with the disadvantage that they 'bite in'. This strategy paid off, though, and the Geordie Pantsman announced at the climax of his feat, 'It feels pretty sore at the minute but I'm just absolutely delighted . . .' as he sprayed a bottle of fizz over some of his friends.

But this might not be the end of things, because the Geordie Pantsman showed few signs of flagging at the end. Speaking afterwards, he said, 'I looked like a giant tennis ball . . . but if I'd had more pants I could have carried on'. Now I call that typically British fighting spirit. It makes you proud.

The Alton Giant and the disappearing giantess

Robert Pershing Wadlow (1918–40) was born at Alton, Illinois, on 22 February 1918. He was the tallest (properly documented) person in history. On 27 June 1940, less than three weeks before his death at the age of twenty-two, doctors at Washington University School of Medicine in St Louis measured Robert Wadlow at 8 foot 11 inches. (2.72 m), his weight was 485 lb (220 kg) and he was still growing.

Sometimes known as the Alton Giant or the Giant of Illinois, Wadlow's great size was caused by abnormal enlargement (hypertrophy) of his pituitary gland, which resulting in an overproduction of human growth hormone. His father, Harold F. Wadlow, later Mayor of Alton, was a normal 5 foot 11 inches (1.8 m) in height, and weighed 170 lb (77 kg). But by the age of nine, Robert was able to carry him up the stairs of the family home.

The term for Robert Wadlow's condition is gigantism, which causes abnormal growth of the hands, face and feet, along with the extreme height. The clothes of people with the condition must be specially made, and a pair of shoes can often be as long as a normal person's forearm. Wadlow's were 18½ inches (47 cm) long. The condition is usually the result of a tumour on the pituitary gland – the pea-size gland in the brain which controls growth, blood pressure and breast-milk production, amongst other things. Gigantism causes a variety of health problems in addition to abnormal height, including headaches and circulatory and skeletal problems. It also results in a greatly reduced lifespan, with most sufferers dying in their youth or middle age.

As a result of his extraordinary height, Robert Wadlow became an American celebrity and was well known in 1936 when he smiled his way around the country with Ringling Brothers Circus, being much photographed, interviewed and observed – medically, as well as by the curious onlooker. He did another tour two years later.

Wadlow's hands measured 12¾ inches (32.4 cm) from the wrist to the tip of the middle finger and he was so tall that he required custom-designed leg braces to enable him to walk. His extreme height resulted in poor circulation and reduced feeling in his long legs and feet, and on July 4 1940, while appearing at the Manistee National Forest Festival, one of his leg braces, which had been imperfectly fitted just a week earlier, injured his ankle without his feeling it. The blister became ulcerated and after emergency surgery his condition deteriorated. He died in his sleep in his hotel room in Manistee, Michigan, on 15 July 1940. He was twenty-two.

Wadlow was buried in Oakwood Cemetery, Alton, in a coffin 10 feet 9 inches (3.28 m) long, 32 inches (81 cm) wide and 30 inches (76 cm) deep. The thing weighed half a ton with him in it and required twelve pallbearers to carry it. Thousands of people attended the funeral.

The British equivalent of Robert Wadlow was Jane 'Jinny' Bunford (1895–1922), who, while she was alive anyway, was the tallest person in the world. When she died, she was the tallest woman in medical history, a record that remained unbroken for the next sixty years. She remains the second-tallest Briton ever recorded, and it is likely that she also held the record for having the longest hair in the country.

Very little is known of Jinny, who was born when Robert Wadlow was a toddler. She was listed for many years in *The Guinness Book of Records* and a photograph of her skeleton was published by that august annual in 1972, which is where I first saw it. Apart from this picture, no photographs of her are known to exist.

Jinny Bunford came from Bartley Green, Northfield, in Birmingham and was a quiet child, who, in 1906, at the age of eleven, measured a perfectly normal 5 feet (1.52 m) in height. But in October of that year she is said to have fallen off her bicycle and hit her head on the pavement, fracturing her skull and presumably damaging her pituitary gland.

Whatever the cause, Jinny now started to grow at an alarming rate.

As she continued to grow, she began to be teased at school, while finding it increasingly difficult to sit at her at school desk. During her life, no treatment was available for the overproduction of growth hormone and the role of the pituitary gland was not yet fully understood, so there was little to do to stop the bullying. In the end, she left school before her thirteenth birthday, on which date she measured about 6 feet 6 inches (1.98 m) in height. Two years later she came in at 7 feet (2.13 m) and on 26 July 1914, two days before the outbreak of the First World War, she was measured at 7 feet 8 inches (2.33 m) tall. By the age of twenty-one she was a towering 7 feet 10 inches (2.39 m) tall, and was often to be seen standing on the pavement, cleaning the upstairs windows of her cottage without recourse to a ladder.

Being of independent character, Jinny declined invitations to show herself off as a freak and instead briefly earned a wage at Cadbury's chocolate factory, growing her hair until it was 8 feet 1 inch long. Plaited, it came down to her ankles and, when untied, reached down to the ground, draped around her like a cloak. You wouldn't want one of *her* hairs in your Curly Wurly, would you?

As the years passed, she developed a severe spinal curvature and towards the end of her days could not stand erect. In March 1922 she was measured at 7 feet 7 inch (2.31 m) tall, her final measurement while alive; she died the following month. If she could have stood up properly she would have been some four inches taller (before she died, *obviously*). Her coffin was 8 feet 2 inches (2.46 m) long but the four schoolboys who carried it from the church to the graveyard said that it felt remarkably light.

After her interment Jinny Bunford was forgotten, except by her friends and family, of course, and she remained so for nearly half a century. Then, in 1972, *The Guinness Book of Records* published a photograph of an 'unidentified giantess who died in Northfield, Birmingham, England in 1921 aged *c*.24 years . . . The most recent research into the identity of the Northfield giantess indicates that she died in 1922.'

Not being entirely dense, people who remembered Jinny Bunford realized that, unless there were two giants living in the same town at the same time, these bones were hers. But how had Birmingham University, which had possession of the skeleton, got hold of them? Had she been dug up or was there more (less) to that light coffin than met the eye? In a spirit of openness, the university initially declined to reveal either the identity of the skeleton or the way in which it had come into their possession. But, faced with the facts, they soon had to agree that it was indeed Jinny Bunford.

The bones remained at Birmingham University until 2005, when they were returned to her family and, after a private funeral (her second), Jinny's skeleton was buried. No headstone marks the plot, though her mother's is clearly identified nearby. Most of those who might know exactly what happened to the corpse of Jinny Bunford in April 1922 are long dead and it remains a tantalizing mystery.

The real 'Deep Throat'

On the evening of 17 June 1972, a security guard at the Watergate residential and office complex in Washington, DC, noticed tapes covering the latches of several doors, preventing them from locking. He called the police who arrested five men inside the Democratic National Committee's office. The five were eventually convicted, along with two others, of conspiracy, burglary and wiretapping.

Revelatory coverage by *Washington Post* reporters Bob Woodward and Carl Bernstein revealed that knowledge of the break-in, and attempts to cover it up, led deep into the bowels of the Justice Department, the FBI, the CIA and, crucially, Richard Nixon's White House. The burglars were linked to the official Committee to Re-elect the President (CREEP).

FBI agents were amazed to see information in the *Washington Post* articles lifted almost verbatim from their recent reports: where were the reporters getting their red-hot stuff? In fact, the *Post*'s main whistle-blower was a man charmingly nicknamed 'Deep Throat' by Howard Simons, the newspaper's editor (in honour of a porn film of that name), owing to his understandable wish to remain anonymous. Bob Woodward later described him as 'an incurable gossip . . . in a unique position to observe the Executive Branch'. When Woodward wanted to meet Deep Throat, he would put a flowerpot containing a red flag into position on his apartment balcony, and if Deep Throat felt like a chat, Woodward would find his copy of the *New York Times* on the steps of his apartment, with a page number circled, and a little clock drawn in, signalling the meeting time. The two met secretly in the early hours in an unromantic underground car park in Washington, where Deep Throat gave Woodward high-quality tip-offs and warned him that he might be followed and that his phone might be tapped. It was all rather exciting.

Under this scrutiny, a Senate Watergate Committee was formed to investigate the scandal and it soon discovered that President Nixon had been tape-recording conversations in his office, implicating himself in the cover-up of the break-in. The US Supreme Court instructed Nixon to hand over the tapes, which he did rather grudgingly. The tapes also revealed that the President knew some choice swearwords and it was clear from the recordings that he was also well aware of what the five burglars and their associates had been up to. Indeed, the team were known informally as 'The Plumbers', and various of them had been involved with all kinds of informal shenanigans for some time. Things were starting to look really bad and, fearing impeachment, Nixon resigned as President on 9 August 1974.

Three decades later, on 31 May 2005, after the death of many of those involved in the Watergate scandal, and following decades of lively speculation over the identity of Deep Throat, his real name was finally revealed by *Vanity Fair*. Deep Throat, it seemed, was a former FBI Deputy Director named Mark Felt. Interestingly, Nixon's White House Chief of Staff at the time of the Watergate scandal, Alexander M. Haig, had suspected that Felt was talking to the press, but aides had advised that, 'If we move on him, he'll go out and unload everything. He knows everything that's to be known in the FBI. He has access to absolutely everything.' Quite what 'everything' meant was unclear.

Woodward had first met Felt at the White House in 1969 or 1970. He described him as a commanding man, 'with perfectly combed gray hair'. He was ambitious and had personal reasons for feeling ill-will towards the White House after being passed over for the job of FBI boss. He had been much admired by, and had risen under, long-time FBI supremo J. Edgar Hoover, and had been referred to by others as 'the latest blond young man', in reference to Hoover's partiality for this kind of person.

Hoover's number two at the FBI had for years been a blond young – and then old – man, Clyde Tolson, whom Hoover described as his alter ego. The two worked closely together during the day, had lunch and dinner together, went to nightclubs together and lay sunning themselves on the beach together. This relationship continued into old age, right up to Hoover's death. Mark Felt described the relationship as 'brotherly', though it must be remembered that for years he also denied being Deep Throat. It's worth noting, also, that the always beautifully turned out Hoover mercilessly sought out and menaced anyone who made remarks about his sexuality. This did not, however, stop the nicknames 'J. Edna Hoover' and 'Gay Edgar Hoover' gaining popularity.

After more than three decades with the FBI, Felt finally left the Bureau on 22 June 1973 and, following a long period of retirement, he died in his sleep at a California hospice on 18 December 2008.

Felt was an odd chap, and goodness knows what his motives had been. I don't think I'd have trusted him farther than I could have thrown him, personally. But the whole Watergate/Deep Throat thing would have made a good book or film. And in fact it did both. In 1976, *All the President's Men*, a film thriller loosely based on the 1974 book by Bob Woodward and Carl Bernstein, became a huge hit. It starred Robert Redford and Dustin Hoffman as much more handsome versions of Woodward and Bernstein. The wonderful Hal Holbrook played a less handsome version of Deep Throat. Luckily he was seen only in silhouette and deep shadow.

Dr Johnson: a man, his dictionary and his Tourette's

Dr Samuel Johnson (1709–84) was the quintessential English man of letters. He was an amusingly opinionated author, poet, essayist, literary critic, biographer, editor and lexicographer, and was said to know 'more books than any man alive'. He was also devoutly religious, politically conservative, strange and sickly.

Johnson suffered from a really good selection of illnesses, including childhood tuberculosis, poor eyesight, scrofula, gout, pulmonary fibrosis and testicular cancer. His somewhat gigantic stature and peculiar mannerisms, twitches and tics caused many to think he was deranged or foolish.

Born in Lichfield, Staffordshire, Johnson went to Pembroke College, Oxford, but left after a year because he couldn't afford the fees. He moved to London, where he wrote a biography, poems, magazine pieces and a rotten play, *Irene*, which, bad though it was, took him twenty-three years to finish.

By contrast, his *Dictionary of the English Language* took him and a few recruits sitting in an attic room off the bottom of Fleet Street just nine years to complete. It was published in 1755 and was an enormous success. Until the publication of the huge *Oxford English Dictionary*, 150 years later, Johnson's dictionary was regarded as the best English dictionary available.

Johnson's dictionary is imbued with the personality of its compiler and he takes a few liberties that would not today be permitted. He seems to have had a prejudice, for example, against the Scots and this is evident in his amusing definition of the word 'oats', which his dictionary defines as 'a grain which in England is generally given to horses, but in Scotland supports the people'. A few Johnsonian definitions have also gone down in history as a bit over the top. For example, 'network', which his dictionary defines as 'anything reticulated or decussated at equal distances, with interstices between the intersections'. He also made a few mistakes in the dictionary but defended himself admirably. When a lady asked him why he had incorrectly defined 'pastern' as the knee of a horse, he replied, 'Ignorance, madam, pure ignorance.'

Johnson's great friend and scribe James Boswell described the doctor, warts and all, in his *Life of Samuel Johnson*. Boswell says that Johnson was often depressed, feeling himself 'overwhelmed with an horrible melancholia, with perpetual irritation, fretfulness, and impatience; and with a dejection, gloom, and despair, which made existence misery'. Sounds like a barrel of laughs. And this was on top of his tics.

At the thresholds of rooms he was said to go through compulsive routines and when the artist William Hogarth first saw Johnson 'shaking his head and rolling himself about in a strange ridiculous manner', he thought him an 'ideot'. Boswell reported that:

While talking or even musing as he sat in his chair, he commonly held his head to one side towards his right shoulder, and shook it in a tremulous manner, moving his body backwards and forwards, and rubbing his left knee in the same direction, with the palm of his hand. In the intervals of articulating he made various sounds with his mouth; sometimes giving a half whistle, sometimes making his tongue play backwards from the roof of his mouth, as if clucking like a hen, and sometimes protruding it against his upper gums in front, as if pronouncing quickly under his breath, 'Too, too, too.' All this accompanied sometimes with a thoughtful look, but more frequently with a smile. Generally when he had concluded a period, in the course of a dispute, by which time he was a good deal exhausted by violence and vociferation, he used to blow out his breath like a whale.

Boswell's detailed account of Johnson's outlandish gesticulations and vocal tics has resulted in a generally accepted post-mortem diagnosis of Tourette's syndrome. Along with the liabilities, compulsions and tics of the condition, many Tourette's sufferers are creatively gifted, characteristically quick, spontaneous, imaginative and bright, which Dr Johnson was in spades, but since Tourette's syndrome had not yet been given a name – indeed, neurologist Georges Gilles de la Tourette was not born until seventy-three years after Johnson's death – it was a condition that Johnson did not know he was allowed to have. When asked, he said his curious mannerisms were the result of, as he put it, 'bad habit'.

Dr Johnson is a nice example of the power of a gifted human being to overcome a supremely annoying affliction and he worked successfully in spite of – maybe even because of – his condition. Unhappily, a stroke in the last year of his life left Johnson unable to speak and he died on 13 December 1784. He is buried in Westminster Abbey, twitching no more.

The man who posted himself

Do you know the song that starts 'I'm gonna sit right down and write myself a letter'? Well, one day a twenty-five-year-old crate-packer from New York, Charles D. McKinley, sat down and sang 'I'm gonna sit right down and mail myself to my parents', and then he did.

Using expertise accumulated over nine years in the packing industry, Mr McKinley sent himself across the United States from Brooklyn to Desoto, Texas, in a crate. After packing himself up, he managed to travel the entire way without being discovered, enjoying part of the journey by plane. It wasn't until a bemused deliveryman witnessed him emerging like a duckling from its egg, on the doorstep of his startled parents' home, that anyone realized what was going on. 'While I was in the crate I felt a little boxed in if you know what I mean,' said McKinley. 'I'm sitting there thinking, "Oh God, I don't know why I'm doing this." I'm sitting there thinking like any minute somebody will notice that there's somebody sitting inside this crate. No one did.'

The contrite McKinley was arrested and, speaking from jail, the crate-packer told a TV station that he had been feeling homesick when 'a friend' had suggested that it would be a lot cheaper to fly cargo than to pay for a seat like a normal person. 'All I wanted to do was save a few bucks,' he said, neglecting to add that he had been aiming to charge the shipping costs to his employer. 'The plan was foolproof,' he added, unconvincingly. The authorities were certainly unimpressed. 'This office is taking swift action on this case through the immediate filing of the most readily apparent federal violation against this individual, which is the "stowaway" charge,' said US Attorney Boyle in a long and muddled sentence.

Asked for his reaction to the unorthodox package, Richard G. Phillips, chief executive of Pilot Air Freight, whose firm had unknowingly flown Mr McKinley in his box, said that he thought he was lucky to be alive, maintaining that he had been blessed with good fortune by being carried in pressurized and heated cabins instead of unpressurized, airless, frozen ones. 'He could easily have died,' said Mr Phillips, bluntly, pointing out that in any case for $550, the cost of freighting himself, 'he could have flown first-class'.

Embarrassed airline officials said they found it baffling that a huge box with a human being rolling about inside it could get through customs with such apparent ease. They announced that security was to be tightened to stop human mail becoming any more popular than it already was.

'Obviously it's something we are investigating aggressively,' said a spokeswoman for the federal Transportation Security Administration (TSA). Cargo planes deal with a huge amount of airfreight every day – millions of shipments – and inanimate packages get less attention perhaps than passengers. FBI Director Robert Mueller was asked for his thoughts on this. 'The fact of the matter is you cannot open and examine every one of those,' he said, somewhat obviously.

The security guard whose responsibility it had been to check the crate inside which Mr McKinley was lurking said it was an easy mistake to make. He was fired.